Studies in Childhood and Youth

Series Editors

Allison James
Department of Sociological Studies
University of Sheffield
Sheffield, UK

Adrian James
Department of Sociological Studies
University of Sheffield
Sheffield, UK

Aim of the series

This series offers a multi-disciplinary perspective on exploring childhood and youth as social phenomena that are culturally located, articulating children's and young people's perspectives on their everyday lives. The aim of the series will be to continue to develop these theoretical perspectives through publishing both monographs and edited collections that present cutting-edge research within the area of childhood studies. It will provide a key locus for work within the field that is currently published across a diverse range of outlets and will help consolidate and develop childhood studies as a discrete field of scholarship.

More information about this series at
http://www.springer.com/series/14474

Sam Frankel

Negotiating Childhoods

Applying a Moral Filter to Children's
Everyday Lives

Sam Frankel
King's University College, Western University
London, ON, Canada

Studies in Childhood and Youth
ISBN 978-1-137-32348-4   ISBN 978-1-137-32349-1   (eBook)
DOI 10.1057/978-1-137-32349-1

Library of Congress Control Number: 2016947039

Cover image © rangepuppies / Getty

Printed on acid-free paper

This Palgrave Macmillan imprint is published by Springer Nature
The registered company is Macmillan Publishers Ltd.
The registered company address is: The Campus, 4 Crinan Street, London, N1 9XW, United Kingdom

To my wife, Moira, esbl

Acknowledgements

This book has been a number of years in its development. Along the way I have been very grateful for the support of many people whose help has been a staging post in finding ways to express the ideas that I felt so passionate about sharing. Thanks to Kate Bacon for the long conversations that saw the emergence of the framework of this book. It is a framework, however, that has only taken on real meaning during my time at King's University College, Western University, Ontario. I want to thank Alan Pomfret for the freedom to explore my ideas and for the opportunity to be part of a dialogue with him, Pat Ryan and other scholars that certainly informed this work. I want to say a special thank you to a wonderful group of students who patiently let me test out my ideas on them. Thank you for the blank faces and for letting me know when it didn't make sense, but most of all for your encouragement that these ideas are of value to people like you, who are ambitious about drawing off childhood studies to make a difference in the world.

Thank you to the team at Palgrave Macmillan for their patience and encouragement. As always, I am grateful to Allison and Adrian James for their words of wisdom and ongoing inspiration.

This book would not be what it is without the input of Sally McNamee, her friendship, encouragement, counsel and spell checking has been invaluable.

I would also like to excpress my thanks to friends and family: to Terry and Gill Over whose support has given me opportunities like this, as well as to both sets of parents. Finally to those who have had to put up with the day-to-day reality of me trying to write – to Ruari, Roise, Maria and most of all Moira – thank you.

Contents

1   Introduction   1

Step 1   A Theoretical Foundation   9

2   Structure '&' Agency   11

Step 2   Establishing a Framework   41

3   Engaging with Structure   47

4   Engaging with Agency   69

Step 3   Deconstructing Dominant Discourses   103

5   Reason   105

6   Virtue   133

7   Social Harmony   163

Step 4   Recognising Agency in Action   193

8   Negotiating the Everyday   195

Step 5   Re-positioning Children Within Structure   229

9   Restructuring Moral Discourses   233

Bibliography   265

Index   287

List of Figures

Fig. 2.1	Uni-directional arrow	24
Fig. 2.2	Bi-directional arrow	32
Fig. 1	Framework overview	43
Fig. 3.1	Framework: part 1	56
Fig. 4.1		96
Fig. 4.2	Framework: part 2	98
Fig. 4.3	Reflecting structure and agency	99
Fig. 1	The framework	104
Fig. 1	The framework	194
Fig. 1	The framework	230
Fig. 9.1	Inverted participation triangles	254

1

Introduction

In January 2016, a 10-year-old boy, probably like many other children his age in primary schools across the United Kingdom, and no doubt in other countries as well, was providing an account of life at home. The point of the exercise was for the children to practise their writing skills and to put into effect the phonetic method of spelling that they had been taught. In describing his house, the 10-year-old, who happened to be Muslim, labelled his home a 'terror-ist house', which using the phonetic technique is not a bad attempt in spelling the word 'terrace'. Rather than this being seen just as a product of the spelling approach adopted in the education system, and simply corrected by the teacher with a wry grin, this boy and his family became the subject of a counter-terrorist investigation (BBC, 20/1/16).

This example has obvious features that make it particularly notable, but it reflects a process that forms part of every child's every day, one in which a constructed understanding of morality is used to inform an image of the child that, as a consequence, leads to certain adult-defined practices that shape the child's experience. It is in relation to this backdrop that children interact with the social world, creating meanings that

© The Editor(s) (if applicable) and The Author(s) 2017
S. Frankel, *Negotiating Childhoods*, Studies in Childhood and Youth,
DOI 10.1057/978-1-137-32349-1_1

inform their behaviours. It reflects a multi-tiered moral dimension that forms part of both our understanding of childhoods and of the individual child. It is the desire to bring these together that forms the focus for this book which presents a framework for exploring this moral dimension and recognising its relevance in children's lives.

1.1   The Moral Status of Childhood

Perhaps the moral status of childhood provides the most dramatic instance of misfit between the adult structuring of childhood and young people's own knowledge and experience. Young people find that adults routinely reject or ignore their moral competence, yet they do engage with moral issues…A further twist to this tangle is that adults also expect young people to take moral responsibility both at home and at school [and also increasingly within the wider social and virtual spaces that make up the neighbourhood]. This adult neglect and indeed conceptual misunderstanding accounts for one of the strongest findings…that children find their participation rights are not respected. This misfit between experience and societal concepts has to be explained. (Mayall 2002: 138)

Children, Morality and Society (Frankel 2012) was written to promote discussion and in order to raise the profile of an area of thinking that had for too long been under-acknowledged (Mayall 2002). Its aim was simply to contribute to a dialogue that placed children within discourses of morality. At the time it was a conscious decision to focus on children's agency and to consider this as the starting point. There was no intention to be 'dismissive' (Robb 2014) of the wider moral framework, rather it was a decision of priorities.

This work reflects the next step. To fully understand the way in which children demonstrate their engagement with morality it is important that this is seen within a wider theoretical framework. These ideas had yet to fully mature in that original work. However, here I hope to put that thinking into a far stronger context that will not only promote dialogue but will actively support the researcher in asking more questions and discovering more answers. Are these the updated views of an earlier piece of writing? No. They are to be seen as an addition to what has already been set out, strengthening those arguments by establishing a more defined model for engagement. The aim of this work, therefore, is to flesh out an enlarged conceptual framework that will not only support this consideration of children and morality, but can also aid the way in which we consider the processes that make up agentic action. As will be suggested, these processes must not be seen outside of the social web in which interaction takes place. It is, therefore, a fundamental concern of this work to make sense of the relationship between structure and agency, and how that helps to further our ability as adults to understand children and to engage with them more effectively.

But why morality? Morality remains a significant stronghold of thought from which adults are able to manage children's position in society. Drawing from notions of the minority group (see Mayall 2002), this work recognises the extent to which morality has acted as a choker through which society has sought to keep control of children. The result has been a misrepresentation of children at all levels of society, with implications for all aspects of their everyday lives. The following quote, although marking an extreme case, has significant resonance. It comes from an interview in which the child murderer, Mary Bell, reflects, some 30 years later, on her trial as an 11-year-old.

'In the court while they were talking and talking, I remember thinking of what I would say when it was my turn. I'd tell them I want my dog. I wanted him with me when they sent me to be hanged. That's what I thought would happen: I'd be sent to the gallows and they might just as well have said that right away because it was just as meaningless as life imprisonment or …well…death. None of it meant a damned thing, not a thing…'

But you were frightened just the same?

'I think probably more of the whole thing, the kind of hushed atmosphere, the reaction from the adults…adults…' She repeated her words as always in moments of stress, losing all structure, rhythm and pattern of speech '…adults, you know, literally avoiding me…looking at me like… like…like a specimen'. (Sereney 1998: 125)

It was the thinking provoked by this case that encouraged me to write *Children, Morality and Society*. Despite this account being a reflection on an incident that happened some time ago, it continues to mirror many of the dominant discourses that form around children and morality. It is the way in which it draws out the child as a 'specimen' that is most compelling, a theme that continues to sum up children's relationships within moral discourses. This book, therefore, sets out to establish a foundation on which a challenge to these dominant ways of thinking can be based on recognising the extent to which 'morality' must be seen as a more overt feature of the way in which we view the social world.

1.2   This Book

The original aim of this book was simply to try and look at children and morality as a social construction. However, as the process of writing moved on, it became clear that the constructed nature of this model was only part of the story, one that could only be fully understood if an examination of structure sat alongside the way in which the individual comes to relate to it. This, therefore, ties the work directly into examining the relationship between structure *and* agency. From this base, this work proposes that childhood studies has much to offer in providing a foundation through which we can challenge the dominant attitudes that have shaped so much of our thinking in relation to children and morality in the past. In order to mount this campaign this book focuses on five key steps,

1. A theoretical foundation
2. Establishing a framework
3. Framing a contextual backdrop
4. Recognising agency in action
5. Repositioning children within structure

I have used the term 'step' to identify these sections because I want to avoid confusion with the term 'part', which might be seen as a more appropriate phrase. 'Part' will be used solely to refer to the three different 'parts' of the framework that will pull together the ideas in this book.

1.2.1   Step 1: Chapter 2 : A Theoretical Foundation

Chapter 2 presents the case for a framework to aid the way in which we are able to analyse structure and agency, and by doing this reflect on a moral dimension that forms part of both. Morality is presented as nothing new to sociological thought in relation to children, rather as a focus for thinking that has lost its emphasis. In doing so, the traditional notion of socialisation is challenged, and it is suggested that if we are interested in understanding the transmission of social order then this should be seen in a far more dynamic way. This brings together structure and agency and the active nature of the relationship between the two because it suggests that the researcher needs to move away from the unidirectional focus on causality (the individual being defined as a product of both their biology and environment) to a bidirectional recognition of the interrelationship that exists between the social agent and the structure in which they find themselves. Drawing from the ideas of Adrian James (2010) that 'wove' together an approach to structure and agency, this chapter illustrates the relevance of recognising the potential this union offers for challenging the way children have, for too long, been positioned in relation to morality.

1.2.2   Step 2: Chapters 3 and 4: Establishing a Framework

Here the framework is introduced. Chapters 3 and 4 focus on the structural and agentic aspects of the framework, respectively. In both chapters a presentation of the theory precedes a consideration of what it means in terms of offering a practical framework that can be used to understand the way in which children negotiate their everyday lives. What is significant about this framework is that it is not a tool that is simply for those who are interested in 'morality'. Rather, the framework suggests that, whatever our engagement with children, a moral dimension cannot be ignored, because it is simply a part of both the structural way in which children's lives are ordered and an intrinsic element of how they, as social agents, make meanings in the context of the interactional settings in which they find themselves. Through the framework one can start to consider the nature of the contextual backdrop, how it is influenced, how it comes to be shaped and the extent to which it establishes (moral) images of the child that inform practices. It is a direct engagement with this contextual backdrop that sees the child demonstrating their agency. The processes of agency that inform this are explored in Chap. 4, with a consideration of those aspects of self that the individual brings to interaction, and the extent to which these impact on individual meaning making.

1.2.3   Step 3: Chapters, 5, 6 and 7: Deconstructing Dominant Discourses

Engaging with the framework initially means focusing on a filter that allows constructed images of the child to be made visible and then to be examined. Each chapter in this section seeks explore the relevance of these filters to a consideration of home, school and the neighbourhood. The filters are reason, virtue and social harmony, and are introduced in Chap. 3. Here they are shown to offer a means of deconstructing social thought in relation to children through a partial historical investigation. Recognising the application of these filters within history shows just how settled society is on positioning children in relation to morality. These chapters show change through time, but they also reflect on similarities that continue to be identifiable, with relevance for how we engage with children today.

In this way it is possible to start to understand the fabric out of which contemporary moral images of the child come to be constructed. As a result of establishing analysis based on the framework, they reflect on how a search for a moral image can illuminate further the nature of adult and child roles and relationships within key settings and the intrinsic place of a moral perception of the child in framing the very processes by which the practices of childhood (for example, in school) are carried out.

1.2.4   Step 4: Chapter 8: Recognising Agency in Action

This section provides a contrast to the images of the child considered in the previous section. Through seeking to illustrate the second part of the framework, this chapter demonstrates not only the differences from the constructed images above but also the practical way in which children engage with morality within their everyday lives. Those differences are illustrated using examples from *Children, Morality and Society* (Frankel 2012) in combination with a continued use of the filters from the last section. Also, through a focus on children's voices, it is possible to highlight the active and dynamic way in which children are continually engaging with everyday morality as they seek to navigate the social world around them. As such it demonstrates the central place of moral assessment as a feature of their agency. The discussions around emotions, the processes of learning and collaboration are examined through the lens of home, school and the neighbourhood, and directly challenge those dominant discourses that are too often relied upon to shape our understandings of children and morality. The themes identified raise questions that demand we acknowledge children's moral learning journey as one that is socially and relationally situated, adding to the case for seeing socialisation as a process that is multilayered, complex and nuanced.

1.2.5 Step 5: Chapter 9: Repositioning Children Within Structure

At the end of Chap. 4 a definition of agency is presented. This definition highlights that morality is simply a feature of structure and agency, that an engagement with morality should therefore be seen as a necessary and regular part of our desire to understand children. The moral dimension should not be seen as a niche area of investigation, but rather as a relevant feature of any consideration of childhoods and children's everyday lives. This final section, building on earlier themes, first seeks to acknowledge that structure is not static, but that the individual through their engagement with it can be part of establishing 'structural' change. It is on the basis of the child as a change agent that this chapter concludes by reflecting on some of the dominant attitudes presented in Chaps. 5, 6 and 7 and contrasting these with the images that are reflected in Chaps. 8 and 9. As a result, this final chapter presents alternative images which reflect ways of thinking about the child that challenge the dominant discourses that have for too long informed how we have approached children and morality.

My hope is that this book moves beyond a discourse that is dominated by the voice of 'adults' and, rather than children being 'specimens', offers a framework through which they can be seen as active partners in a shared discourse on morality. This framework not only adds to the way in which we are able to make sense of childhoods, but it also extends our capacity to understand agency and therefore to make sense of children's interactions within the different settings of their everyday lives.

Step 1

A Theoretical Foundation

In the introduction to the book *No Way: the nature of the impossible*, Davis and Park (1987) explore those who have set their sights on taking on some of the most extraordinary physical challenges known to man, summed up by the endeavour of climbing Mount Everest. It is a journey that can only begin when someone sees a way to move beyond the sign marked 'impossible' that has prohibited previous attempts. It is only by questioning the impossibility of the challenge that what is possible might emerge.

To demand a revolution in the way in which we position children in moral discourses presents a conceptual challenge that is not totally dissimilar. Children's place in society has been defined with reference to their perceived biological maturity which has marked them as being without the capacity to engage with morality, resulting in children's role being little more than as the focus of an adult driven project. The implications of this have seen society after society build institutions from this foundation, held together by ongoing constructions of the child which, although they may differ, reaffirm adult dominance over children through an ownership of these discourses. To demand that we dismantle the understandings of the child that flow through these institutions and society more widely changing the way in which we as adults come to 'practice' in our dealings with children, might appear at first impossible. However, embracing the illustration above, it is only by engaging with the impossibility of the challenge, that one canstart to de-construct and consder taking on the challenge at alll. As ones perspective starts to shift, the next question then becomes, what 'tools'might we use to take on the 'impossible'.

This opening chapter of this book moves beyond these analogies to identify a theoretical base from which one can begin to take on this conceptual challenge. It will introduce key theories that invite us to reconsider the way in which we position both childhoods and the individual child in relation to morality as it introduces structure and agency, and how these are relevant to engaging with children's everyday lives.

2

Structure '&' Agency

Why do children do what they do? What was it, this morning, that led to my ten-year-old son telling his three-year-old sister that, uncharacteristically, he 'hated her' after she had tried spinning his chair around while he, after many hours of 'training', was on the verge of reaching the next level on an iPad game?

Is this a silly question? For some, surely the answer is that it's just what children do? It is part of family life, sibling interaction, it is part of childhood. A slightly more in-depth reflection might focus on the fact that children do these things because they have not got the ability (yet) to avoid them. They are driven by a hungry pursuit of their own self-interests rather than an awareness of the other. They lack a moral maturity, a moral competence, that with age will allow them to frame their actions differently. Was it a lack of effective teaching on the part of their parents that caused this scene? Are these children lacking clarity in terms of what behaviours are acceptable, both within this home and in the social spaces beyond? Should the parents be the sole focus of any blame? Should it not also include their teachers, or maybe other family members or friends of the family with whom they spend time? Or does

S. Frankel, *Negotiating Childhoods*, Studies in Childhood and Youth,
DOI 10.1057/978-1-137-32349-1_2

this example reflect the combustible reality of a child as they teeter on a boundary between order (the adult world of reason) and chaos (where children are driven by impulse)?

Of course there are other possible answers that might emerge from the moral philosopher, the faith leader, psychologist, educationalist, politician and more. Uniting these perspectives, although they will differ, is the centrality of hypotheses that are adult-constructed, based on adult-defined 'understandings' of the child. Notably, missing in the repertoire of our responses to the way children act and behave is an approach that draws from knowledge that has been created through direct and explicit engagement with children themselves. It is a desire to provide such a perspective that we are concerned with in this book. Childhood studies has already proved its ability to open windows into areas of children's lives, here through a focus on children's everyday the place of morality as a feature of the individuals negotiation with the world around them will emerge. As such morality moves on from being a theme linked to discourses around nature and nurture to be seen as a feature for examination within the day to day processes that result in individuals making meanings that inform their actions.

2.1   A Theoretical Starting Point

The relationship between children, morality and everyday life is a topic that, as suggested above, has seen the psychologist, politician, lawyer, writer, philosopher and preacher (and more) all vying for a voice. This has seen morality defined and presented in many different ways, with reference to many big questions about the way in which the human being 'is'. Whether evolution or creation, obligation or contract, will or reason, discourses of morality are played out on a battlefield that resounds to ongoing canon fire from many different encampments. Each encampment reinforces its position with numerous arguments and 'evidence', justifying and motivating the need to maintain and defend their position in the continuing fight. So entrenched is the field of battle that the room for manoeuvre is limited, and the scope for fresh positions to be established is restricted. However, the argument of this book is that there is an element of this debate that has yet to be fully heard or recognised. Despite childhood studies not presenting such visible colours on the battlefield as other disciplines, its emerging ideas offer an opportunity for a fresh campaign of engagement. Childhood studies has drawn from sociological concepts that were founded in explorations for truth that included a search for understandings of morality, leading to the evolution of views that, it will be argued, are now ideally placed to be reapplied to this investigation of morality. It is a recognition of both the multi-disciplinary nature of childhood studies and the relevance of the conceptual definition of the child and its relationship with wider society that demands that it is time for these questions about children and morality to be heard, as we seek to position a new force within moral discourses.

In 1791 Thomas Paine, in his pamphlet 'Rights of Man' wrote:

> Freedom had been hunted round the globe; reason was considered as rebellion; and the slavery of fear had made men afraid to think. But such is the irresistible nature of truth, that all it asks, and all it wants, is the liberty of appearing.

It was as much a statement of the time as a prophecy for the future because the battle for truth has been a central tenet of the human story. As I am writing (2016), the most powerful country in the world is toying with the idea of electing a woman to the role of President, following its first black leader. Both minority representatives represent battles in which 'truth' simply wanted the 'liberty of appearing', the chance for race or gender to no longer be used to mask the capability and potential of the individual. These examples can be aligned with moral discourses in which gender and race both provided markers of competency. However, there is another fundamental truth that needs the opportunity to emerge, a truth that has been missed by thousands of years of philosophical enquiry and one that places childhood studies scholars firmly in the role of revolutionaries as they seek to challenge some defining bastions of human intellect and nature. For, although discussing 'morality' it is not controversial to say that children have simply been outside of moral discourse throughout its rich journey.

Thus presenting arguments that seek to re-position the child within moral discourses does not mark an attempt to overturn previous thought, rather to addd to it by including a truth that has for too long been left out. To explore how we might acknowledge children in such discourses, it is important to start by establishing a sense of how 'morality' is to be seen within this work.

Moral philosophy is and always has been heavily interconnected with the social. Indeed, notions of right and wrong carry little value outside of a context that places individuals in some form of communion with others. The derivation of the word – *ethikos,* which in Latin became *moralis* – means 'pertaining to character'. As such, 'morality' starts from a desire to think about and understand the individual and how he or she comes to express themselves or position themselves within society. Unsurprisingly this is a central theme in the earliest of shared stories and accounts, as well as being the subject for the first examples of philosophical writing. Such themes are reflected in religious traditions, for example in the monotheistic faiths where bad 'character' is the cause of social disharmony and discord, from which believers seek to distance themselves and eventually escape altogether. In its purest sense, before the layers of thought were added to it, 'morality' was simply about how the individual's actions were seen and perceived by themselves and others.

Homer exemplifies this in the formative works for Western literature, as his listeners (and later readers) are asked to reflect on different characters brought together through conflict as they engage in aspects of their lives. Throughout, Homer seeks to provoke his audience to consider what individual actions have most impact in the context of such discord, opening the debate (for this is how his audience would have engaged with his work) about the values people sought to espouse within their own lives. Homer's work, as a result, tests out a range of 'characters' as he invites the audience to search for some sense of harmony in their relationships with one another. This is reflected poignantly in the home-coming of Odysseus at the end of Homer's second work, *The Odyssey.* Here in this climatic moment there was the potential for more blood to be spilt (as had been the ongoing theme) but as the 'much enduring good Odysseus' prepared to strike his countrymen once again with his sword, Athene called on him to hold. And, after two volumes of conflict, Homer ends with:

Odysseus obeyed her, and his heart rejoiced. Then Pallas Athene, daughter of aegis-bearing Zeus, still using Mentor's form and voice for disguise, established peace between the two sides. (Homer 1991: 370)

It is the centrality of a search for harmony that is so characteristic of this work and the philosophical ideas that followed as links were made between the actions of the individual and their impact on society in the search for an effective code by which to live. This original application of 'morality' – as a means through which we can consider the understandings and behaviours that emerge within society to allow individuals to manage co-operatively through searching to do what is acceptable – is to be the overriding definition used within this work.

The ways in which questions of acceptability have been engaged with have been played out in the subjective laboratory conditions of philosophers' minds. It is not to disabuse the principal aim, in many of these cases, of establishing a universal position,[1] noble as this is, but simply to recognise that such a position does need to reflect the context and indeed reality of individuals as they act out their everyday lives. For it is here that the piece of the jigsaw that is the central motivation for this book has been missed: all of these universal principles have simply underestimated the role of children. It is therefore only by asking questions about the relationship between children, society and morality that one can start to offer a view of morality that is inclusive of this key social group. In an effort to seek to establish a backdrop in front of which more applicable musings around morality might take place in relation to children, this work places the individual into a social web in which the acceptability of one's actions is a reflection of a social process in which both internal and external reflections of the self as I and Me play a part. As such, the application of morality must be seen from the individual's perspective, but it also demands that we look at how understandings of morality come to influence and 'structure' how social efforts to manage what is and is not acceptable come to be practised.

It is though looking at the dual themes of structure and agency that childhood studies has the potential to offer a significant contribution to these discourses on morality. For to extend our understanding it is important to look beyond a sole consideration of the social forces that influence all children, on the one hand, and the individual child, on the other. Rather we need to engage with both. In relation to children this has seen a divide between those who recognise a 'singularity' to childhood (James 2010) and those who pursue the 'plurality' of childhoods. It is a divide that is marked by an emphasis on the key concepts of structure and agency. James illustrates this by drawing from the work of Qvortrup, who has provided a consistent voice in favour of a structural approach that recognises the universality, and thus the singularity, of childhood. It is a direct attack on the desire to pursue a 'complex uniqueness' that sees Qvortrup seek to distinguish the need for an ongoing 'singular' focus on that which makes childhood studies, childhood studies: that power divide between adults and children. It is, thus, within a political discourse that 'plurality' is seen as a weak partner because it shifts the focus away from what makes childhood the same, to what makes *them* different.

The singularity of childhood offers focus but in so doing, as James suggests, it hides realities. It denies the importance of the everyday particularities of children's lives, although not denying that these are played out in structural frameworks that carry an element of universality. Indeed, as the argument builds, so it becomes clear that structure alone cannot provide an effective explanation of the relationship between children and adults, let alone other aspects of children's lives. The former is an approach that is firmly connected to the positioning of children in relation to 'age' yet, as James argues, age alone carries with it socially-constructed features that impact on the role that adults and children take up in different spaces,

> To engage with such age based distinctions, which vary from culture to culture, does not mean that we must accede to the influence of developmentalism; however, to ignore the social reality of such distinctions by seeking theoretical refuse in the singularity thesis would be to side step a major theoretical challenge that clearly faces childhood studies. Instead, we must move beyond the struggle between competing theoretical positions and engage in the task of developing a conceptual framework that will enable the integration of what are, all too often, presented as oppositional perspectives. (491)

James, therefore, makes the case for a 'fabric of childhood studies' (492) in which the different theoretical elements can be woven together, with the threads of the 'fabric' reflecting a number of dimensions of the conceptual debate. In short, because I will return to this later, James takes those commonalities – those singular dimensions of childhood – and argues that they become the weft, the stronger threads that run lengthwise. These sit in contrast to the warp, which interlace with the weft and reflect the uniqueness of children's lives.

> In terms of constructing research and of analysing social policies and social practices in relation to children and childhood, this has some important implications. Rather than simply focusing on and exploring the experiences, relationships and agency of a child or group of children at a micro level and charting what differentiates these from those of other children, such an approach would require us to chart how that child's experiences are framed at a macro level by the commonalities of childhood – social stratification, culture, gender, generational relations etc – that set them aside from adults, before exploring the impact of their agency and of the many other factors that create the diversity of their daily lives in different social, cultural, religious, political or economic contexts. The importance of this lies in the fact that it enables us to focus upon and understand the ways in which children's agency is not only constrained but can also be enabled by structural and other influences and that, although children may be set aside from adults, they are not, should not and cannot be set apart from adults. (494)

It is this hybrid version of structure and agency that is to be the driving force behind this investigation in which both structure and agency come to be seen to inform each other and are far more than separate entities. It is a desire to explore the application of these ideas and to see what they look like in practice that offers a framework for an investigation of children and morality.

In many ways, our engagement with morality reflects elements of this model that James applies to childhood. There is the constructed and universal understanding of morality that informs ways in which practice has been done, is done and will be done. This then needs to be contrasted with the application by the individual of moral decision-making in children's day-to-day lives. It is a desire to recognise the need for these different dimensions, a structural perspective and an awareness of individual agency, and particularly to understand the relationship between the two in the context of children's lives that provides the following chapters with their focus.

2.2   Structuring of Morality

By using structure and agency as analytical vehicles it is possible to start considering the relationship between children and morality and how this plays out in their everyday lives. These themes will continue to emerge as the chapters develop. The focus within this chapter, however will be to consider this relationships between children, structure, agency and morality as it has developed over the last 100 or so years, before considering more directly how one might come to apply the lessons from this journey.

2.2.1   Structure as the Source of Causality: Durkheim

The desire to make sense of morality was a dominant theme in the formative years of sociology as a discipline. Sociology, in contrast to other areas of philosophical thought, was asking questions about how communities, in their broadest sense, present, preserve and perpetuate a social order that defines and shapes a society, and it was with reference to the 'structure' of society that answers were offered. It was at the start of the twentieth century, in the context of a disparate and chaotic French society, that Emile Durkheim set to work, with a particular focus on 'morality' and a desire to test out this emerging discipline by exploring the impact of social forces on people's everyday lives. In contrast to Marx and Weber, Durkheim sought to develop an understanding of society that could bring about positive change (Lee and Newby 1983). He offered a 'scientific' model that could provide direction to a society searching for answers.

Durkheim's intervention into the discourse on morality was taking place as 'morality' itself was going through one of its many regenerations. Freud had been seeking to place morality only in the realm of the subconscious as, for him, early experiences alone were to be relied on to shape one's moral direction, with obvious limitations for the social scientist. This sat alongside Kantian thinking, which was also shaking up the previously accepted sources for moral thought because it gave the individual (not children) capacity for moral decision-making. This challenged a domain that had been closely guarded by the church (Lukes 1973) in which the voice of the 'outsider' was not to be encouraged. Durkhiem, a man who did not disguise his differences with the Catholic church, believed that he was in a position to offer a moral approach that was more grounded in the realm of the people rather than that of mystery (Lukes 1973).

At the heart of Durkheim's approach were his efforts to construct thinking on morality that saw it framed within the fabric of society itself, as a product of social structure. This link between structure and the nature of moral action is illustrated particularly clearly in his study of suicide (Durkheim 1951), which paved the way for thinking that impacted areas such as crime and deviance. Here, Durkheim argued that human action should be considered with reference to a social dimension rather than an ongoing reliance on biology and psychology, and that this understanding could be framed with reference to the way in which various social structures exerted a moral force on the actions of the individual. This is highlighted by the way he defines mechanical and organic solidarity – two forms of social cohesion that were separated by the coming of industrialisation. Mechanic solidarity saw societies forming a 'conscience collective' as a response to their deeply held place in small identifiable communities. The norms and values of these communities being clear and easily transmitted, 'although this constraining moral force was external to the individual – in the form of "social facts"[2] – through a process of socialisation it came to be internalised' (Tierney 1996: 83). Not only does this point to the transmission of morality through a structural force ('social facts'), it also suggests that the way of engaging with these facts is through a process of social inculcation, one that welcomes those who conform and punishes those that do not.

This way of thinking sits in contrast to 'organic' solidarity in which the transmission of moral forces is not as clearly defined. Organic solidarity becomes marked by the individual's growing sense of wishing to act outside of a shared solidarity as they demonstrate a new-found sense of being an individual. Notably this sense of freedom is structurally created, rather than reflecting any particular additional competence on the part of the individual. Organic solidarity thus saw the individual moving away from that easily defined sense of their 'moral' roots, neatly structured in the model of the past, as they became party to a greater variety of structural patterns which could influence the transmission of moral order in different ways. This change in structure was a weakness which left Durkheim demanding that society needed to re-establish that sense of moral direction in order to maintain social order, otherwise it would result in 'anomie' (a society of no moral constraints). Here, moral forces remained as important, they were just not so explicit. Each of Durkheim's interpretations of suicide[3] highlighted a sense in which morality drew from a wider sense of the structure that surrounded the individual, impacting on their actions.

Because Durkheim saw morality as a product of social structures it was, therefore, a tool for society to use in order to manage its congregation. It gave meaning to opportunities for action that allowed members to demonstrate solidarity and cohesiveness, whilst at the same time providing markers to regulate because personal ambition was restrained. For Durkheim, the moral processes of the individual were 'set apart', definable and identifiable, whilst at the same time being a completely unconscious aspect of daily action (in keeping with a Freudian approach).

These [moral] judgements are instilled in normal adult consciousness; we find them fully formed within us…faced with a moral or immoral act the individual reacts spontaneously and even unconsciously. It seems to him that this reaction springs from the depths of his nature; we praise or we blame by instinct, as if we could not know otherwise. That is why we so often imagine moral consciousness as a sort of voice within us, without our knowing as a rule what this voice is or whence its authority derives. (Durkheim 1978: 191–192)

Morality, significantly, was something that happens to the individual (notably those of normal adult mind), such that actions can be defined as 'predetermined' (Lukes 1973: 112), as a system of distinct rules, or structures, within which norms are created and actions regulated.

As such, a capacity for 'moral' engagement was recognised in each 'normal' adult who, as a result of their presence within society, was instilled with this 'unconscious' yet definable attribute that provided the individual with a constant tool through which to assess action and therefore frame reactions within the everyday. Framing these processes of morality was 'structure'. Jenks (1996) comments that:

> [Durkheim] marked out their [sociologists] identifiable characteristics and the conceptual space that they occupied as he sought to devalue all other attempts to explain 'social reality'. Thus we arrive at a kernel idea for sociology, that of 'social structure'; it is from this concept that the discipline proceeds. (Jenks 1996: 34)

To engage sociologically with themes of morality, those 'rules' that shape and give meaning to our interactions, one must, therefore, engage with structure and through this also recognise its relationship with the individual. As Durkheim suggests, structure is instrumental in transmitting morality and instilling this in the individual. As a result of the preeminence of structure within this model, if society was structured correctly, then the individual would receive and also emit the commonly held values of that society, creating the desired harmony that Durkheim believed was possible.

Durkheim's structural model demanded that effective transmission be based on certain psychological and physiological criteria. Not all members of society, therefore, were seen as being capable of engaging with the 'moral consciousness' mentioned above. Using a present-day analogy, it meant that there was a subsection of society that could be characterised as 'hardware' that was not yet configured to support the necessary 'operating systems' required to allow it to respond to the challenges of the social world. Without the correct software, it could not receive the 'structural' cues that were required in order to be seen as 'morally' competent. Children fitted into this category: they were asocial, and as a result stood outside of a Durkheimian model of social order. To Durkheim, the child was beset by a natural 'weakness' in body and mind and an inner compulsion for change which he called 'mobility'. The result was that Durkheim summed up the child's moral ability as follows:

> The child's expressions of will are the faintest of impressions and are scarcely traces. As a rule, neither good nor evil is very deep-rooted in his nature; he is incapable of great and sustained effort; good resolutions are no sooner made than forgotten. But, at the same time, what eagerness greets every novelty! This diminutive conscience is a veritable kaleidoscope. The most varied mental state, the most contradictory passions and attitudes follow one another in succession; laughter gives way to tears, playful submissiveness to stubborn resistance, outbursts of tenderness to explosions of anger. These passions and enthusiasms wane just as quickly as they are aroused. Nothing is ever definitive. Everything is continually made and unmade. (Durkheim 1978: 148)

As a result, the child becomes a project through which society can fulfil its mission for sustainability. A predisposition for habit forming and suggestibility (see Wyness 2012) meant that society had a particular role to play in bringing 'order' into the lives of its children because the child still needed to 'learn to regulate and co-ordinate his actions' (Durkheim 1978: 149). The child is therefore, a weak link in society's efforts to establish a collective sense of values. Structure offers a framework that, for Durkheim, transmitted morality to its functioning members. Those members then had a responsibility to ensure that children were exposed to the proper structures so that in time they would receive and understand the collective values of society.

Durkheim highlighted clearly the association between the social 'context' and moral action. As a result it offered a starting point that not only impacted sociology and the different foci within it, but it also directly influenced criminology as seen in the early work of the Chicago School, as it sought to make sense of individual action as a response to social structure.

2.2.2 Inculcation Through Socialisation

Durkheim had established a very clear model in which structure played the dominant role in framing the moral order on behalf of the members of that society. Although Durkheim did mention children, it was the work of Talcott Parsons (1951) which really explored how this structural approach to social order related to children. Parsons also believed in structure as the key means through which society reproduced itself. As a result, children needed to be drawn into these social structures, a process by which 'volatility is stabilised, its [the child's] riotousness quelled' (Jenks 1996: 13). Thus the child retains that sense of being asocial (and to differing extents amoral), of being unpredictable and, as a result, a threat to the efficient maintenance of social norms. In this model social order remained the constant, drawing on Durkheimian roots by which 'society becomes the monitor for all order and it further inculcates a set of rules of conduct, which are enforced less by individual will and political sovereignty, than by society's own pre-existence' (Jenks 1996: 13).

In order to be 'inculcated', the child needed to be part of society, to 'learn' from the structures that society had so 'effectively' created. For children 'socialisation' was the means through which those value patterns were 'laid down' as norms were set. Indeed, the mechanistic processes of transformation that Parsons identified demanded that the child went through a 'change', a distinct step as they were brought into the 'adult' world. In defining the stages of socialisation, Parsons refers to terms such as 'extinction' and 'substitution' as children learn to reframe the meaning they attach to action by drawing on different cues. Reward and punishment clearly play an important part because the adult, as enforcer, controls this process which, if successfully completed, sees 'common values internalised in ego's personality' (Parsons 1951: 142). In effect, what Parsons offers to Durkheim's original approach is a vehicle – 'socialisation' – which imparts those moral codes to children, preparing them for the role of effective adult. Throughout, children are seen as nothing more than cogs in a machine (Jenks 1996), as they are shaped and moulded to fit within a defined structure.

Parsons offers a model for understanding morality that places the spotlight firmly on the composition of the different spaces within which children live their lives. The child's role within this was to absorb the appropriate cues that that structure offered, allowing them to 'learn' how to participate in society. Indeed, Parsons' approach had taken him further than Durkheim in stressing the power of structure over the individual.

For Parsons, social norms were therefore not only regulative but, ultimately, constitutive of human nature, a process that took place through the individual internalising sets of norms. In Parsons' hands it was the internalisation of social norms and values that became therefore, the explanatory lynchpin for solving the big question of the time (Musgrave 1987): how is social order maintained and how are social structures perpetuated. (James 2013: 27)

This focus, as James (2013) assesses through the eyes of Dennis Wrong (1961), presented the individual in a very particular way, one that was argued to misrepresent the very nature of human beings. At the centre of this was Parsons' approach to 'internalisation'. For Parsons this was a process that was linked to 'learning' in its blandest sense and 'habit formation' (James 2013). As a result, norms were adopted without going through any process of self-reflection and assessment. It created a model in which structure becomes the defining factor in shaping that sense of 'social order' that the individual child carries into the 'adult world'. Morality, as reflected in the transmission of norms for example, is a product of this positioning of the individual within structure. It offers a uni-directional relationship between structure and the individual child, and, consequently, their adoption of moral understandings. This is reflected in Fig. 2.1.

The significance of this 'one way' model becomes more clear when it is contrasted to later ways of thinking. However, it highlights an important approach that reflects ongoing dominant attitudes towards children that haunt our engagement with children and morality. Within this, the role of adults is to ensure that children are experiencing their childhood within the confines of spaces that have been effectively created by adults.

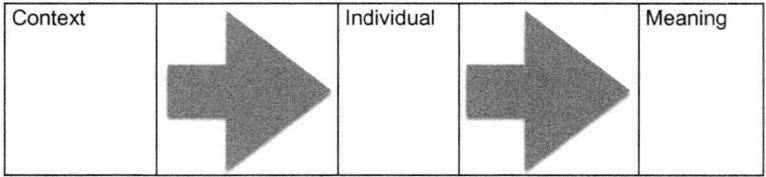

Fig. 2.1 Uni-directional arrow

If these institutions have been created correctly then they should result in the right kind of adult in the future. It highlights the importance of the institution as a defining feature of a child's moral journey, a theme that is ever present in discourses today. Notably, it is the amount of weight that is given to the one-directional nature of these institutions that becomes key, and as will be seen in later chapters, it is a model that has been used, and is still used, to emphasise an adult-centric approach to moral engagement that maintains the child as a project rather than a partner.

2.2.3   Children as Rational Thinkers?

As Parsons' model of socialisation evolved questions started to emerge about the total reliance on this uni-directional way of thinking, particularly in relation to self-reflection. The notion of the self-reflective actor is an important one that has implications for the discussion of morality. As we have already seen, the level of engagement that is given to the role of the individual has varied. Durkheim was clear that morality was inextricabbly linked to being social: 'we are moral beings only to the extent to which we are social beings' (Durkheim 1979). However, it was the collective that was shaping and defining that sense of order, a process of constructing meaning over which the individual had little influence. As Jenks (1996) notes, because of the attention given to structure within sociological investigation as the 'supra-individual source of causality' (Jenks 1996: 35) the individual was sidelined, their importance rejected in light of the weight of structural forces that govern their actions. The result was the habit forming, rule-following creature that Parsons created. However, despite all this, the individual continued to have an awkward presence and therefore what emerges is a qualified view of the child and their capacity for moral engagement that is linked to stages of their development.

Indeed Elkin's *The Child and Society* (1960) examined this theme of self-reflection in the context of socialisation. Drawing on Parsons' broad model that children lived within structures which came to socialise them into society, Elkin presented a version of the child which, although remaining limited, did acknowledge some of these themes of self-reflection.

In sum the child learns roles and socialised behaviour through a combination of techniques, but the direction of development depends basically on the reaction of others and the development of a self. (1960: 35)

The key here is that socialisation takes place as part of a process of development in which the child goes through certain levels of competence before reaching their final goal. For Elkin, in his initial work, socialisation was seen as a 'process by which someone learns the ways of a given society or social group, so that he can function within it' (1960: 4). This model, therefore, provided a means for the 'normal' child to 'learn' the ways of the adult and in time to take up their role as an acolyte of social order as they embraced the 'patterns, symbols, expectations and feelings of the surrounding world' (1960: 5) and ultimately passed them on to another generation. Throughout, this 'learning' is presented as nothing more than a natural awakening or realisation. Indeed, in suggesting the 'stages of socialisation', Elkin draws directly from the work of psychologist, Jean Piaget.

Piaget had, some years previously, begun to look directly at themes around morality and rules through his study of children playing marbles (Piaget 1935). As were others at the time, Piaget was seeking a way to explain moral processes within children. Kant had helpfully provided a model of morality that recognised the individual, but he had stopped short of considering what this meant in relation to children. And despite the fact that others within his discipline (Freud for example) were considering morality from a very different perspective, Piaget sought to make sense of this obvious gap in understanding, notably by engaging with children themselves (this is considered in more detail in Chap. 5). However, there was an important theme within Piaget's work that socialisation theorists and others relied upon to support a staged assessment of children's competence, and consequently their capacity for moral engagement. The heart of Piaget's argument was that it was only at a certain point (in a universal, predictable and biological journey through life) that the child developed an ability to 'reason'. Reason had an established place within moral discourses as a marker of moral capacity, and its application to different groups within society had been fought over for many thousands of years. Despite the gift of reason being granted to other groups within society, the child in Piaget's assessment continued to remain 'without reason' until they were 12 years old. Again this raises many wider discussions, which have also been dealt with elsewhere (see also Archard 2004) and will be revisited later, but ultimately it created a position that excluded the child from playing any active part in moral discourses.

For Elkin this meant that the child was to be seen not in the context of an adult mind yet to develop, but as operating in a world of their own within which certain biological stages impacted on their moral awareness and a gradual recognition of the self and others.

> A child until he adequately matures is not able to realise that moral judgements of behaviour need not be absolute. At first the young child views right as the will of the adult, later he judges behaviour in terms of its consequences and only still later is he capable of placing himself in the position of others and judging by their motives or intentions. (1960: 22–23)

The limitations on children as moral meaning-makers results in the transmission of morality being seen through a restricted focus on the adoption of rules and norms which promotes the child as passively imitating rather than actively processing. Thus it is experiences of predictable patterns that will bring the child within society's sense of social order. Framed by a recognition of 'norms' (patterns of behaviour) and an ability to make sense of their status (their position in the structure) and role (expected behaviour as a result of status), a child with an 'adequate biological nature' (Elkin 1960: 10) could/would be socialised. This ability to learn through others is an important part of Elkin's position because the purpose of relationships, and indeed (to some extent) feelings and emotions, is recognised in shaping an understanding of the social rules. It is by placing these relationships into 'key agencies' (with 'agencies' here referring to 'spaces') that children are able to gather a range of different and varied information that equips them for their role in society.

> Each agency socialises the child into its own patterns and its own values. The family has certain rituals, the school its rules of order, the child peer group its codes and games, and the media of mass communication their traditional forms and story plots. Moreover, each agency – and this is more

significant for our purposes – helps to socialise the child into the larger world. Parents, teachers, peers, and mass media are surrogates of wider social and cultural orders, and their impact extends beyond their own organisational limits. (Elkin 1960: 45)

Ultimately we are left with a model that offers a staged approach to children's engagement in the world around them as they gather and build understandings (through this process of socialisation). Although aspects of Elkin's case reflect a greater sense of the individual, the child is still limited in their capacity to engage with, rather than simply to respond to, structure.

Five decades later, socialisation as a concept remains but Elkin and others (Handel et al. 2007) present the notion of a rather more competent child. Here greater reference is made to the child reflecting on the social world around them. However, significantly, this analysis of socialisation does not mention 'morality', although implied throughout. It is, therefore, important first to consider *why* this change and *how* this affects, or not, our conception of socialisation as a tool for understanding children, and second to explore *where* 'morality' is now as a focus within such sociological approaches.

2.3   Agency '&' Structure

For both Parsons and Piaget (although perhaps to a lesser extent), children's 'moral' development was based on them being shaped by a force that was beyond their control (structural or biological, respectively). However, outside of these investigations into children, questions had already begun to be asked about the pre-eminence of structure. Turner reflects on this gradual journey to thinking about smaller and smaller groups, moving from Marx to Durkheim to Simnel to Goffman (Turner 1986). As these arguments continued to build, what emerged was recognised by some as being nothing short of a revolution in which the old school's notion of the 'mechanistic' man (Crick 1976) came to be redefined and recharacterised in favour of a competence for meaning-making that had been ignored. Crick, writing in relation to language, was not alone in calling for researchers to re-engage with the causes of behaviour (Crick 1976: 93). Were these causes structurally determined or individually constructed? For Crick, it was the latter. He argued that social life must be seen in terms of 'the creation and negotiation of meaning' where 'in the new paradigm, human beings are convention making, theory constructing, rule following creatures' (Crick 1976: 88).

This shift in emphasis cannot be overstated. Giddens (1979) and others (see Thompson and Tunstall 1971) from within sociology, also looked to support this challenge by increasing attention on the reflective, interactive ability of the individual to engage with, indeed even shape, structure as defined by the process of 'agency'. Here the 'cultural' dope of the past was replaced by an active social player. Structure, therefore, was not seen to be defining in and of itself. For Giddens, structure developed out of the actions and interactions of the individual, creating a 'system' of rules and resources that could easily be reproduced. The individual was being characterised as a feature in the creation and re-creation of meaning. This was not to dismiss structure or to promote agency ahead of it, rather it was a call for agency and structure to be recognised as mutually dependent. For Giddens, this meant a 'duality' to structure and agency such that they could not be separated. Such a position was not without challenge, notably, this contrasts with the work of Margaret Archer (1982) who, rather than arguing for a duality, called for a 'dualism' (Ritzer 2011). She proposed that structure and agency must and should be separated because, without that, one was not able to look effectively at the relationship between the two.

Giddens, as noted above, was not the only one looking to redefine this relationship.[4] For Bourdieu (1977) the relationship between structure and agency came to impact on the individual, both in terms of their internalised sense of 'habitus' but also in relation to the fields (or networks) in which they found themselves. For Habermas (1987), this was played out through a consideration of the 'life world' – the space for interaction – and the systems that emerge from it which ultimately come to frame or 'colonise' the life world itself, with implications for individual agency. Despite differences in these perspectives, the unifying factor was that structure and agency were being considered alongside one another. This sits in contrast to so much earlier sociological thinking that was characterised by a mutually exclusive division between structure and agency. Kirchberg (2007) typifies this through the terms *homo oeconomicus* and *homo sociologicus*. The latter is 'compelled to operate in light of strong role expectation' (2007: 116), a product of theorists such as Durkheim and Parsons, as the actor comes to be driven by 'norms'. Here peer relationships are key as the individual seeks for and finds guidance in understanding and drawing from those norms. *Homo oeconmicus* is not constrained by those norms but is in 'full' control: 'on this micro sociological view, rational actors freely and self consciously exercise decision making capacities' (2007: 117). However, what is really interesting about this discussion is not the way in which these two views are held at arms' length, but the extent to which Kirchberg draws them together, emphasising their similarities. He places Bourdieu's work and Giddens' work side by side. However, the defining product of this placement is the extent to which neither theory works by simply championing structure or agency, rather structure and agency must be acknowledged in both.

2.3.1 Positioning Children

In relation to children, however, the argument for the coming together of structure and agency still needed to be made. The work of Parsons, Piaget and others had created an approach in which children remained the product of structure. Part of the challenge to get children's agency recognised lay in the way in which reason was perceived. Reason, as we have seen above (and which is discussed in more detail in Chap. 5), was a focus not only for the psychologists but also the sociologists, and offered a shared perspective on children's capacity that was linked to their journey through the life course. Since Darwin (1877), and indeed before (and continuing to this day), biology had offered a staged view of children's lives in which competence was attached to their position at each step of their life journey. In its simplest form, competence (as defined by the developmental model) was not fully achieved until one reached adulthood, thereby marking childhood as a time summed up by children's 'lack' and resulting in a limited and partial view of the developing future adult. The stranglehold of this view would need to be broken if any sense of agency was to be acknowledged for children.

However, pulled along by a particular head of steam that started to build towards the end of the 1970s, scholars were asking questions that challenged the notion of the child as simply a product of structure (Donaldson and McGarrigle 1975; Donaldson and Hughes 1979). International events, such as the Year of the Child in 1979 and the introduction of the United Nations Convention on the Rights of the Child (1989), offered a platform to reassess the way in which we thought about the child, a position for which anthropologist Charlotte Hardman (and many others, notably Bluebond-Langner (1978)) had been pressing by arguing that the child should 'be studied in their own right, and not just as receptacles of adult teaching' (1973: 87). It was about moving beyond the universal and passive child to seeing the child interacting with their social world in shaping and constructing meanings. This approach sees children as 'beings', having a role to play in the here and now, and not simply as 'becomings', a product being prepared for the future (Lee 2001). The notions of being and becoming and their reference to 'lack' are highly significant within a broader discussion around children and morality. For so long, indeed even before Piaget, reason had been used as a theme to place children outside of such discourses. In practice, children were regarded as 'lacking' because they were not 'ready' to engage with such issues (Short 1999). The challenge, therefore, was to question this sense of 'lack' and with it our very understandings of children and childhood.

The developing work around children established that 'reason' as a defining factor needed to be questioned (Hardman 1973; Bluebond-Langner 1978; James and Prout 1990). As the case for the child's active nature within social relations took on greater prominence, the idea that children were only capable of a higher level of thought on reaching a certain age or having passed through a set of experiences, no longer made sense. Rather, reason needed to be reconsidered alongside an understanding of children's agency.

2.3.2 Reconsidering Socialisation

In the Parsonian model, structure was presented as clear and distinct from the individual. It meant that, the 'normal' child placed into 'normal' agencies (noting again the definition of 'agencies' as relating to institutions), will result, as is society's aim, in that individual becoming a law-abiding citizen (Handel et al. 2007). This model, however, sits in opposition to the 'new paradigm' (see Fig. 2.2). As part of challenging the sense of children's competence through acknowledging their active role in social interaction, it recognised them as 'agents'. If, as argued earlier, the result of the work of Giddens and others was to establish a new association between the individual and structure, then if children were agents why would this not apply to them? James and James (2004) (see also James 2013) respond directly to this by drawing from Giddens' structuration theory as they highlight the need for thinking on children and the relationship between structure and agency by considering time and individual action. In relation to the former, an acceptance of time as creating a moment for analysis limits the extent to which individuals can be separated from the social structures they are seen to reproduce. For children, the temporal aspect is particularly nuanced because their experiences are taking place within the wider context of an enduring social construct that is childhood. It leads James and James to conclude:

> This twin temporal framing of each individual who passes through 'childhood' has therefore to be taken into account, we argue, in terms of both agency and structure and as an ongoing and interwoven experience. (James and James 2004: 39)

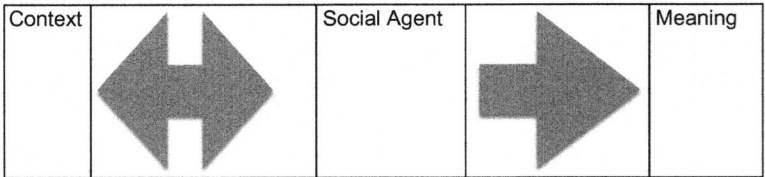

Fig. 2.2 Bi-directional arrow

The second factor – individual action – focuses on Gidden's view of the reflective nature of individual consciousness in which actions reaffirm social reproduction through the individual's choices. James and James thereby establish a marker that emphasises the interaction between structure and the individual, specifically in relation to children. In direct contrast to Parsons, the need for the individual to be engaged in and responding to the world around them forms a significant part of the process for agentic action. It is a position that sits uncomfortably alongside the traditional notion of socialisation. However, in her book, *Socialising Children*, Allison James (2013) asks whether the perspective of socialisation can be looked at more from the point of view of the child. In so doing, James continues to acknowledge 'context', as previous socialisation theorists had done, but she does this by suggesting a more interactive engagement between structure and the individual as an agent.

As such, structure effectively offers a backdrop with which the individual connects as part of framing their own 'performance'. The agent is seen as someone who is actively processing their identity or sense of 'personal life' in the context of the interactional settings in which they find themselves. The emergence of a sociology of 'personal life' (Smart 2007; May 2010) presents the idea that the individual has a set of personal 'elements' that they bring to a process of meaning-making as the individual acts or reacts in response to the wider contexts of the settings within which everyday life is experienced. Personal life, therefore, seeks to characterise and legitimise (for the sake of our arguments here) the need to recognise the formation and re-formation of the self in the context of interaction, as the individual responds to those different 'elements' that make up *their* personal life, forming a very individualised basis for meaning-making.

Smart (2007) summarises 'personal life' as follows:

> To live a personal life is to have agency and to make choices, but the personhood implicit in the concept requires the presence of others to respond to and to contextualise those actions and choices. Personal life is a reflexive state, but it is not private and it is lived out in relation to one's class position, ethnicity, gender and so on. (Smart 2007: 28)

As such we are presented with a different model to the uni-directional approach highlighted earlier, one that sees the individual processing and re-processing the 'context' in relation to what they, as an individual, bring to a particular setting.

It is arguably the addition of the double-headed arrow (see Fig. 2.2) that highlights the most significant contribution of childhood studies to our understandings of children. It illustrates the extent to which the individual must be seen to be bringing 'something' to structure. It is seeking to understand what it is that the individual brings to structure, and how this has implications for the way in which they respond to it, that offers a significant reinterpretation of children and the part they play in society.

It is a change that, according to James, allows for more nuanced questions around socialisation to be asked. James sums this up:

> In brief, it [analysis of a child-centered approach to socialisation] means trying to see from children's perspectives – from their status position as children in society – what the experience of growing up is like. It means asking about the things that are regarded by them as important in their lives and why; it means showing how, in the course of their everyday lives, children encounter people, ideas, events and policy interventions that in some way or another have an effect on them, or not, as the case may be, and asking why they do or don't. It means assuming that children grow up in society, not outside it and in some marginal and separated childhood zone. It also entails recognising that because children are participants in the social world, what they do or say can have an effect on other people, ideas, events and also on the ways in which policy interventions in their lives take root or not. It means acknowledging too that it is most often through the mundane and pedestrian pattern of everyday life, rather than through dramatic biographical events, that children get to know how the social world works and the parts they can play in it. Taking a child centred perspective to socialisation, as can be seen from all the above, means therefore also embracing the uncertainty and ambiguity of the growing up process and, in the end, having perhaps to wait and see how it is that children do eventually turn out (Davis 2011). There are no certainties to rely on. (James 2013: 174)

As well as giving a sense of what James means when she refers to socialisation, the bi-directional approach also provides a challenge. It is a particular way of thinking that stands in contrast to the approach of Parsonian socialisation. Within this model, James is suggesting that socialisation needs to take greater account of the way in which the individual develops meaning, recognising the range of characteristics they bring to interaction and the different settings in which these interactions take place. It suggests that what the individual brings to socialisation 'matters' because this has an impact on the type and nature of the meanings that come to be created. It is this dynamic interpretation of socialisation that will be implied whenever this term is used in this book.

2.4   Implications for Children and Morality

The bi-directional model offers a focus on how we must come to engage with morality in the context of children's lives. It demands that we consider both a structural and an agentic dimension to morality. Although the link between children, morality and structure has been strong, the connection to agency has not been as distinct. A consequence of this in relation to the child is that it maintains the dominance of structure as a defining feature of children's moral 'development'. It is only by establishing a case for a link between the social agent and morality that this imbalance can be challenged. Part of the problem, as Mayall notes, is that society struggles with the concept of children having the capacity to be 'moral'.

> [T]he idea of the child as a moral agent is one we (we adults in the UK) have been taught to find difficult, even a contradiction in terms. The dominant discipline providing knowledge about childhood – developmental psychology – has proposed childhood as a series of stages…though adults who live with children are daily confronted by their moral agency and their lively discussions of moral issues, these adult experiences and these child activities do not form part of the common culture of UK understanding about children. (2002: 87–88)

Mayall here makes a number of points to reflect on. The first is the use of the term 'moral agents', which leads to further questions. What makes someone a moral agent? How does that differ from being a social agent? Is the moral agent different from the social agent, or are these terms indivisible, such that social agency and moral agency are but one, with morality being an expression of the social agent in action? Mayall's second point is that, despite our lack of formal recognition, children are, in their day to day interactions, relying on moral meanings as part of making sense of the social world around them: in their interactions with parents, their siblings, in their routine at school or when they go to the local park or indeed share a photo on Instagram or Facebook. Morality in each of these settings offers meanings that define the actions and behaviours that result.

Despite a seeming reluctance to engage with the notion of morality from those perhaps closest to James and Prout's 'new paradigm', others have sought to wrestle with some of the limitations that have been placed on children in the past. Haste (1999) refers to Vygotsky (see Chap. 4) as providing a bridge to link the social with discourses such as morality by recognising the importance of interaction in shaping the individual's 'development'. Subsequently the focus has been on interaction, and the extent to which morality can be a valid and credible feature in which children are actively involved. This sense of children as participants in the different settings in which they live their lives is a constant feature of investigations of morality (Haste 1999), as it looks at, for example, caring and sharing (Kagan 1986; Dunn 1988; Damon 1990).[5]

Sociology has also sought to address this focus on interaction.[6] In a really interesting body of work that draws originally from Goffman and the desire to understand interaction, research has been developed which provides an insight that pointedly situates morality in the everyday world of the child (Killen and Smetna 2010). Morality in such research has been validated as 'practical', as an integral part of the everyday. Indeed, in laying a foundation on which others have built (Goodwin 2006), Bergmann (1998) presented a powerful case for combining the social and the moral. He argues that the birth of modern science sought, in the context of discourse (here relating to processes of conversation-building), to separate morality from the social. The resulting danger is that social interaction is seen as outside of this moral dimension.

> There is an inevitable and uncomfortable tension between the moral quality of everyday life and the social sciences that strive to study social interaction without taking a moral stance. Within modern moral philosophy this tension is often dissolved by projecting the is and ought dichotomy, which is a constitutive feature of scientific discourse, onto the discourse of ordinary persons in everyday life. One implication of this conception is that it ascribes morality a theory-like status with logically interconnected and hierarchically organised statements of an evaluative or normative kind. But the idea of extracting a grammar of moral judgements from single isolated sentences inevitably leads to a decontextualised notion of morality, which leaves out the most salient feature of the 'lived' morality of everyday life – its practical character. If one wants to get access to the actual practices in which morality comes to life, one has to abandon the philosophical idea of an independent logic of moral language. (Bergmann 1998: 281)

Not only is Bergmann providing some explanation of why morality has been excluded from investigations of children, but he is also suggesting why it should be considered. In the context of his own focus on the meanings within language, Bergmann points to the need to consider the extent to which language has the potential to convey morality through its constant draw on 'lived' morality. Following this lead, this growing body of work (referred to above) (Danby and Theobald 2012; Cromdal and Theolander 2016) is reflecting on the extent to which morality is a meaningful process within children's everyday lives. Here, children are engaged with on the basis that they are 'agents' and, through practical examples, it is shown how morality forms part of the agentic process. These examples take ethnographic research and examine the detail of interactions, and from this they have highlighted the continuous way in which morality is demonstrated in children's lives. An illustration is Sterponi's (2009) study of meal times in Italian families. Through an analysis of a particular aspect of dinner-time conversation, she was able to show how parents through their comments drew an expectation of their child's agency in attaching moral meanings to behaviours. Notably, she places this into a concept of 'socialisation', and refers to the scaffolding that is put in place through children experiencing these interactions. This framework provides a grounding for an ongoing recognition of social order and the norms through which the children can demonstrate their commitment to their family.

This body of work is offering new insights into the moral world that children inhabit. Its focus is on definable aspects of interaction. However, there is also a need for a deeper understanding of what Bergmann called 'lived' morality. In many of the studies, the focus is specific to a given scenario, such as Sterponi's dinner table. Although this grants insight into a particular interaction, it does not paint the full picture. Rather, as is being suggested here, morality needs to be seen within the context of a process of socialisation, one that requires a wider recognition of the relationship between structure and agency.

One must, therefore, engage with the bi-directional exchange between structure and the individual as a social agent. Each social agent will come to a setting with the individualised baggage of personhood, which will then shape how structure comes to be interpreted and meanings come to be made. As a result of engaging with personhood, one comes to consider the layers of meaning that are linked to the individual's sense of self and how that comes to be interpreted in relation to others.

2.5   Conclusion

The 'new paradigm' (James and Prout 1990) offers an examination of what sits behind everyday interactions, the 'context' in which they take place and how it is interpreted in light of those elements that make up a 'personal life'. As such, childhood studies provides a basis for an analysis of the interrelationship of structure and agency as one engages with the notion of a bi-directional arrow representing individuals actively processing the structure around them. It results in structure and agency holding moral dimensions that need to be considered. From a structural perspective, constructed images of the child are imbued with dominant discourses about children and morality. This sits alongside a social agent which, in constructing meanings, searches for ways of acting that recognise the need to perform in a manner that is seen as acceptable. As such the notion of everyday morality places the formation of moral meanings at the centre of a model of identity construction and reconstruction. As such it sees the individual as an agent pulling from and engaging with a whole range of different structural influences to arrive at meanings.

It is, therefore, only by bringing together structure and agency that one can really start to understand children's everyday lives and the practical place of morality within them. This book examines the roles of structure and agency alongside one another in offering a perspective on the relationship between children and morality. It is the application of James' (2010) approach, considered earlier, that demonstrates the importance of childhood studies as a vehicle for investigating the social layers that surround our ability to understand children and morality. It is only by recognising and then analysing these layers that one can start to challenge the dominant discourses around children and morality that have shaped children's experiences for millennia.

Notes

1. Iris Murdoch (1971: 76) suggests that scholarship should encourage the purity of moral philosophy in the same way as 'pointless' historical research. The arguments in this book are not denying the importance of this, however they are marked out from it.
2. Social facts are defined as:

   [a] way of acting, fixed or not, capable of exercising on the individual an influence, or an external constraint; or again, every way of acting which is general throughout a given society, while at the same time existing in its own right independent of its individual manifestations. (Durkheim and Lukes 1982: 59)

3. Egoistic suicide, altruistic suicide, anomic suicide and fatalistic suicide.
4. Ritzer (2011) explores structure and agency in the context of alternative, albeit related, approaches that consider a 'micro–macro integration' and the levels of analysis it offered, alongside efforts to synthesise the theoretical perspectives within sociology in order to heal wounds that had arguably impacted on the development of sociology as a discipline. It highlights how structure and agency must, within childhood studies, be clear in terms of the

theoretical definitions it adopts as it draws from, but distinguishes itself from, alternative ways of engaging with both structure and agency.

5. From a psychological standpoint Schaffer (1996) recognises such actions but defines them as children's recognition of 'social rules'. He distinguishes them from 'moral rules': 'rules relating to morality...are universal...whether there is a social consciousness or not, for they refer to ethical standards common to humanity and are thus obligatory' (268).

6. Wilson (1966) investigates the individual's relationships to rules and treats social relationships as key. The role of the sociologist is then to understand the 'context' within which interaction is happening, and the implications of how those rules come to take on meaning.

Step 2

Establishing a Framework

This part of the book lays out a framework to order an investigation of a moral dimension to children's everyday lives. After this introduction, Chaps. 3 and 4, focused on structure and agency, respectively, will engage in theoretical 'discussions', followed by practical considerations of what each element of the framework might look like when 'applied'.

Chapter 2 showed how Durkheim and others had used the notion of morality as a filter for understanding society. In this approach, the individual is dominated by the force of structure, and the child in particular by their limited capacity, such that an individual's moral journey is determined by forces that are outside of their control. However, if we are to embrace the 'new paradigm' that was presented in the previous chapter, and accept that children's social agency is practised within the context of a given social structure, then how should we think about the child, morality and society?

In this book, morality is being treated as a filter for analysis which, when applied, reveals a layer of the social workings of everyday life that are too often hidden. It challenges a long established notion of traditional socialisation as the recognised means through which the child comes to follow, practise and maintain moral (social) norms. By seeking to identify a backdrop for children's interactions we are encouraged to consider morality as a feature in shaping children's experiences. Here, socialisation becomes the journey of an individual child within which the researcher is asked to pay attention to a wide variety of factors in seeking to investigate that relationship between structure and agency. Notably, the union of structure and agency demands a recognition of the way in which adult musings on children and morality have shaped the context for children's experiences alongside the practical ways in which children, as social agents, engage with morality in negotiating the realities of everyday life.

1.1   Creating a Framework

One of the interesting questions that remains many years after the birth of childhood studies, is 'why is morality as a filter for understanding children and childhood not more prominent?' The 'new paradigm' has provided researchers with a framework to enter children's worlds and search for meanings, which has resulted in research on a multitude of different areas. However, morality as a specific focus in these investigations is not so obvious. The aims of the new framework presented in this book are to recognise the centrality of discourses around morality to the way in which we (as adults) come to both engage with children and also to understand how children themselves make meanings as part of their everyday interactions. The framework (see figure 1 below), therefore, seeks to reflect the idea of the interwoven 'fabric' (James 2010) that results when structure and agency come together (as highlighted at the start of Chap. 2). What the framework offers is a model for viewing morality, both in terms of the structural impact it has on shaping the backdrop for children's experiences, and also as a means to make sense of the experience itself. The framework thus comprises, in Part 1, structure and, in Part 2, agency. However, there is also a third part. It is an element that is not so obvious in the model considered at the start of Chap. 2. Part 3 thus reflects the extent to which children are involved in reinforming structure, so that they can be recognised as agents of potential change (this will be considered in Step 5).

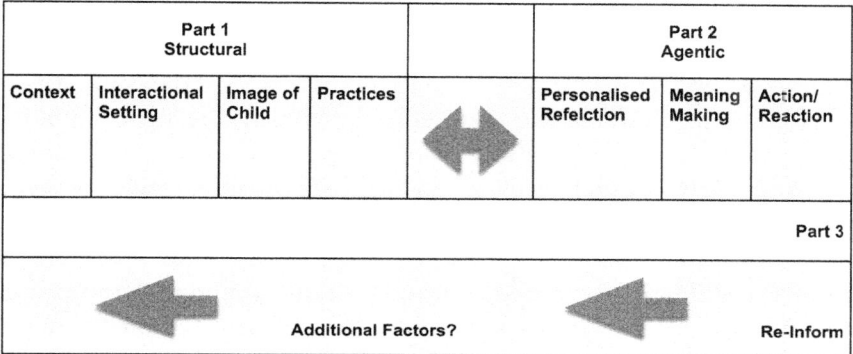

Fig. 1   Framework overview

Despite being presented in parts, the framework is interlinked. In order to make sense of children's everyday lives it is important to consider the way in which the wider context of society comes to inform the setting in which the child finds themselves (Part 1). The argument is that this setting will hold (albeit in a dynamic fashion) a moral image of the child which will shape the way in which the individual comes to be positioned in that space with implications for the design and implementation of any practices that involve the child. It is into this context that the individual in Part 2 finds themselves having to make meaning which leads to their responses (both active and passive). It is a model that can change continually because children's actions and reactions, as well as a similar process in adults, have the potential to reinform the structural dimension (Part 3), changing the backdrop with implications for the basis on which meanings are made.

Chapters 3 and 4 focus on Parts 1 and 2 of the framework.

In making the case for Part 1 of the framework, one must, therefore, recognise the socially constructed nature of childhood and the extent to which within this there are moral understandings which shape the way in which the child comes to be represented. It is the desire to identify this that sits behind the way in which the model is drawn up. It recognises that children interact in a range of settings. These settings will be influenced in different ways by the wider context that is society, but, notably, as a result of this within each setting a particular 'moral' image of the child will be constructed. This framework, therefore, encourages the researcher to look at the relationship between the social forces that inform an interactional space, the constructed images of the child that are established within them and the practices to which this way of thinking leads. The result is that children perform their agency within a context that is defined by socially engineered images of the moral child. By looking to understand this, one can get a sense of what informs practices that develop within certain settings and, as we add Part 2, how this comes to influence children's meaning-making. The model acknowledges that different interactional settings will see different constructed moral images of the child. Although each setting is exposed to the wider context and the forces that it holds, the arenas within which interactions take place will draw from that context, uniquely creating a micro structure that is informed and informing a moral image of the child. Although this image is not static, it does offer a means through which adults can establish practices which will have an effect on children's experiences.

The second part of the framework focuses on the processes involved in agency. Having considered the way in which practices for children come to be established through constructed moral images, one then needs to consider how children act as social agents in front of this backdrop. Indeed, it will be suggested that an integral aspect of the agentic process involves the individual seeking to manage meanings through reflecting on questions of everyday morality. It will be argued that within this process of meaning-making children are actively involved in making 'moral' decisions as they 'weigh up' the elements of both structure and agency, and seek to perform an action or reaction that, within that context, carries an assessment of its social acceptability. This part of the framework reflects the extent to which the individual child is processing meaning as a response to the structural context in which they find themselves. This process of meaning-making draws directly from the personal 'elements' that they bring with them into an interaction. As the individual responds to the 'context' through the 'personal elements', a moral dimension comes to inform meaning-making and the subsequent action or reaction. Fundamentally this part of the model seeks to personalise the way in which the individual responds to the structure around them. It is a view of the agentic process that provides the means through which to consider more fully the individual nuances that affect meaning-making and the moral interpretations, judgements and understandings that the individual brings to their day-to-day life.

3

Engaging with Structure

3.1 Discussion

Part 1 of the framework suggests that an engagement with structure provides a starting point from which to consider individual action. This chapter examines the backdrop that the social agent comes to engage with as part of negotiating interactions. It is a backdrop that reflects the extent to which understandings around the child are based on constructed images which have been shaped by a range of social factors. Our intial focus, therefore is on the socially constructed nature of childhoods, with specific reference to the moral images of the child that this process creates.

3.1.1 Establishing a Context

In order to establish a sense of 'context' for structure and recognise this moral dimension, one must acknowledge the constructed nature of childhood.

> [C]hildhood is understood as a social construction. As such it provides an interpretive frame for contextualising the early years of human life.

© The Editor(s) (if applicable) and The Author(s) 2017

S. Frankel, *Negotiating Childhoods*, Studies in Childhood and Youth,
DOI 10.1057/978-1-137-32349-1_3

Childhood, as distinct from biological immaturity, is neither a natural or universal feature of human groups but appears as a specific structural and cultural component of many societies. (James and Prout 1997: 8)

Therefore, childhood as a term demands that we position children through an understanding that both their experience of being a child and our understanding of what a child is (with the range of etcetera's that might be linked to this) is shaped by the particular context that the child or adult finds themselves in.

The realisation of the contextual importance is strongly highlighted by Jenk's efforts to deconstruct childhood (1996) as he looks at the relationship between structure and social order and how this frames thinking towards the child.[1] Jenks argues that for too long we have been sidetracked by the idea that growing up is the point of being a child. However, he suggests that we need to move beyond this and to recognise the 'context' of childhood.

[C]hildhood is not a brief physical inhibition of a Lilliputian world owned and ruled by others, childhood is rather a historical and cultural experience and its meaning, its interpretations and its interests reside within such contexts. These contexts, these social structures, become our topic. (1996: 61)

That call to explore and to capture that 'context' in some way is our initial focus. It is not surprising that, in making the case for 'context', Jenks draws from the work of historians who have offered a range of literature that has enriched and furthered the way in which we understand the relationship between the child and the social setting. By looking at this research, themes quickly emerge that show not only the wider contextual dimension of childhood but also the extent to which morality is a feature of such discussions.

That sense in which childhood is impacted by 'context', as it is culturally defined within time and space, is one of the important contributions of Aries' *The Centuries of Childhood* (1962). Aries suggested that it was not until after the Middle Ages that the notion of 'childhood' came into existence as a recognised stage in the individual's journey through life. Although acknowledging the criticism placed at Aries' door in relation to this (Jenks 1996), one must at least acknowledge the two important contributions made by his work. One was in claiming the term 'childhood' and establishing it as a concept through which this moment of the individual's life can be considered. The second is the extent to which his work draws on the cultural diversity of time and space, with the result that children can be seen to have very different experiences as a result of that context. Aries illustrates this, for example, through attitudes to games and pastimes, and how these reflected certain moral attitudes to which parents aligned themselves (or not).

> The high regard in which games of chance were still held in the seventeenth century enables us to gauge the extent of the old attitude of moral indifference. Nowadays we regard games of chance as suspect and dangerous, and the proceeds of gambling as the least moral and least respectable revenues. We still play games of chance, but with an uneasy conscience. This was not yet the case in the seventeenth century: the uneasy conscience is the result of a thoroughgoing process of moralisation which made the nineteenth century a society of 'right-minded people'. (Aries 1962: 82)

This example provides a useful illustration of differing contexts and the implications for the construction of an image of the child and, as a result, the meanings given to certain practices. It reflects the extent to which certain discourses come to carry particular weight and meaning, and how these affect the everyday experiences of the child through a focus on what is seen to be acceptable or not. It is a theme that has been repeated in the evolving work of historians since Aries (de Mause 1974; Shorter 1976; Pollock 1983).

A significant conclusion Jenks draws from his review of history is the extent to which the link between childhood and social order has been maintained through the dominance of certain ways of thinking, or discourses. Different groups may draw from different discourses, so that a variety of 'discourses' can be seen to exist alongside one another. The ways in which these discourses emerge and take prominence is defined and shaped by the 'context'.

Thus the way we treat our children is indicative of the state of our social structure, a measure of the achievement of our civilisation or even an index of the degree to which humanism has outstripped the economic motive in everyday life. Similarly the way that we control our children reflects, perhaps as a continuous microcosm, the strategies through which we exercise power and constraint in the wider society. (Jenks 1996: 69)

However, it is the direct impact that Jenks mentions in relation to these structural forces that is particularly important. His reflections suggest that the way we engage with children is driven by the context that in effect creates an image of the child from which emerge adult efforts to control and manage children. Practice towards children at every level, therefore, comes to be ordered by blocks of constructed understandings from which one can extract a particular moral dimension.

3.1.2 Constructing Morality

The desire to place morality within our thinking about the constructed nature of childhood is not without precedent. Jordanova (1989, 1999), using the lens of a cultural historian, linking childhood to both the natural and moral sciences. Her work shows the interrelationship between these developing ways of thinking and their impact on framing the context in front of which children came to experience their everyday lives. Reflecting on the family, Jordonova paints a picture of how the way children were thought of was directly linked to evolving perceptions of the moral and social world. The sense in which childhood is framed by the wider philosophy of society is noted by others[2] (Hendrick 2005). More recently, Garnier (2014) has sought to develop the way in which we consider childhood and adulthood by considering the moral and political order that surround them. Her work touches on the limitations of Bourdieu's approach (considered in Chap. 4) and how it is rooted in more 'classical conceptions of socialisation' (2014: 448). Instead, she cites the work of French sociologist, Luc Boltanksi. This allows the construction of a model that offers a means to consider the differences between groups by relying on six (or more) philosophically based perspectives, that reflect ways of evaluating individuals as part of establishing social order. Garnier pursues this line of argument to the point of suggesting that one of the orders through which society can be helpfully understood is the relation- ship between children and adults. It is a perspective that flags up themes of the common good, justice and domination, to name a few. In short, it raises the awareness that there is a hidden moral dimension to childhood that has not been fully exploited. It is further evidence for the importance of reinstating morality as a theme for enquiry, and reason to suggest that it should be a fundamental element of how we come to look at the con- structed nature of childhoods.

In reflecting on the constructed nature of childhoods, one must also consider the extent to which morality itself has taken on different con- structed forms. In *A Short History of Ethics*, MacIntyre (1998[1966]) presents a case that in some sense combines the philosophical traditions of the absolute and relativist positions.[3] MacIntyre sought to assess the extent to which the way we think about morality is influenced by social factors. In opening his book, MacIntyre states:

> Moral philosophy is often written as though the history of the subject were only of secondary and incidental importance. This attitude seems to be the outcome of a belief that moral concepts can be examined and understood apart from history. Some philosophers have even written as if moral concepts were a timeless, limited, unchanging, determinate species of concept, necessarily having the same features throughout their his- tory...in fact, of course, moral concepts change as social life changes. (MacIntyre 1998[1966]: 1)

He also highlights the intricate way in which society and morality must be viewed together: 'moral concepts are embodied in and are partially con- stitutive of forms of social life' (MacIntrye 1998: 2). Indeed, 'one key way in which we may identify one form of social life as distinct from another is by identifying differences in moral concepts' (ibid.). Morality and soci- ety therefore must be seen together. By placing this in the broader context of western moral philosophy, Macintyre shows, through a chronological investigation, the different flavours of morality present at different times as he seeks to connect those cultural influences with a constructed pre- sentation of a moral position.

However, MacIntyre came to question his own thesis. His explanations were explored within defined brackets of time and, as such, a particular construction was restricted to a given time and place. Indeed, there is a similar danger with the way in which notions of childhood have come to be presented (for example, with notions of the evil child being tied to the Reformation and Puritanism in the sixteenth century – see James et al. 1998). In an honest preface to a later edition (1998) of his book, he documents the exact nature of the way in which a perception about the chronology can impact on our engagement and indeed our presentation of the substance that surrounds the discourse. MacIntyre considers how his position was suggested by some to have reflected a relativist view, one in which morality is shaped by and defined within a culture. However, MacIntyre responds that his stance, although reflecting his ongoing understanding, was limited by a lack of explanation. As he suggests, it would have provided clarity had he acknowledged the extent to which, within each culture, there remains an underlying objective that is the search for an ethical truth. The way in which that comes to be shaped or presented is, however, culturally defined.[4]

MacIntyre's later work reflects this development, as he continues to touch on the relationship between what are seen to be the universal truths of ethical theory and the extent to which they may be shaped by culture. Indeed his work *After Virtue* (2007) reflects the extent to which there may be some strands that hold ethical theory together, but nonetheless it cannot be disengaged from the social world within which it is understood. This sense of cultural relativity can be seen in the way moral images of the child are presented within childhood studies. Indeed, the early texts in childhood studies offered representations of children that were intrinsically linked to moral attitudes, exemplified by the contrast between the 'evil' and the 'innocent' child. As part of these texts, these images were deeply rooted in the time and space to which they belonged, and reflected not only that society had different views on morality, but how this impacted on their views of children. As such, social attitudes to morality can be seen as changing, and also linked to the constructed way in which we view images of the child.

3.1.3   A Framework for Analysis

Carol Gilligan's work (1982) highlighted some important factors in thinking about the constructed nature of morality. In reflecting on morality from the perspective of women, she highlighted how it was dominated by the thinking of men: 'mens morality has been mistaken for the only, universal morality and women have been measured against this standard and found wanting' (cited in Lee 2005: 84). It is a view that can be just as easily applied to children. However, if we are to challenge adult (male)-dominated moralities in relation to children, we must be clear about the measures that have been used to assess the child's place within such discourses.

The link to women studies is strong. Indeed, it is only in the last 100 years that the voice of women has become a more established part of the relationship between adults themselves. Through looking at women's studies, therefore, it is possible to start to gather a sense of some of the themes that have kept women, and children, apart in the context of accepted understandings of morality. In considering some of the links between women and children, Oakley (1994) offers a definition of a minority group.

> Membership of a social minority group results from the physical or cultural characteristics of individuals being used to single them out and to justify their receiving different and unequal treatment, in other words collective discrimination. (1994: 14)

Based on this definition, children, as well as women and many other groups, can be linked to the status of a minority. What is particularly important here are the characteristics that are assigned to this group. Oakley talks about these characteristics being framed by the need for a majority group and the limited political access of the minority, both of which are relevant and important. However, two further themes are particularly significant here. First, in separating the minority from the majority, one of the roles of the majority is to 'de-competence' the minority. As a result, the minority is portrayed as being lesser in comparison to the majority. The second theme is that the majority provides a focus on the 'volatile' nature of the minority. This volatility is perceived in different ways, including the sense that the minority is often the bearer of 'negatively critical and even hostile attitudes' (Oakley, 1994: 15). Both themes are of particular relevance to the positioning of the child in society. However, a further characteristic of minorities is needed to bring the two themes together: a belief that the majority is designed by human nature (however that is defined) to control the minority. With reference to women, Dobash and Dobash (1992) highlight this directly:

> [Rousseau, Hegel, Kant, Fichte, Blackstone, St Augustine, John Knox, Calvin, Martin Luther] believed that men had the right to dominate and control women and that women were by their nature subservient to men. This relationship was deemed natural, sacred, unproblematic and such beliefs resulted in long periods of disregard or denial of the husband's abuses of his economic, political and physical power. (1992: 7)

Not only does this quote reinforce the male-dominated approach to morality, but it also demonstrates the extent to which this domination has been used as a means of maintaining the interests of a majority over those of a minority on the grounds of nature. It is from this starting point that the additional themes of ensuring that the minority remains 'lesser' and defined as 'volatile' start to take on greater form.

Indeed these themes reflect clearly some central tenets of philosophical thought so, by extracting elements of these discussions, one is presented with a set of lenses that can be used to explore the way in which moral thought comes to infect constructed images of the child. As such, reason (and its consideration of natural capabilities and competence), virtue (and a focus on lack and directed moral education) and social harmony (where control is used to manage a wider volatility) offer three filters that can be applied to challenging the deep-rooted implications of children's place as a minority group.

Chapters 5, 6 and 7 will focus on these recurring themes of reason, virtue and social harmony as means of framing these discourses around childhood and providing vehicles through which one can assess the images of the moral child.

3.1.4 Contextualising Structure

Consideration of a 'generational order' has also proved to be a significant area of study in promoting the importance of structure (as well as its relationship with agency) as a backdrop for framing children's experiences. 'Generationing' will be considered in more detail in Chap. 4, because it offers useful support to the interactive way in which children respond to structure. However, here it is important to acknowledge the extent to which this work contributes to our understanding of how structure is created in the first place. It looks at the extent to which social order is reflected in and through a social world that is marked by the differences between the adult and child (Alanen and Mayall 2001). As such, it allows consideration of those forces or parameters that come to influence these relationships, and the extent to which they impact the institutions within which childhoods are experienced.

Part 1 of the framework, as the following section will show, acknowledges this particular focus on the contextual understanding of structure as it seeks to extend a level of analysis beyond generations and leads into a consideration of the way in which moral discourses inform children's experiences. It highlights the extent to which moral discourses form part of the social forces that influence the settings within which children interact as well as the practices that come to be created. By engaging with this part of the framework one can start to understand the backdrop (and how this is infused with moral discourses) that children are interacting with as they negotiate their everyday lives.

3.2 Application

Part 1 of the framework is shown in Fig. 3.1. It draws from the last section's themes, offering a means to examine the constructed nature of those images, their moral dimension and their influence on the practices that shape children's everyday experiences.

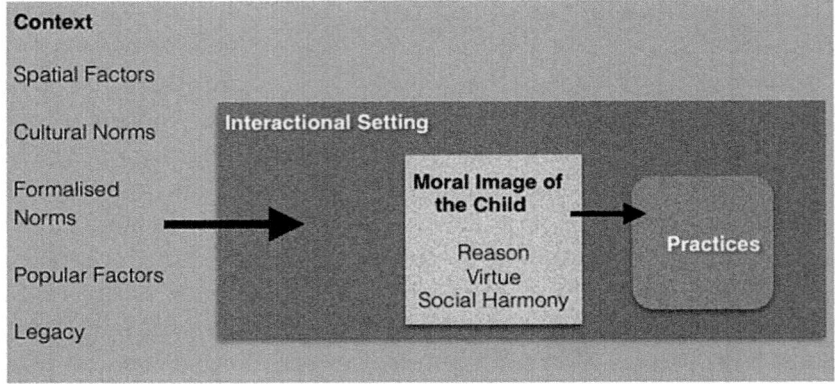

Fig. 3.1 Framework: part 1

This part of the framework, as well as being a first step in offering a wider understanding of children's engagement with morality as it comes to be seen as integrated with agency, can also stand alone. Indeed, this aspect of the framework can simply provide a means to consider the constructed nature of childhoods as it reflects on the extent to which different settings establish particular images of the child that then inform practice. This investigation on its own gives an insight into the backdrops for children's experiences such that it has potential application in contemporary research as well as historical investigations.

3.2.1 Context

Part 1 presents the backdrop in front of which interactions take place. It highlights the importance of recognising the context and the different forces or parameters that might influence the 'structure' that is then reflected in a given interactional setting within which a unique image of the child comes to inform practice.

Engaging with context emphasises that constructed images of the child are by definition products of social forces. Therefore, any effort to extract that moral image must begin by recognising its wider context. In practical terms, the focus is not on the need to have a complete picture of the context because, as discussed below, this is an impossible task. Rather, the researcher is seeking to build up enough of a picture to establish the 'backdrop' as it will apply in the context of their research. As such, in seeking to draw out the forces that are most relevant, the researcher will be directed to an extent by the interactional setting they are considering and, of course, the objectives of the research itself. Qvortrup (2011) defines these forces as parameters. Although he acknowledges that the parameters are easy to name, it is a much greater task to identify them in their entirety. The following headings provide a starting point, offering a direction for the researcher to build the backdrop in front of which agency will be practised:

Spatial Factors: Environmental, Economic, Health, Stability
Cultural Norms: Customs, Conventions, Religion, Institutional
Formalised Norms: Laws and Policies
Popular Factors: Media, Literature, Internet, Consumerism
Legacy: History

The significance of these contextual forces is that, rather than simply offering them as an influence on the child (as, for example, in Brofrenbrenner's ecological model (1994)), they are first being presented as features that inform a constructed image of the child, before recognising the extent to which children themselves come to engage with context as part of practicing their agency. For example, James and James (2004) reflect on the extent to which the law forms a defining feature in institutionalising childhood and the way in which it is expressed in key spaces that children inhabit. They suggest that law, as well as a number of other features, are part of this wider context, and what becomes significant is the way in which these forces affect the setting itself. As will be argued below, the forces do not impact each setting, and as a result each child, in the same way. Rather, each interactional setting will see different weight being given to these forces, with one result being uniquely constructed images of the child.

3.2.2 Interactional Setting

Where, Who, When

Recognising a uniqueness to childhoods does not devalue the themes that relate to the generalities of childhood. Indeed, the model must acknowledge the extent to which certain generalised factors influence the specific understandings of the child that develop within certain settings. That said, the way in which the model engages with context in practice will be defined by the interactional setting under investigation. For each interactional setting will be structured by different people, at different times, with the result that the images that come to be created will, to varying extents, be unique to those people and that time. A consequence of Giddens' theories on structure and agency is the recognition that structure is a social product. For anything to be social requires the interaction of individuals. As such, structure becomes a product of individual interaction. An interactional setting, therefore, is effectively shaped by individuals, albeit, in many instances, within a defined physical building or geographical space. However, what is important is that it is not the building that shapes the structure of that space, it is the individuals within that space, albeit framed by wider contextual forces. An example of this is a school, which is surrounded by a range of contextual forces. However, the way in which a particular school comes to interpret those forces is shaped by the individuals within it, such that each school is a unique community, although there are commonalities with other schools. The process whereby individuals shape the structure of that setting is ordered with reference to those forces – with law, policies, culture and so on – all playing a part in defining the constructed understandings that are held within that space. The socially designed model of school, therefore, means that the head teacher becomes a significant portal through which wider contextual features take on meaning in the structuring of a particular school.

By recognising that the setting is inanimate (that is, non-social), it is easier to see the extent to which those that inhabit a setting become a membrane that controls the flow of social forces. It is the dynamic process of meaning-making in relation to this interactional space that is significant here because the setting will reflect a changing structure, one that should be constantly under review, and in which certain changes to the external context can impact on how meanings come to be created within the setting itself. The question of 'who?' is therefore important because to some extent it will shape the nature of the structure created within that setting. This is relevant to established institutions such as schools – where the role of individuals contributes to shaping the unique structure of each school – as well as less definable spaces such as, for example, a skate park or other areas used for play or informal recreation.

In practical terms, when applying the framework, a natural starting point would therefore be a consideration of the interactional setting, and from this a consideration of its relationship with the context. So although the 'setting' sits inside the 'context', the 'setting' under investigation will shape the way in which this part of the framework is applied. For example, a child's home will be a space that is uniquely structured because it draws from a range of social forces in creating a unique understanding of that child. This will have consequences for the way in which adults establish practices within that space, and subsequently how the child comes to experience and interact with that setting. As will be shown, this structuring carries with it a moral dimension which is reflected in the specific construction of a 'childhood', as represented in that space. Each setting will relate to the wider context in different ways, with a figurative membrane that will control the extent to which those forces will influence the image of the child that the space comes to adopt.

This model offers a means for the researcher to consider the relationship between the wider context and the setting itself. The structure that develops within a setting must be seen to reflect the uniqueness of that setting, both in relation to the where and who, but also in relation to time. As will become clear, the search for a moral image of the child is not restricted to contemporary analysis but is highly relevant in historical settings as well. Therefore, in establishing the structural element, the researcher is interested in the 'when', and the realisation that this offers opportunities for considering settings that would have impacted on the experiences of a child in third-century Rome just as much as it might allow consideration of a child in contemporary China.

3.2.3 Images of the Child

Having recognised those wider forces or parameters and the extent to which they are uniquely adopted to differing degrees in a given interactional setting, one can then consider how these features come to inform constructed images of the child. These images, which carry a moral dimension, are defined within the given distinctions of a particular interactional setting (noting the when, where and who) and therefore will vary and change.

This approach is somewhat different from the 'off the shelf' representations of the child that are so commonly explored within childhood studies (James, Jenks and Prout 1998). As such, it demands that the researcher should not simply be interested in associating the child with the generalised representation of 'evil' or 'innocent', to name but two, but in the particular characterisation of an image as it takes shape within the context of a given interactional setting. Although there will be commonalities between images the stability of these images will be impacted by the nature of the setting (for example, a more fixed image in adult-controlled institutions, such as a hospital, to a more fluid image in settings where children are more autonomous, such as a playground), with the result that any image must be seen as specific and unique.

A focus on images, rather than image, does not restrict this model's application to international or national attempts to create a generalised image of the child, but it also means that this wider view needs to be sat alongside its application in the context of, for example, a particular home. The way in which the family in one half of a semi-detached building sees a child could be very different from that of the family in the other half. One family may be driven by a traditional view that rewards and punishments are the most effective way to support their children's future place in society, while the other family might recognise children as partners in a system of ongoing negotiation and renegotiation about the nature of home itself. These two homes will be exposed to similar parameters, but the way in which those parameters have come to influence the setting are different and, as a result, two alternative images of the child will be established, with implications for the practices within that space.

In order to help explore these images, the framework relies on the filters of reason, virtue and social harmony, which were introduced earlier. These themes have played, and continue to play, a role in framing the way we think about children and morality. They form part of literary narrative, religious dictates, parenting advice, educational practice, legal policy, media reports and so on. They are there in many different forms and presented in many different ways in social life. Sometimes they fuse together, at other times they are engaged with separately, but they remain talismans for society's appreciation and consideration of children's behaviour. Reason reflects the desire to understand behaviour in the context of 'knowledge', asking questions about competence and understanding. It provides a marker from which judgements can be made about whether the child knew what they were doing. Virtue is not only about placing the 'act' into a box marked 'acceptable' or 'not acceptable', it is also about society defining and preserving behaviours that reflect membership. Virtue, therefore, is about reflecting, reinforcing and reasserting key characteristics that mark a sense of belonging in communities – it is about stating society's ambitions for its members. Social harmony is the protecting, by a society, of a perceived ideal, a sense in which moral norms are followed and respected. The threat that certain behaviours pose, therefore, becomes very real, leading to active steps to hold on to what is seen to be the status quo.

Considering these three filters adds an important layer of enquiry to the way in which we seek to make sense of constructed images of the child. As questions are asked about reason, virtue and social harmony, so we, the researchers, are encouraged to consider the subtle understandings that are built into this construction as it is shaped by a certain group within a given interactional setting. That setting, of course, will hold certain streams of thought, extracted from the wider social context, as the connection is made between the context, interactional setting and images of the child that are constructed. It is notable that these three themes have application both in contemporary investigations and in historical analyses.[5] Chapters 5, 6 and 7 will consider this more specifically, but this section has shown the extent to which images of the child have been and continue to be created with reference to a moral agenda. Thus, it is impossible to fully understand the constructed nature of childhoods without reference to morality.

3.2.4 Practices

What James and James (2004) show with reference to the institutionalisation of childhood is the link between the way in which we view the child and the practices or policies that develop as a result. This is what the final part of the model (see Fig. 3.1) highlights: the extent to which the image of the child that is created within a given interactional setting leads to particular practices that will directly shape children's everyday experiences.

An investigation of practices can simply be considered in light of the relationship between the setting, the moral image and the practices themselves. However, practices can also provide a starting point as one considers the nature of a practice in a given setting. For example, the researcher might ask why one home or one country accepts the smacking of children, while another does not. Either way, practices must be seen in relation to an image. This is the key which, once identified, offers the opportunity to compare, contrast, challenge and change.

One example of the way in which an image of the child impacts on practices relates to how children with disabilities are included within practices that reflect their participation. The theme of participation will be discussed more fully in Chap. 9, but what is relevant here is the extent to which one acknowledges that children with disabilities are not only challenged by images that reflect their status as children, but also by images that reflect their status as 'disabled' (Russel 2003). This has implications for the way in which opportunities for their involvement in society are presented. The image of the disabled child that Martin and Franklin (2010) note with reference to children's representation in policy-making is one that highlights the themes of reason and virtue: the disabled child is seen first as incompetent and second as lacking value. What is significant is that this image, balanced alongside a broader moral discourse around the place of disability within society, is reflected in practice by the lack of opportunities for disabled children. The invisibility of the disabled child is summed up by Martin and Franklin with reference to the Every Child Matters criteria.[6] These, they argue, are constructed to reflect (amongst other themes) children's future effectiveness within the work place. As such, they demand that one considers how this objective 'values' the child with disabilities because, if 'value is being placed on children primarily for their potential future economic contribution, what implication does this hold for the value placed on disabled children who will not be part of the future workforce' (2010: 100)? This image places children outside of meaningful participation because their '"needs" are often primarily defined by non-disabled adults' perceptions of what they need' (ibid.: 101). This lack of meaningful practices, which is connected with an image that was built around perceptions of incompetence and a lack of value, offers just a brief example of the extent to which image has implications for the practices that are established.

The example of disability reiterates the broad definition of morality that is being presented within this book. It is the question of acceptability that sits at the heart of how the disabled child is positioned in relation to participation. It is a debate that directly reflects themes of competence and social ambition, and the way in which society as a whole feels comfortable about making visible the issue of disability. As such, a moral consideration of the image of the child is as relevant here as it is to the image of a child who has committed a crime. The point is that in fact we cannot disassociate the moral aspects from the construction of any images of the child.

A further applied example is presented as Appendix 1. It reflects the connection between the different aspects of the framework using an example that looks at images of the child within school (as seen through the work of Paul Connolly, 1998).

3.3   Wider Application

The framework does not sit in isolation from other vehicles that illustrate a moral dimension. The notion of moral panics has perhaps been the most prominent in asserting a moral component to the way in which social issues can be analysed, and will be looked at more in Chap. 7. Using the concept of a moral panic, one can investigate the interconnection between some of those structural forces and the type of image and practices that are created as a result. It highlights very particularly the power dynamics that are played out between certain groups within society (McRobbie 1994; Cohen 2002).

The aim here, however, is to spread this moral dimension more widely in relation to how we see children in the settings of their everyday lives. My argument is that an analysis of the image of the child, and particularly the moral aspect of it, offers explanations, or at least a focus, through which it is possible to start making sense of how 'practices' are designed and carried out. As such, it represents a framework for investigating issues within a wider setting (for example, the law) as well as the narrow settings (for example, children's place in the court room). It offers an opportunity to consider the past as much as the present. However, what is significant in its application is that it is no longer acceptable to simply draw from pre-constructed images, such as that of the 'evil child', as a means of explanation. The themes around children as evil might be of relevance to a particular construction, but simply categorising with broad brush-strokes will not create the rich tapestry or backdrop within which children's experiences are interwoven. Without asking questions about reason, virtue and social harmony, it becomes accepted that the 'evil' or the 'innocent' child can be taken from one era and one setting and placed into another. It is an effort that brings some value of comparison, but has the potential to mask both the specific way in which an image is constructed in a given interactional setting and the nature of the image itself. This has implications for how an image comes to be connected to certain practices, a connection that is very relevant in seeking to understand children's experiences.

If we accept that an image of a child is very far from fixed, but rather is dynamic and changing, then this invites greater investigation of other areas. Engaging in more depth with a moral dimension might first support understanding and second establish a better basis for examining the specific practices that are shaping children's experiences. For example, in 2015 the Canadian province of Ontario introduced a sex education programme for its schools (Ministry of Education 2015). It was a policy that polarised opinions (Parents as First Educators 2016) as people took up positions in relation to the moral themes that were made explicit through a discussion about 'sex'. Much of this discussion was driven by the desire of groups to assess how being educated about 'sex' fitted with their constructed images of the child. As such, it was a debate that, in the first instance, can be considered with direct regard to the question of 'reason' because it discusses the child's competence to be privy to such knowledge and the extent to which the sex education programme does or does not challenge a fundamental perception of innocence. However, the framework offers more than a consideration of the image of the child in relation to 'reason'. It also provides a means for considering, with reference to the other elements of the framework, the relationship between the image and the practices proposed, in the wider context of political action. Indeed one might argue that, at a surface level, the move to ensure that five-year-old children are introduced to sexual terminology is one that reflects a desire to recognise children as competent. But when these practices are sat alongside wider contextual factors (for example, the political problem (both in terms of cost and support) of teenage pregnancy), then it offers another dynamic that might play a part in one's analysis. Is the construction of this policy about children's autonomy and choice or is it a smoke-screen for an ongoing model of education by which children can be effectively educated into appropriate behaviour (recognising the traditional model of socialisation in Chap. 2)? Could one be even more cynical and suggest that the image of the child, with reference to reason, virtue and social harmony, is in fact one that allows the politicians to appear both as progressive and also deeply traditional? On the one hand they show their desire for action by 'skilling children up' through providing them with information, whilst on the other they are passing the responsibility of any future behaviour to the child, thereby removing themselves from future blame which will be seen to rest with children and, by extension, their families.

The importance of recognising the application of this model can be seen in many different arenas within children's lives. The framework offers a challenge to explicit moral discourses. An example is the training of children to be extremist fighters (*Guardian* 5/3/2015) and the extent to which commentary continues to view these children through a lens of traditional socialisation, by which being trained must result in indoctrination, and comes to a one-dimensional conclusion regarding the children's fixed and enduring moral understandings. The model also offers a means for analysing the connection between a wider social context and images of the child that result in an acceptance of practices such as female genital mutilation (WHO 2016). By engaging with the very particular construction of womanhood, and fears around the threat that women pose to social harmony, one is in a stronger position to challenge those embedded social attitudes as the problem is seen as something more than just an act of mutilation but as a multi-layered social phenomenon (as images are constructed in certain settings, drawing from that wider context, resulting in a particular set of meanings around a given action).

Not only is it useful to be able to recognise the application of the framework in relation to high profile issues, such as extremism (BBC 13/7/2015), child euthanasia (*National Post* 14/12/2015), gender violence (Das et al. 2015) and more, it is also vital in shaping how we think about more mundane aspects of children's everyday lives. It provides an opportunity to investigate particular practices, but most importantly, it establishes a backdrop with which children interact as they shape meanings in negotiating the complexities of the social world around them. This backdrop is far more than a one-dimensional 'stage set' in front of which the individual performs. As we shall see in the next chapter through a consideration of the social agent, this backdrop offers a basis with which individuals engage to make meanings as they seek to position themselves (in the fullest sense) in the world around them. The next step in promoting the framework is to consider the child and agency.

Notes

1. Jenks (2005), in considering an explanation for cultural reproduction and social organisation reflects on the work of Basil Bernstein. He uses a quote from Douglas to summarise the importance of engaging with and defining those layers that surround the context for social life, 'whatever he does, whether analysing how a mother controls her child, how a teacher teaches, how a patient confronts a psychoanalyst, how the curriculum is worked out in a school or college, he looks at four elements in the social process. First, the system of control; second, the boundaries it sets up; third, the justification or ideology which sanctifies the boundaries; and fourth, the power itself which is hidden by the rest. The analysis always ends by revealing the distribution of power. This is the trick of demystification' (cited in Jenks, 2005: 59 from Douglas, 1972).

2. Steedman's work (1994), for example, reflects on the extent to which the way we perceive childhood today is deeply rooted in 'the natural sciences, such as physiology and medicine' (Oswell 2013: 23).

3. Moral philosophy represents a variety of thought, although each perspective will to some extent have a view on how the morality of the individual is shaped by the social. In its simplest form this translates into the difference between two approaches, the absolute and relativist positions. The former focuses on the universal nature of moral thinking and its potential to guide the individual no matter where. The individual is thus equipped naturally with the capacity to frame moral judgements. This contrasts with relativist theories that see the individual's moral understanding to be shaped by the culture within which they find themselves. The individual therefore is not able to stand outside of this culture in presenting moral findings because those findings are merely the product of the culture itself.

The way we engage with these positions clearly has relevance when considered in the context of a structural exploration. An absolute position rejects the influence of contextual factors on the way in which moral meanings are created. Although a consequence of this natural ability to define morality is that it will lead to certain practices, which will then 'structure' to a greater or lesser degree other people's – significantly, children's – experiences. A relativist position reflects the importance of the social, not just in terms of how meanings structure the experiences of others, but also in recognising that the source for the construction of those meanings is society itself.

Although it might be easy for a work such as this to be categorised as taking a relativist position, it is important to note, first, that, no matter how we come to think about these positions, both will result in meanings leading to actions that will impact on people's experiences. Second, a relativist position carries too much of that Durkheimian reliance on structure providing causality for it to offer a definitive model that works. For example, child A is part of a gang. This gang has a culture 'normalising' certain behaviours. To what extent are the stealing and violence that are associated with this gang to be seen simply in the context of that culture? To approach this with the limitation that moral meaning is simply the product of the gang limits our ability to analyse this, and, therefore, must be kept more open. Indeed, the framework in this book does not deny absolutism – it does not reject a universal ambition to find the 'right' way of acting. However, it does emphasise the importance of how that moral ambition is played out as a response to the structure in which the individual finds themselves. It is, therefore, the relationship between structure and agency that is important.

4. Cf. Ayer (1997/8) – see Chap. 6.

5. As Hendrick (2000) notes, 'the little children of long ago, they only speak when they are spoken to, and they will not talk to strangers' (42). This framework will provide a chance to examine those structures that positioned children in relation to adults and as a result will 'illustrate their significance for the varying concepts of childhood' (ibid.: 46).

6. Being healthy, staying safe, enjoying and achieving, making a positive contribution and achieving economic well being are the criteria of Every Child Matters, a programme for children and families that has been supported by succesive UK governments since 2003.

4

Engaging with Agency

4.1 Discussion

The frameworkset out in Chap. 2 reflected how the investigation of morality and children must be seen in relation to both structure and agency. Chapter 3 concentrated on the extent to which context forms a backdrop against which moral images of the child emerge. These images come to inform practice within different interactional spaces but, importantly, this is only one part of the model. The second part of the model will allow us to consider the extent to which the individual responds to structure and what this means for a process of meaning-making and subsequent action.

This chapter will, therefore, seek to draw out those aspects of the agentic process. As one considers the relationship between structure and agency, it becomes necessary to recognise that childhood studies has not engaged deeply enough with the processes of agency. By breaking agency down, one can start to see where a moral dimension fits by considering the particularities of the agentic process on any one individual. This chapter highlights the personal elements that the individual brings to interactions because these become filters through which the individ-

S. Frankel, *Negotiating Childhoods*, Studies in Childhood and Youth,
DOI 10.1057/978-1-137-32349-1_4

ual interprets the structural backdrop identified in Chap. 3, forming the basis on which meaning and action are constructed.

4.1.1 Reflecting on Agency

In order to reflect on the processes mentioned above, we must try to break down the way in which we think about agency. 'Agency' is a term that we have frequently attached to our understanding of children's competence (Oswell 2013). However, it remains a term that we seem to be more comfortable in applying at a theoretical level than at a practical, research-based level. Why is that? One reason is that we are not sure how to make agency visible, with the consequence that it is both harder to define and, as a result, harder to record (and, therefore, analyse). Valentine (2011) asks the pointed question of whether childhood studies needs a theory of agency at all. She suggests three answers to this question:

1. No, as we already have one and everyone understands it.
2. No, because we can 'advocate for children's rights and participation without it' (347).
3. It is of interest to theorists but not beyond.

These responses offer a very effective summary of our attitude towards agency: we remain unaware of its capacity as a tool for research because some of us presume that we understand it, others feel that we don't actually need it, and finally, that its place is simply in those ivory towers of our academic institutions. Valentine argues that what we need to move towards a 'social' model if we are to further our understanding of agency.

This means a move away from a 'liberal' definition, which can be characterised through its focus on using agency as an equaliser, putting different social groups on the same footing. We must not underestimate the extent to which the 'liberal' perception of agency has created challenges for how we might take the notion of agency forward. Presenting agency in terms of its ability to create equality and to challenge the barriers between adults and children has given it a profile, but one that has offered a target for attack rather than fully progressing a desire for engagement. As Wyness (2012) notes, it is that increased sense of self-determination for which 'agency' has been seen to be a battle cry that has resulted in the more powerful voice of the adult finding ways to discredit and ignore children's claims for competence. An emphasis on self determination does not sit easily alongside those dominant discourses presented in earlier chapters, a tension that provides an explanation as to why agency has not found a more constructive place in our ongoing desire to make sense of children's lives. As such it is an approach that sits uncomfortably alongside psychological and biological considerations.

In his efforts to offer some direction to our thinking around agency, Oswell (2013) touches on this awkward relationship. He notes the challenge it presents to the childhood sociologist because it questions a body of thought that has built up through recognised medical and scientific practice and has then been shared with the general population as fact (see Steedman 1994). However, as James and Prout note, 'the immaturity of children is a biological fact of life but the way in which immaturity is understood and made meaningful is a fact of culture' (1997: 7). This highlights the influential role played by the structures we have been discussing in shaping an image of the child that attaches meaning to words such as 'immaturity' and indeed 'morality'. Part of the reason why the medical professions have been more effective in claiming a definition for competence stems from the fact that, as can be seen from the work of Piaget, they have made efforts to apply their theory. Here the argument is that, if our understanding of competence, and by extension agency, is truly to be meaningful, then social scientists also need to be in a position where they can more fully apply, measure and evaluate[1] their theories (Hutchby and Moran Ellis 1998). It is a sense of action that James and Prout's 1990 [1997] work encouraged. However, rather than simply questioning the structural meaning behind these terms, they should be examined from the perspective of the individual, as we move towards Valentine's notion of 'social' agency.

This means that our focus should not rest on establishing a universal conception of agency, which in many ways has been done (Valentine

2011), but rather in seeking to make sense of what it looks like at an individual level. This is given further direction through the need for the discussion to focus on the agent, rather than the actor. James (2011), reflecting on Mayall's (2002) position, suggests that the actor 'is someone who does something; the agent is someone who does something with other people' (2011: 41). What James suggests, pursuing Mayall's position, is that 'to see children as agents is to regard them as also having a part to play "in the lives of those around them" in the societies in which they live' and as forming independent 'social relationships and cultures' (ibid). The need is, therefore, for a move from seeing the individual as a topic of inquiry to recognising them as a catalyst for action. This shift demands a more research-based approach to the notion of agency rather than treating it as a theoretical standard behind which we can gather in arguing for some sense of self-determination. Indeed, even if self-determination is where we are going, then surely a 'liberal' definition should not be the starting point? We need to establish a sense of what children's agency actually looks like, and how it comes to be applied, and from this further discussions might then extend, in much more concrete terms, to a more rounded discussion on self-determination.

The Elements of Agency

Emirbayer and Mische (1998) reflect on how 'many theorists have failed to distinguish agency as an analytical category in its own right – with distinctive theoretical dimensions and temporally variable social manifestations' (1998: 962–3). This statement marks the need to move agency away from being a theoretical tool that we use to try and assert children's competence and sense of equality, to seeing it as a means through which we can analyse and make sense of interactions. In challenging us to develop how we think about and, therefore, come to apply agency, Emirbrayer and Mische seek to remove what they argue are the limitations of both Giddens and Bourdieu who, they suggest, 'have given selective attention to the role of habitus and routinised practices: their perspective sees human agency as habitual and taken for granted' (ibid). As a result of these limitations we have come to accept understandings of agency without being prepared to break it down into component parts, to recognise its dimensions and to reflect on what that means for research (ibid.). Significantly, it is by re-examining the relationship between structure and agency that Emirbayer and Mische seek to present their case. They reflect on a number of theorists, including Jeffrey Alexander (1998) whose work 'shows how human agency engages with its structural contexts' (Emirbayer and Mische, 1998: 967). Alexander, a proponent of Social Action Theory, identifies two terms of agency in action: 'interpretations' and 'strategisation'. Both terms promote active and engaged processes that see the individual taking part in the meanings and actions that result as a response to the social structure that surrounds them. The result is an incredibly dynamic process which results in a definition of agency as:

> temporarily constructed engagement by actors of different structural environments – the temporal-relational contexts of action, which through the interplay of habit, imagination and judgement, both produces and transforms those structures in interactive responses to the problem posed by changing historical situations. (ibid.: 970)

This definition, albeit wordy, reflects the interplay between structure and agency and points to the extent to which the individual responds to structure through active and creative considerations which are temporally situated (see an alternative definition of agency, based on the model in this book, in section 4.1.6.). Emirbayer and Mische argue that it is by combining a sense of the past with perceptions of the future that the individual acts in the present. They offer three elements that inform the meaning-making process that is part of agency and which provide certain filters through which we can assess agency. These are iteration – the selective use of past patterns of thought or action, giving stability and order, projection – the use of imagination to shape possible future trajectories, and practical evaluation – which the individual uses to make judgements about a range of trajectories of action in response to the 'demands, dilemmas and ambiguities of presently evolving situations' (Emirbayer and Mische 1998: 971). Each of these filters forms part of meaning-making (to varying degrees), with time and space having an impact that can affect inventiveness and reflexivity but which throughout refelct processes that are intrinsically social.

However, this definition does not give a sense of what the individual is setting alongside structure in order to reach the point of being able to process meaning. Also, there is a further dimension to the process of meaning-making that we must recognise. In establishing the link between structure and agency, Emirbayer and Mische note that this must include a consideration of a connection with everyday morality (as introduced in Chap. 2). As such it forces the question of whether agentic action and moral meaning-making can be divided or whether an intrinsic part of agency is a process of moral assessment, which then has an implication for action?

4.1.2   Reflexivity: Processing Structure

The nuances of agency are played out as part of a relationship with structure. The sense in which the individual is responding to a social order that has been created is explored in a number of theories including in work focused on a generational order. In a similar way to Durkheim's work, generationing focuses on the nature of social order and how this comes to be transmitted (Mayall 2002). Mayall reflects on how the difference between child and adult is passed on, 'in individual transactions between children and adults; in group transactions, as between pupils and teachers, in individual relations between people born at different points in history; in social policies handed down from an earlier cohort to a later one' (2002: 35). This perspective is helpful in considering the range of settings and the nature of the interactions through which social order comes to be transmitted, as framed by adult–child relationships.

As well as encouraging a wider structural analysis, a particularly important contribution of this work has been the extent to which it has narrowed the divide between structure and agency, and shown how the interplay between the two takes on a particular form in shaping children's daily lives. Alanen highlights the extent to which the generational order places relationships at the heart of a developed means of researching and understanding children's lives (drawing from the work of Fitz and Hood-Williams – see Alanen 2011: 160), She defines it as:

a system [in modern societies] of social ordering that specifically pertains to children as a social category, and circumscribes for them particular social locations from which they act and thereby participate in ongoing social life. Children are thus involved in the daily 'construction' of their own and other people's everyday relationships and life trajectories. (2011: 161)

It is Alanen's recognition of the active and dynamic nature of generation-ing that is so compelling to the framework being offered in this book.[2] At the heart of this definition is the sense in which the individual comes to engage with and interpret 'structure' as part of constructing mean-ings that shape their interactions. It highlights the need for structure to be seen as more than a one-dimensional backdrop in front of which the child *performs*, but rather as a backdrop with which they *interact* as a social agent in the daily processes of making sense and contributing to the world around them.

In an earlier effort to make sense of social order and the way in which it impacted on the individual, Mary Douglas had offered the notion of grid-group. She sought to show how the individual's actions could be defined by the pressure of society, through structural forces, with this having an implicit impact on private systems or codes, thus shaping the production of individual meaning (1973: 85–86). Although Douglas' model offered a means to think about the individual's relationship to structure in different spaces, James and Prout (1995) questioned whether it was effective in the context of thinking about children. Instead, they presented the idea of hierarchy and boundary which addresses 'both structure and agency at the same time' (James and Prout 1995: 81). They sought, therefore, to offer a model that moved beyond the social group as a point of analysis and, in keeping with the nature of children's every-day lives, focused on the individual. Social environments, they suggested, could be understood in relation to varying combinations of hierarchy and boundary. Hierarchy, as a continuum, reflected cultures that at one end were highly structured with lots of rules and little negotiation and at the other end, where the structure was loose, were characterised by fewer rules and lots of negotiation. This concept could be set against 'bound-ary', which referred to whether a group was open or closed. A closed group is one that is highly regulated and difficult to leave, in contrast to the open group which is more freely constituted.

Hierarchies and boundaries thus present children with various opportunities and constraints for practicing their social agency and facilitate different modes of social action or different ways of being an agent. (Bacon and Frankel 2013: 15)

As a result, James and Prout's model offers not only a means to follow children through their everyday lives and to recognise the different settings, but also to consider the children's 'strategic flexibility in moving between different environments'(James and Prout 1995: 86) as different modes of action are employed in different settings. The dynamic and ever-changing nature of the relationship between structure and agency becomes clear, therefore, as children respond to each setting. Although highlighting the relevance of the structural context, the hierarchy and boundary model lacks a means to understand what actual processes of agentic reflection and assessment shape the production of meaning. It is, therefore, necessary to look in more detail at agency and whether those elements of the processes of meaning-making can be identified.

Research on Morality

This theme of the individual engaging with the wider context in order to shape meanings is reflected directly in research that deals explicitly with morality. In the context of 'moral' development, Burman (1999) focuses on how Piaget's and Kholberg's approaches maintained a 'tunnel vision' that did not allow them to consider morality in a more applied (in terms of the everyday) way, such that morality was fixed. She critiques Kholberg:

morality as moral reasoning cannot engage with issues of moral commitment, and individual priorities or differences of moral salience of particular issues. Nor does it address the subjective experience of feelings of guilt and shame which, as Kagan (1984) notes, children exhibit from an early age. (Burman 1999: 173)

Burman had also noted this partial approach to defining morality in relation to Piaget who, for example, judged naughtiness on the damage it caused rather than any consideration of the meaning that sat behind it. It led her to conclude that a developmental view that does not engage with 'culture, class, gender and history' (ibid.: 177) is limited in the depth of analysis that it can provide and the extent to which a universal developmental model of moral reasoning is appropriate.

As such, we see, at best, only a partial connection between structure and a consideration of the individual as a meaning-maker. Ongoing acceptance of this view of development separates out the I (an inward perception of self) and the Me (a socially projected image of the self) (Haste 1999). (For a further discussion of I and Me, see Frankel 2012.) However, Haste considers that such barriers should be broken down as interaction adds to moral development and the social must therefore be seen as part of our understandings of mental functioning. Here she draws on the work of Vygotsky (1978) in making the case for the 'ongoing dialectic' (Haste 1999: 194) that is moral development. Vygotsky's notion of the 'zone of proximal development' provided a link between the I and the Me, and reflected the extent to which 'sense-making' was connected with interaction on the one hand and wider social and cultural themes on the other. It is through recognising children's ability to engage with these frameworks for social and cultural attitudes (schemes) that, Haste suggests, one can make greater sense of children's moral development. As she observes, children are able to draw from these schemas or scripts in 'managing the moral expectations of one's culture' (ibid.: 186). As such, it offers an alternative way to see children as part of a discourse of morality (see Gilligan 1982),[3] one that questions the notion of reason and the competence levels that have been required in the past.

Haste's position presents a view that is aligned with the idea that structure and agency can not be seperated. As thinking has evolved, it has increasingly acknowledged that the individual cannot be disconnected from the social world of which they are a part. As argued in Chap. 2, the divide between the social agent and the moral agent thus becomes blurred (Bergmann 1998). As Danby and Theobald (2012) reflect in relation to disputes:

> disputes can accomplish the negotiation of social practices, and the alignment and realignment of social identities through the building and monitoring of social orders that are always in flux, existing only in the instance of the practice being done. (Danby and Theobald 2012: xvi)

This perspective reflects the need to bring a sense of the wider social context, as refined in relation to a given interactional setting, into focus alongside the individual's sense of self. As such, morality forms part of the individual's negotiation of social life, as moral order becomes defined and redefined by the individual rather than being an invisible set of structural forces. It is a desire to explore the interrelationship between the individual and the wider social context that sits behind the model presented in this book, with particular reference in this chapter to the processes of agency. In order to make an effective case for everyday morality and its absolute integration with a process of social agency, then one needs to establish a stronger sense of what those processes involve. It is by focusing on those elements of agency that this chapter seeks to draw out some of the themes connected with the way in which the self comes to be positioned vis-à-vis others in a given interactional setting, with implications for (moral) meaning-making.

The remainder of this chapter therefore seeks to engage with morality in terms of its place within a process of agency. Indeed, I argue that managing a personal sense of social order is a constant process of assessment and reassessment that takes the form of everyday morality. Within this, the processes of agency are key. It is, therefore, crucial for the individual as a social agent to develop expertise in understanding everyday morality because it offers them a level of social skill and knowledge that can only help them to navigate their day-to-day lives.

4.1.3 Personalising Agency

A limitation to research on children and morality is that, although it demonstrates the capacity of the child to engage with morality, it does not provide researchers with much more to go on as we seek to make sense of what shapes that meaning and how it sits in relation to the surrounding structure. As such, an investigation of agency and moral meaning-making is hollow unless it is specifically tied to an individual. This might sound rather counter-intuitive, but if the aim is to make the processes of agency visible then it is fundamentally important that the individual is deconstructed in the same way as the structure that surrounds them. Valentine

(2011) (whose work led us into this discussion) defines agency in terms of 'competence, strategy and awareness' (2011: 347), all of which stress the personal nature of agency. Indeed the personal dimension that must be attributed to agentic meaning-making is reflected in a range of work (James 1993; Mayall 2002; Connolly 2004; Corsaro 2005; Bacon 2010), of which each author highlights the subtleties and nuances that form an essential part of how we come to make sense of the individual's place within this process.

There are two areas of work that offer a means for shaping the analytical framework: identity and personal life. Both were referred to in Chap. 2 but we need to consider them in more detail here. Despite arguments that identity and personal life should be kept apart, there is value in looking at them together in an effort recognise as fully as possible those elements that personalise agency.

Identity

Handel et al. (2007) are very clear that symbolic interactionism and the construction of the self are key to the traditional socialisation process. However, in their model (see Chap. 2) the driving force is socialisation itself: 'a baby is not born with the ability to engage in interpretation but develops it in the course of socialisation by developing a self' (2007: 83). The self is, therefore, a product of socialisation and is categorised most essentially as the ability for the individual to be seen as the 'other' and to have the opportunity to reflect the social order through the capacity to distinguish themselves from someone else. As such, 'the self is, then, a form that gives the person the capacity to function and participate in society by distinguishing different relationships and responding with appropriate differences' (ibid.: 103). The notion of the self as the formulating factor in how the individual experiences society is helpful, but the sense in which the self is simply a transmitter which is formed and then directed by the processes of socialisation sits uncomfortably alongside the notion of children as agents. It implies that the capacity of the 'biologically proper child' is limited – they simply absorb and are formed by processes that they find themselves within. Socialisation, the 'process by which we learn and adapt' (ibid.: 2), then becomes a definable tool that is measured by whether the child becomes a law-abiding adult. Those who do not conform are seen as having 'dropped out' of society. Parsonian socialisation, working through the aspects of the individual with self at the centre (as well as themes such as attachment, communication, language and self esteem), drives an understanding of a process that is limited in nature and which positions morality simply in terms of children recognising a defined social order set by adults.

Can we extend the way in which we view the process of socialisation, and thus the relationship between children and morality, by engaging more deeply with the individual themselves? For this to be considered it is necessary to think more on those aspects of self-identity and the reflective process which are at its heart. Not only does that invite consideration of the interplay between the individual and the 'context', but it also allows us to explore further those elements that the individual brings to interaction.

One of the themes raised above is the extent to which the redefinition of agency, that took place within sociology, has recognised the self-reflective aspect of the individual in terms of how they not only respond but also influence their social worlds. Rapport (2003), in his compelling book *I am Dynamite*, challenges the reader to be more aware of the social definitions that inform and shape us as individuals because they have implications for our emotions and actions. In this wide-reaching work that is so full of powerful examples, Rapport focuses on the reflective nature of human meaning-making. At the centre of this is an ongoing dialogue between the individual and their sense of self, and how they seek to position this in the context of the world around them. This dialogue, which Mead (1934) refers to as 'I and Me', reflects the inner and outer sense of self and the personal understanding which is presented as a response to the wider social world. Cooley (1964) refers to it as 'the looking glass self', an illustration that is helpful because it underlines the sense in which the individual is managing perceptions of themselves in shaping, creating and presenting an identity. It is through an ongoing dialogue with the structural 'context' that the individual reflecting on 'self' then acts. Rapport considers this in relation to those in the concentration camps of the Second World War. He argues that, in the awful strictness of that setting, it was not the structure per se that defined how the individual acted, but it was the individual, as a consequence of ongoing reflection, that chose to act in a particular way. Action therefore, is not a 'deterministic' result of the 'context', but rather it is a process of the individual, as a social agent, forming a conclusion in dialogue between the 'context' and the 'self'. He reinforces this by referring to Cohen's (1994) work and the extent to which individuals reject identities that are given to them. This idea of taking on a given role is part of the traditional socialisation model. However Rapport rejects this. Drawing from Cohen's work, he argues that the researcher should focus on the processes of reflection and refraction that form part of the individual's engagement with their interactional setting: 'Cohen concludes, social scientists should work towards "giving people back" their individual consciousness, their selfhoods' (Rapport 2003: 253). It is, Rapport suggests, fundamental that we engage with these processes of self because we cannot understand our lives except 'through an appreciation of the interpretations, meanings, intentions of their individual owners, their construers and creators' (ibid.: 253). Rapport argues that it is not only through the researcher recognising the individual in these terms but also the individual recognising *themselves* in these terms that one is in a position to set a 'moral' example. It is through knowing the self, a self who responds to and engages with the 'context' that it finds itself in, that meanings are created that form the basis of action.

The extent to which we are able to see people (in general) and children (in particular) has certainly been added to by the developing discourse around the sociology of personal life (James 2013). These debates have enabled us to recognise the micro processes that inform individuals' meaning-making, but placed within a wider 'structural' context. It marks a coming together of agency and structure that allows for greater consideration of the relationship between the two. Smart (2007) recognises that part of the challenge for sociology is the extent to which it has had to move away from searching for a grand overarching answer, to recognise and to engage with the mundaneness of everyday life. This is crucial for the developing themes within this book because it suggests that morality is a response to the everyday and to the relationships that are experienced.

Smart unpacks her approach through reference to the 'cultural turn' which offers a means for considering how those elements of identity, which will be considered in more detail below, take on meaning. She refers to a set of five overlapping themes: imaginary, memory, biography, embeddedness, and relationality (Smart 2007: 37). Examined primarily in the context of the family, she makes the case for the way in which each offers a pool out of which the individual carries/ brings certain elements that frame and shape the meanings that they compose. For example, the recall of a memory may be a 'conscious process, what is recalled may come with layers of meaning and significance, of emotions and desires, which go beyond the simply rational or conscious' (Smart 2007: 39). She refers to the home as a site where the individual recognises what to remember and what to forget, learning to weigh up the value of certain experiences. It is an approach that demonstrates that these processes of meaning-making must be contextualised because the individual manages those personal elements, on the way to making meanings, in light of the particular setting that they find themselves in.

Like Rapport, an interesting theme in Smart's work is the extent to which it encourages sociology to take a greater stake in the notion of the individual, which is more generally seen as the domain of psychology and psychoanalysis (Smart 2007: 41). Smart suggests that 'for sociology to start to be interested in individuals requires the overcoming of a long standing dispute' (ibid.: 41). It means getting to the heart of the relational nature of socio-cultural interaction and the extent to which this impacts the debate around agency. We are being encouraged to take account of emotions and of personal narratives. By recognising the everyday (also see May 2011), this focus on personal life provides a means for detailing the workings of structure and agency. It reflects the extent to which different people who have had similar experiences will reflect a variety of personal lives which, in the context of children, result in multiple childhoods amongst children in the same communities (Morgan 2011). It means that, as well as considering structural themes, they need to be broken down in the reality of the everyday interactions and histories of an individual's personal life.

4.1.4   Elements of Identity

In order to examine these personal lives effectively we need to have some sense of what it is that the individual brings to the process. The following section, therefore, draws from previous research in establishing some key elements that can act as markers or filters through which the researcher can look into the processes of meaning-making that were introduced earlier. Doing this adds to the tools for analysis in seeking to make sense of the individual's place within a given interactional setting.

Jenkins' (2004) work on identity offers some direction in helping to consider the elements through which the individual comes to engage in an interactional setting. I have considered this relationship elsewhere (Frankel 2012). Here, however, the intention is to highlight some areas of interest that might then form part of our framework as we consider the extent to which the process of moral meaning-making becomes tied into our sense of identity and our personal lives.

It is through the essential recognition of the self, within an ongoing and dynamic process of identity formation, that one starts to establish the relevance of defining that what the individual takes into the interaction impacts on the meanings that come to be formed. Jenkins reflects on identities in the following way.

> All human identities are by definition social identities. Identifying ourselves or others is a matter of meaning, and meaning always involves interaction: agreement and disagreement, convention and innovation, communication and negotiation. (Jenkins 2004: 4)

This perspective highlights the extent to which identity formation is a process of negotiation that is fundamentally social. It is only by placing the self into the context of others that meanings follow. Within this, however, one must be aware that each individual will bring certain 'elements', that will be particular to that person (whether adult or child), into the social arena, with implications for the meanings that come to be made. Jenkins, rather than focusing on these elements, concentrated on identities in relation to three orders or zones: individual, interaction and institutional. Each of these orders offers a dimension within which one can look at the active nature of the individual, with implications for children and moral meaning-making (Frankel 2012). In the individual order, Jenkins invites us to think about the extent to which our conception of self-identity includes an embodied element, how we think about ourselves. Jenkins suggests that children take on 'primary identities' with reference to the body, and these identities are more 'robust and resilient to change in later life' (Jenkins 2004: 19). Whether this is the case or not, the extent to which the body is central to children's identity formation is clear because it becomes 'one of the most important signifiers and conceptual filters through which any particular child's childhood and social identity is understood' (James 1993). Through filters such as the body, and later power and capital (with links to the other zones that Jenkins identifies), one can start to consider the personalised 'elements' through which the individual processes interaction and creates meanings.

The discussion below is not an exhaustive examination of the ways in which these personalised 'elements' impact on the individual's engagement with (moral) meaning-making. Rather, it offers an indication of the need for these 'elements' to be considered, recognising the depth of investigation this could lead to, as these headings sit alongside other definable 'themes' from investigations into personal lives in the pursuit of understanding the processes of agency.

Body

Belonging, Language

Douglas suggests that an essential element of social order is the extent to which we are able to distinguish ourselves from others. 'It is only by exaggerating the difference between within and without, above and below, male and female, with and against, that a semblance of order is created' (1966: 4). Our embodied sense of self plays a significant role within this desire for creating a sense of similarity and difference, with the body as 'an index of collective similarity and differentiation, and a canvas upon which identification can play' (James and James 2004: 19). It is thus through the body that 'otherness' can be understood and categorised as children discover the tools to mark out similarity and difference. Frames of reference that children might use in this process include age, gender, the actual body (body shape), the styled body (how the body is made to look, clothes, jewellery) and performance (James 1993; Frankel 2012).

In establishing a recognition of who one is with reference to one's body, the individual is then able to position themselves in relation to others. This can be seen on a range of levels from the one-to-one interaction to developing a group identity. Cohen (1982) focuses on the extent to which the ability to have an identity forms part of the individual taking on culture.

> Firstly, people recognise their culture as that which distinguishes them from others and, thereby, as the source of their own identities. Secondly, that in conditions of frequent contact with other cultures the valuing of such distinctions is a condition of survival. Thirdly, these are processes which occur close to the everyday experience of life, rather than through rare, formalised procedures.

It is the context of the individual taking on a role in framing and shaping culture that is important. This is an interactive process, whereby one's sense of self affects the culture that develops, such that it is not a major event that shapes culture but the day to day. It places belonging and the desire to belong not at a moment of one's development, but from the very initial stages of it.[4] However, belonging is not simply about the individual assessing notions of similarity and difference and then aligning themselves with a particular group. It represents a greater desire within the individual to enhance and underline, in Goffman's (1969) words, a presentation of self. The ability to define oneself through association is an important element of agency, and within the context of belonging, it can also be seen to offer frameworks for meaning-making. Here the notion of the collective or group is significant because, as a product of establishing sameness, whether at home or school, we create cultural units (Cohen 1994). These units play a role in defining our sense of who we are as well as shaping the meanings that we make because judgements are made in the light of maintaining or not maintaining that sense of belonging within the definable context of a given cultural unit. This is made more complicated by the recognition that we belong to many different groups, each which will offer a different context for understanding our identities, with subsequent implications for the way in which we shape and create meanings of acceptability. (This will be discussed again later in relation to capital.)

As experience increases, a sense of self forms the basis from which the individual can draw to create short cuts or cues to meaning through tools such as 'stereotypes' and language more generally. In keeping with this theme of difference, stereotypes reflect an everyday vehicle to help channel understanding. In Rapport's assessment, the traditional view of stereotypes is that they are products of 'hearsay and rumour' (1995: 270) and they are left at that. However, by bringing an element of personalisation into this concept, stereotypes can start to reflect so much more about the individual. Although the traditional notion of stereotypes is shared, they come to be practised by individuals and, as such, the individual draws from them in creating 'a short cut to generalise' through which they find a 'foundation [which] is very necessary not only as a bulwark against the expected randomness of future events in our entropic western conceptions, but also as an encouragement to action' (1995: 280). The nature of these short cuts must also be seen in the context of language and the way in which language in itself becomes an element that an individual brings to interactions.

An interesting feature of the practice of stereotyping, in the work of James (1993), Thorne (1993) and Frankel (2012), is the extent to which these short cuts to meaning, built on efforts to establish similarity and difference with direct reference to the body, carry with them explicit moral meanings. As mentioned above, Douglas (1966) asserts that our ability to place ourselves in relation to others is essential to establishing social order. She considers this through the prism of 'pollution' which encapsulates the centrality of the body and uses it as a marker on which to construct moral meanings. 'A polluted person is always wrong. He has developed some wrong condition or simply crossed some line, which should not have been crossed and this displacement unleashes danger for someone' (1966: 113). This approach frames the idea of the unacceptable body being linked with an essence of moral deviance. For James, this was characterised through body size, as the body becomes a filter through which to assess right and wrong. She cites an example that stemmed from a discussion on bullying with reference to a poem and a picture with a child, a child that was 'far from fat' (1993: 119):

Allison: So what do you think about him in the picture?
Gareth: He's pulling her hair
Tony: He's a bully
Gareth: He's a fat bully
Allison: He's not fat though.
Tony: He looks like a fat pig.
Gareth: Thin pig. [They all laugh] (ibid.)

It is the 'fatness' that becomes the easy marker, not only to identify difference but also to indicate morally unacceptable behaviour, demonstrating a 'clear conceptual link between morality and physical shape' (James 1993: 119). Similarly Thorne (1993) reflects on the extent to which oversexualising the body can result in the label 'slut', as the body is moved away from those accepted childhood notions to a less innocent state. She draws from those themes of pollution that had been a part of Douglas' work. Her work reflects the extent to which our sense of self offers a filter for meaning-making, one that carries with it a moral dimension as we seek to position ourselves in relation to others (see also Frankel 2012, Chapter 4). Here, the body becomes an 'element' that the individual brings to an interaction. This 'element', therefore, acts as a prism through which the 'context' (see Chap. 3) is viewed and, as such, it offers a very personalised basis on which meanings come to be made. However, this process is not supported by simple reliance on one element. Rather, the agentic process sees the individual responding to the 'context' through a range of elements, of which power is another.

Power

Power here reflects the extent to which those embodied notions of self, touched on above, are added to as the individual actively seeks to engage with others. Power rather than taking on a traditional form of structural force (defining children's everday lives) here is presented as a social tool, in which power relates to a set of meanigns that the individual reflects on and uses within the context of shaping and framing how they position themsleves vis-a-vis others (for more see Frankel, 2012). In the past, discourses on power and children have followed a vertical trajectory. Power was something done to children. Whether in terms of managing their bodily functions, shaping their bodies or reforming them, the adult was the distributor of power in a process of domination. How we now think about power has been challenged, such that it now includes a wider recognition that power can be displayed at many levels and in many ways,[5] indeed it is a fixture within our day-to-day interactions.

As Lukes so definitively suggests:

> Social life can only be properly understood as an interplay of power and structure, a web of possibilities for agents, whose nature is both active and structured, to make choices and pursue strategies within given limits, which in consequence expand and contract over time. (Lukes 2005: 68)

What is so important about this position is that, rather than power simply being seen in terms of its horizontal connotations, it becomes something more because it provides an additional filter through which the individual is able to make sense of and draw meaning from the world around them. Power is integral to identity and must be viewed as a further dimension through which all the other elements of self come to be seen. Fingerson (2005) drawing from Foucault[6] (1977) considers the idea of negotiated power. This offers an understanding of power that engages with the vertical dimension and places power at the heart of interactions, with direct implications for the way in which we assess what is and what is not acceptable.

> Power is negotiated through relationships, language and disciplinary practices rather than being an essential element that a person, group or gender does not possess. Power is a fundamental aspect of all social interaction. (Fingerson 2005: 92)

The point here is that, within these layers of identity, power offers a further lens through which to engage with the process of meaning-making.

This power, in its variety of forms, carries moral connotations that form part of children's ongoing everyday interactions. This was illustrated in *Children, Morality and Society* (Frankel 2012) by breaking power down into six categories: the 'mutual other', the 'mutual self', the 'powerful other', the 'powerful self', the 'powerless other', and the 'powerless self'. Within these categories it was possible to look at themes of power in terms of how children reflected on an embedded, although dynamic, sense of power, contrasted with a perception of the power of others, with implications for how this impacted on the moral dimension of their meaning-making. Notably, different interactions showed the children placing themselves and others into different categories. This is an approach that moves power from simply being seen in the context of a structural force and presents it as an 'element' that the individual brings to an interaction and which becomes a filter through which agency is practised and meaning is made.

The following example shows the strategic way in which notions of power are used and reflected on as part of interaction. A group of friends are discussing David, one of their peers, who would like to be part of their friendship group. Despite their efforts to keep David out, he shows how he manages conceptions of 'power' to find ways back in.

Matt: *Well basically if I went and told an adult David would get off.*

Harry: *David always gets off with all the adults.*

Matt: *He always gets off whatever he does.*

Harry: *Because everyone thinks David is so good, so if we go and tell Miss Heater its "I'm sure he didn't mean it, I'm sure he did it by accident" and then if we went and say that Jan McMulling went and did the same thing, I went and told the same Miss, she would say, "now Jan why did you hit Mathew, what was the point in doing that", because all the Misses think that. Because every kind of Miss knows David Jones, Miss Fletcher, Miss Lloyd and all that because they have all had loads of experience with us because mainly its David whose been breaking us up, isn't it.*

Matt: *He went and told Miss Fletcher because he knows that Miss Fletcher doesn't like me, she doesn't really like us…I told her off because she is not allowed to do what she is doing, but now she's*

	much better but she still doesn't like me. So if David wants to play with me or wants to get me in trouble, which he often does, then he goes and tells Miss Fletcher.
SF:	*[How would you react?]*
Harry:	*Well I would ignore it, but normally I, I, I kind of know David if he hits you, you say, David, why do you do that and he's "oh I didn't mean it". We were playing a game um, when we used to play blind man's bluff, and I was blind man. I pulled my hat over my eyes, I was walking around, David, everyone was going in staying about two meters away and then touching them and then running, but David came right up to me, made a noise I turned round but he knew I was going to hit him, and then he said "oh you did that on purpose because you can see".*
Matt:	*And he went off crying and if he doesn't get his way that's it, there is nothing you can do about it, so basically we've got to let him have his way, otherwise it just happens, it just repeats itself, over and over and over again.*

The boys recognise David's power. However, it is not a traditional notion of power exercised through an ability to provide muscle, but rather a power that is practised through David's skill in managing the setting as he plays off his understanding of different relationships to achieve what he is after. Power provides a defining feature in this interaction as David seeks to assume power over his peers, and as his peers recognise their powerlessness in the face of the strategic plays that David is able to employ. By strategically positioning 'others', David is able to engineer an outcome, one that Matt and Harry feel forced to accept. Here the impact of 'power' is not simply a one-dimensional perspective that results from the spatial setting that the boys find themselves in. Rather it is far more subtle, as it reflects a web of understandings that are framed through relationships. Notably, however, David's aim is not to be seen as more powerful, rather he wants this group to acknowledge him as a friend, sharing a mutual relationship.

Such thinking on power flags up the extent to which a relational understanding of the interactional setting is important. Recognising the agentic elements that individuals bring to the interaction is, therefore, significant because it provides a means through which to explore how they seek to position themselves in relation to others, which is essential if one is then to make sense of the meaning-making process. Power offers one dimension through which this can be investigated because moral judgements form part of the strategic actions by which individuals seek to place themselves, or are placed, with and amongst others.

Capital

Experience and Emotions

This section is partly influenced by the earlier discussion about hierarchy and boundary. These ideas offer a means for thinking about the extent to which different spaces have different implications for the way in which the individual is free to demonstrate their agency. Bourdieu's notion of 'habitus' was questioned earlier in this chapter for the less than stringent way in which it is able to engage with detailed elements of agency. It is, however, worth reviewing some of the conclusions that Connolly (1998) reaches because they are valuable in terms of encouraging us to think about *experience* and also about *capital* as elements that can further inform the agentic process. Habitus, as Connolly suggests, 'acts unconsciously to organise our social experiences and encourage us to think and behave in certain ways' (1998: 18, see also Connolly 2006). These experiences, therefore, become important in helping us to make sense of individual meaning-making because it is habitus, this set of 'transposable dispositions', that is seen as the restraining factor on the actions of the individual. '[H]abitus imbues people with a tacit sense of how to become competent social agents, which is realised in practices that are constitutive of social life' (James and James 2004: 40). As such, it reflects an interpretation of social structure (Tomanovic 2004) that responds to individual action and is fundamentally reliant upon it.

> People do not create society…rather society must be regarded as an ensemble of structures, practices and conventions, which individuals reproduce or transform, but which would not exist unless they did so. (James and James 2004: 42)

As Connolly (1998) suggests, habitus guides action but it develops through a desire for capital. A useful aspect of Connolly's discussion is the way in which the presentation of capital, and therefore its value to the individual, is framed by a given context. For example, within peer groups in a particular setting, what might result in capital for boys may be seen to be of low value by girls. Therefore, it is important to account for the 'field' within which the struggle for capital takes place. Significantly, as Connolly works his way through the literature, he comes to the conclusion that, rather than fields which have limitations, it is the concept of figuration that offers the best means to capture the backdrop within which habitus is performed. At the centre of this is a set of relationships and interactions which change as children pass between groups.

> Children therefore, can be seen to have multiple habituses that reflect the complex range of social networks that they are involved in. In this sense there is no one, 'true' identity that each child has as manifest through their habitus but rather multiple identities and ways of being that are contingent and context-specific and that can often be contradictory. (2004: 90)

The result is a dynamic process that moves children's engagement a long way from the passive approach as it takes account of the context within which children's lives are lived, with a defining effect on the way in which meaning comes to be shaped and practised (Connolly 2006). It reaffirms the idea of the 'interactional setting' as a feature of the framework in this book: recognising the extent to which children are practising their agency in a variety of spaces, with each of these requiring a different assessment of how the individual positions themselves in that space, as they draw from 'elements' such as capital.

The extent to which this comes to be played out in a moral context can be seen in the following example as a group of boys seek to establish capital with 'PC'.

PC: You said when they came up to you to start with; you were
         playing with some girls?
Paul: Yeah, I had some fighting but he {Daniel} didn't
Daniel: Yes I did!

Paul: No you didn't

Daniel: Jason {White} pushed me in a puddle!

Paul: Yeah, What did you do? Nothing!

Daniel: No

Paul: So you didn't fight, did you? I did! 'Cos I got, erm, one of them over.

Daniel: Yes I did fight! When I was running, I was going to kick them.

Paul: But missed them, didn't you!

Daniel: What?

Paul: Missed them!

Daniel: No I never!

Paul: Well I got, I got, I had two people over from me.

PC: You had two what, Paul? What did you say – you had two people what?

Paul: Down!

PC: Down?

Paul: Three! – Sean, Craig and Jason

Daniel: Yeah, I, I, you got Sean down by kicking him, didn't ya?

Paul: No! He ran and I got my foot out so he tripped over,

Daniel: Yeah, and then he was going to kick you, weren't he?

Paul: Yeah, but he couldn't – he was running and trying to get me but [gets up to rehearse the actions – Daniel also gets up]

Daniel: But he missed, didn't he?

Paul: I put my foot out and he went over […] Then I tripped Karl {White} down so he was, so he was down.

This discussion shows the extent to which the children are trying to represent a particular identity of themselves in front of 'PC', as each boy vies with those around them to position themselves in relation to each other. This discussion has a particular 'spatial' element in that it is happening with peers, at school, in front of an outsider. It is not a conversation taking place at home, in front of parents (for example). Within this discussion, the children are seeking to attach certain values to their behaviours, behaviours that have particular meaning as a result of the space they are in and the people they are with. These six-year-old boys, in relation to the cut and thrust of the playground, are presenting certain moral meanings that are interconnected with a sense of identity drawn from their experiences as they seek to assert a certain 'part' in the ongoing drama of being at school. This example offers a strong illustration of the boys' agency as they process the 'context' through elements of self, creating accepted ways of acting.

Indeed, the following example, reported by Connolly (1998) extends this illustration. Although it is possible to see how a particular group of individuals creates a set of meanings that position themselves within a given space, it is interesting to recognise that that space can create a range of 'contexts' that frame the way in which children 'perform' as they make sense of it through personalised 'elements' of self. Reflecting on the image that teachers create (considered in Chap. 9, also see Appendix 1) of Black boys, here contrasted with South Asian boys, Connolly demonstrates the extent to which the children themselves react to the teacher's characterisation of them and how that comes to inform the way in which they act and behave. The two groups were approached using contrasting moral images: the Black boys were seen as a potential threat to the harmony of the classroom and, as such, they were responded to through arbitrary and direct discipline. That resulted in the creation of a sense of value around being Black, which led to the children seeking ways in which they could maintain that sense of capital. As a consequence, they played a role that reinforced to some extent the part the teacher was 'directing' them to play. It was a role that saw these Black boys become 'walking symbols of masculinity' (1998: 97). This created markers which had implications for the everyday morality that was practised in school. For example, Connolly notes how it created instances of conflict as White boys 'physically and verbally' confronted Black boys as part of 'reasserting their own identity' (1998: 97). This sat in contrast to South Asian boys, who were seen very differently from Black boys, creating a different 'context' for their interactions. The teachers perceived South Asian families as 'tight knit', 'strict' and 'traditional', so the children were considered to be model pupils because the teachers' moral image of the children reflected a sense of conformity and respect. If these boys did not conform, rather than their behaviour being labelled as 'bad', as with the Black boys, it was interpreted as 'laziness' or 'tiredness'. The South Asian boys were, therefore, not seen 'as a serious threat to order and control, [rather their behaviour] would tend to be downplayed by the use of words such as 'silly' and 'immature' (1998: 119). What is so important about Connolly's work is how this contextual definition of a 'moral image' impacts on the children themselves. It creates an identity issue for the South Asian boys that left them having to find ways to manage the label of 'effeminate'. For them, the question of what was and was not acceptable, that notion of everyday morality with implications for meaning-making and action and reaction, has to be understood through a very particular sense of identity, seen here through personalised reflections on 'capital'.

An accepted part of habitus is the unconscious dimension, which sits uncomfortably next to the desire to make visible the different elements that the individual brings to interaction. Although aspects of identity will remain hidden (Smart 2007) through drawing on a greater awareness about the intricacies of personal life, there is a growing opportunity for the social scientist to explore notions such as 'experience' and to look at it with more specific lenses that allow for a deeper investigation. The inclusion of a more developed understanding of emotions, for example, offers a means by which we can start to fill in some of the gaps that have previously existed. It has been too easy to make assumptions about experiences and their impact. However, a more detailed focus on those elements of agency offers the opportunity to delve into those assumptions and, through this, to establish a means of engaging with them. There are, of course, aspects that can affect interaction which sit outside this structure and agency model. This does not mean that these themes should be ignored, rather it invites a growing understanding of the relationship between the biological, psychological and the social, moving away from the acceptance of assumptions. Here, however, the focus is on making visible the social dimension and the extent to which drawing out these elements of personhood provide a framework that can further our understanding of the individual and their decision-making.

4.1.5 A Definition of Agency

Fusing structure and agency permits more informed discussion on those processes of value orientation to which both Durkheim and Parsons refer. This chapter is not saying that we should reject an interpretation

Emotions Biography Memory Conflict Secrecy Imaginary Experience

Body Belonging Power Capital Language

Fig. 4.1

in which morality is transmitted through the structures of society, but that morality needs to be examined with a greater awareness of what it means to have agency. Each social action is informed and shaped by social structure, however this then comes to be interpreted through the filter of the self and the sociologies of our personal lives, providing a foundation for agentic meaning-making and subsequent action or reaction. The researcher, therefore, needs to recognise a range of tools (as listed in the non-exhaustive list in Fig. 4.1), some more incisive than others, that can be used for eliciting a sense of how those personalised 'elements' might impact on meaning-making.

Engagement with morality, therefore, becomes an interest in interpreting 'personal elements' in relation to structure and within the ongoing processes of agency. It offers a framework which allows one to investigate further an individual's journey to moral judgement, action and reaction. Children are no longer pawns to the power of moral forces, rather they are strategic instigators of action, and their actions are played out in a never-ending game of moral chess against these powerful forces, in which the individual is constantly drawing from complex, multi-layered, personalised 'moral' meanings as a fundamental part of being social.

The purpose of this chapter has been to show that the agency element of our original model needs a certain amount of deconstruction if it is going to constitute a tool for tracking those processes of socialisation to which James (2013) refers (see Chap. 2) and which provide a means to make sense of how 'morality' plays a part in children's everyday lives. As such, agency is considered in relation to a range of themes, of which this chapter has merely offered some examples. Moral agency is, therefore, the day–to-day engagement with the social world, which intrinsically involves a moral element of consideration as meanings come to be produced. It leaves us with a definition of agency as the *contextually mediated capacity of the individual to make meanings that inform their actions, that are relationally situated and morally constituted and which are framed within a range of elements that make up children's personal lives.*[7] By strengthening the way in which we are able to observe the workings of agency, we are presented with a tool for analysing an increasing number of areas within social life. At the heart of such investigations sits this reference to a moral dimension to meaning-making.

4.2   Application

The relationship between Parts 1 and 2 of the framework is relevant in all of the interactional settings that children find themselves in. It is just as relevant in formal settings governed by adults, such as a school or a law court, as it is in informal settings that are constructed by children themselves. For example, even if the interactional setting is a bus stop, there remains a need to make sense of the way in which the individual is drawing from that wider structure if one is then going to be able to make sense of the meanings that they go on to create. Within this, the individual will make meanings with respect to some sense of a moral image (or their interpretation of it) and how that relates to the nature of the practices for that setting.

The framework presented here not only offers a model through which to look at the construction of childhoods (Part 1), it also provides a practical tool that can further the way in which we are able to understand the relationship between structure and agency, and its implications for meaning-making. Part 2 of the framework thus provides an opportunity to consider these processes in action, as they build up a set of lenses through which the child could be seen to engage with structure, making meanings that reflect an ongoing moral dimension rooted in their desire to act in ways that reflect a consideration of what is and is not acceptable (Fig. 4.2).

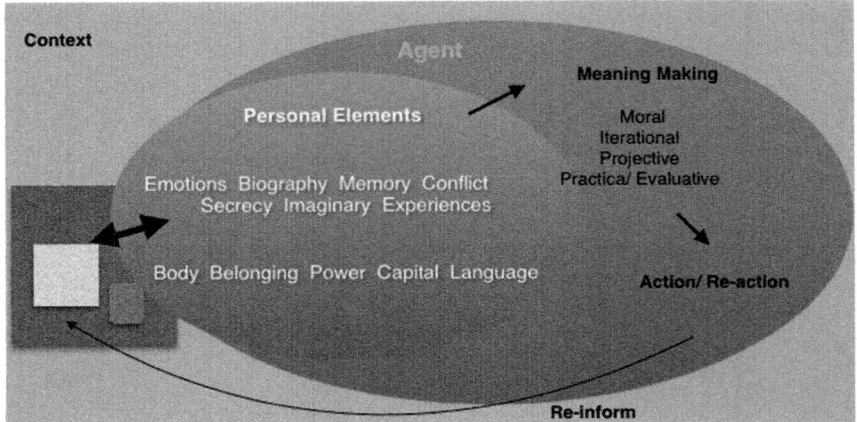

Fig. 4.2 Framework – part 2

4.2.1 Personalised Reflection

The first important feature of Part 2 of the framework is the placement of agentic processes within the contextual themes that were outlined in Chap. 3. It suggests that agency is played out as a dialogue between the agent and those structural themes from which meaning comes to be made. It highlights the bi-directional arrow which, in contrast to traditional models, sees structure as *framing* rather than *defining* as the individual engages with it. Notably, this individual engagement will be directed by the personal elements that the agent brings to interaction, and which will result in a unique response. That does not mean that there is not a commonalty of interpretations, but the way in which interpretation is arrived at must first and foremost be seen as an individual process.

It is, therefore, in response to a range of personal elements that the individual comes to process 'context' as this comes to be framed within particular interactions.

The discussions in the first part of this chapter started to show the active way in which children are engaging with the setting and, in response to this, developing meanings. The active processing of context was presented in relation to different 'elements' that the individual brings into interaction, as considered in relation to the body, power and capital.

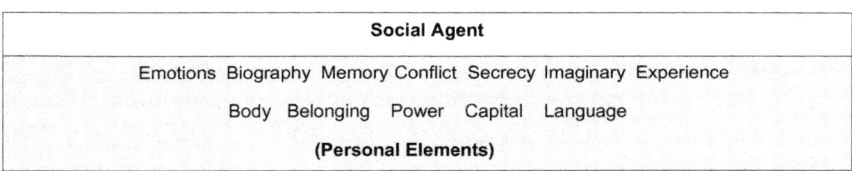

Context	Interactional Setting		
Spatial Factors Cultural Norms Formalised Norms Popular Factors Legacy		**Moral Image of Child** Reason Virtue Social Harmony	**Practice** Policy Defined Practice Informal Practice

Social Agent
Emotions Biography Memory Conflict Secrecy Imaginary Experience
Body   Belonging   Power   Capital   Language
(Personal Elements)

Fig. 4.3   Reflecting structure and agency

Defining these personal elements means that they can be set alongside contextual components for a deeper assessment of the processes that inform meaning-making. Figure 4.3 shows how, in relation to some of these elements, they become filters through which the context is interpreted. Each contextual factor is processed to differing degrees in light of the range of elements that the individual brings to 'moments' of interaction. Naturally, within this, the priority placed on different factors is fluid and dynamic. Through this process of reflection, the individual establishes a foundation for decision-making (Fig. 4.3).

Figure 4.3 shows the bi-directional nature of the relationship between structure and agency and, importantly, how this is processed through a variety of personal elements that reflect considerations of similarity and difference, through to use of language, as well as personal memories or experiences. The assessment of those structural themes (Part 1 of the framework) through consideration of these personal elements provides the basis for meaning-making.

Meaning-making

A theme that emerged from a consideration of these personal elements in the sections above is how, through reflecting on structure, the individual comes to create meanings. The beginning of this chapter considered the steps that form part of meaning-making, with reference to the work of Emirbayer and Mishe (1998). However, it extended the model by suggesting that a fundamental consideration in an individual's response to a structural context is a moral one. Everyday morality is focused on the individual 'weighing up' what is acceptable or not within the context of an interactional space as they seek to negotiate it. Again, definitions of 'acceptable' will differ because the individual makes an assessment with reference to personal elements in light of a particular structure. But nonetheless, meaning-making encompasses an integral moral element that allows the individual to position themselves in relation to others. This aspect of the framework thus shows the extent to which children are processing meanings through these elements of self, with reference to the wider structure in which they find themselves. These meanings notably reflect the extent to which children are weighing questions of everyday morality as part of navigating the social world – a social world that would be impossible to traverse unless children were engaged in asking and answering questions about what was and was not acceptable.

Action/Reaction

The place of a moral dimension within this framework is essential. Without it, our ability to understand meaning and how it relates to action and reaction is significantly restricted. The outcomes from meaning-making are, of course, not always going to be a definable act, such as a punch or sharing a toy, but also include responses such as changing or modifying a behaviour, establishing a memory or simply not doing anything at all. Action and reaction might be reflected in a current action, or they might provide information that will shape future actions.

A significant aspect of action/reaction is the extent to which it reinforms future interactions or, indeed, later parts of an ongoing interaction.

This will be considered in more detail in Chap. 9. Here, however, what the model seeks to illustrate is the connection between a structural dimension and how an individual responds to it. It is with this focus that the following chapters will seek to establish a sense of the 'backdrop' in front of which children are left to negotiate their everyday lives.

4.3   Conclusion

The components of agency add further detail that can support developing understandings of the relationship between structure and agency. In so doing, they provide the basis for a more in-depth analysis of the process of agency itself, from which one gets a clearer sense of how the individual child comes to engage with morality. Having outlined the framework, the next step is to further the case for reason, virtue and social harmony, before looking again at agency and how children engage with notions of morality as part of strategically negotiating their everyday lives.

Notes

1. Oswell sums up the case for the visibility of agency by drawing on the following quote: 'the social competence of children is to be seen as a practical achievement: that is, it is not something which is accorded to children by adults, like a right, and can thus be redefined or removed. Rather, social competence is seen as something children work at possessing in their own right, the display of which is an active, agents achievement (Hutchby and Moran Ellis 1998: 14).
2. The dynamic component of generationing, is reflected in Alanen's comments about what studying it allows,

   By conceptually privileging the asymmetry between children and adults, childhood and adulthood, space is opened for empirically exploring:
       1. The generational structures that are composed of generational categories (positions) of childhood and adulthood…linking them into a reciprocal interdependency, as well as relationship of power;

2. The material, social and cultural processes in which children and adults, as both individual and collective actors, are involved, and in which also their everyday activities are embedded so that generational (re)structuring is recurrently effected; and finally

3. The cultural systems of meanings, symbols and semantics through which existing generational categories and their interrelationships are produced and rendered culturally meaningful.

(Alanen 2011 168–169)

3. Gilligan's (1982) work on women and morality established a sense in which women had a particular perspective on moral understanding.

4. Kantor et al. (1998) observed this in relation to friendship-building amongst children aged five years. Research with even younger children has also noted children's capacity as 'agents'.

5. Lukes (2005) includes the different ways in which communities use power, including collaboratively to create shared values.

6. Foucault in *Discipline and Punish* (1979), as well as in *Madness and Civilisation* (1988), reflects on the way in which power offers a structural dimension that is framed and reframed by society. That wider sense of Foucauldian power is relevant here, but more in relation to the way in which it has an impact on the constructed nature of childhood. This is a more overt theme in Chaps. 5, 6 and 7.

7. This definition draws from the work of Alan Pomfret, Kings University College at University of Western Ontario.

Step 3

Deconstructing Dominant Discourses

The following three chapters will look in detail at reason, virtue and social harmony as they engage with Part 1 of the framework

There is a significant amount that could be said in relation to the themes of reason, virtue and social harmony, therefore, what follows is simply an indication of the extent to which they offer relevant filters through which to consider a moral dimension to the construction of a contextual backdrop with which children engage as they negotiate everyday experiences.

Each chapter loosely associates each of these filters with a consideration of their impact in relation to the settings of the home, school and the neighbourhood. However, as will become clear, there is considerable overlap between them. What is notable about considering the history of these ideas is the extent to which they continue to play a part in projecting strains of thought onto images of the child today. As suggested in Chap. 3, it is not sufficient to simply draw on an image from the past and apply it to the present, but one can consider the similarities and differences, and the extent to which repetition and reapplication of certain moral discourses is prevalent.

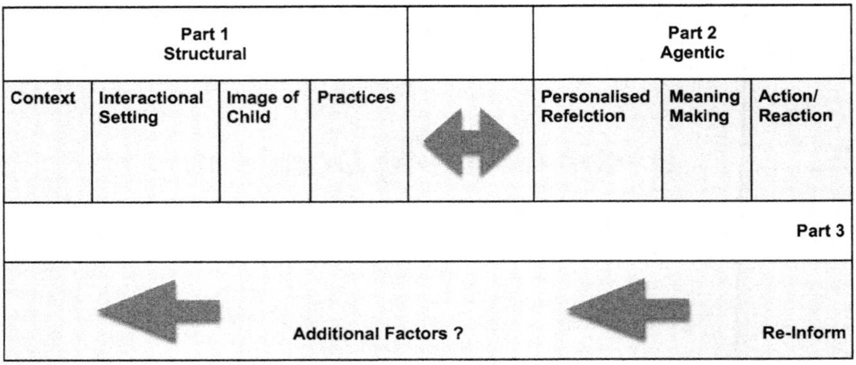

Part 1 Structural					Part 2 Agentic		
Context	Interactional Setting	Image of Child	Practices		Personalised Refelction	Meaning Making	Action/ Reaction

Part 3
Additional Factors ?   Re-Inform

Fig. 1   The framework

It is important to reiterate that the review that is to follow, which draws mainly from Western European examples, does not set out to provide a historical analysis of all relevant evidence. Rather, the aim is to show that, by introducing these moral filters, themes emerge that are helpful in establishing a sense of the backdrop against which the social agent is seen to respond. In creating this backdrop one is also recognising the strength of the constructed nature of childhoods, and the way in which images shape the practices that frame children's experiences.

5

Reason

There was an old woman who lived in a shoe,
she had so many children she didn't know what to do.
She gave them some broth without any bread,
and whipped them all soundly and sent them to bed.

The aim of this chapter is to establish an element of the contextual backdrop by drawing out certain dominant images of the child in relation to reason, and to examine how reason comes to be associated with practices that frame children's everyday experiences. Although the focus is on the past, the themes raised in this chapter not only highlight how deeply rooted our approach to children is, but also the extent to which these themes continue to have an impact on contemporary constructions of childhood. Although this issue is considered here, mainly in relation to children in the home, it has much wider application. In short, it is only by casting one's attention back to the history of thought in this area that one can get a sense of the significant chains that continue to bind adults to particular images of the child, with implications for how children are positioned in relation to moral discourses.

© The Editor(s) (if applicable) and The Author(s) 2017
S. Frankel, *Negotiating Childhoods*, Studies in Childhood and Youth,
DOI 10.1057/978-1-137-32349-1_5

Reason, in this book, is defined with reference to the individual's ability to engage with morality, as it questions an internal capacity for competence. As Plato notes, reason has to be the staring point because, without it, there is no consideration of virtue. Reason thus reflects an assessment of the competence and capacity of the individual, a way of thinking that was not just made explicit in Ancient Greece but in other societies as well.[1] Reason has thus become the key factor in defining access to moral discourses. In relation to children, a model has emerged, and continues today, in which 'reason' is generally framed by a time of ignorance (associated with age) which then comes to be transformed at a moment of enlightenment, empowering them with 'understanding'. It is an approach that, from its early days, has been framed by a sense of hierarchy with questions of gender, class, age and race playing their part in establishing a sense of moral competence (themes that are equally relevant today). In many ways, morality was (and arguably still is) the province of a chosen elite who were marked out by their education, power, gender and wealth and who managed their position with reference to the 'reason' of others (Cockburn 2013). It is that insipid sense of hierarchy that is going to dominate the journey in this chapter as we travel from Ancient Greece through to the psychologists that have shaped so many of our attitudes towards reason today. In short, this chapter demonstrates how constructed images of the child must be understood with reference to the moral dimension, which is central to the structuring of children's lives.

5.1   A Managed Household

For Socrates, the 'city state' as a model offered a means to manage natural human compulsions. He perceived man as being driven by aggression and lust, which was curbed under a model of moral regulation as man came to live amongst others within the city state. Within this model the free born man was morally superior thanks to an advanced capacity to reason, which set them apart from others, such as women and children. The issue was, how was society to ensure order if only a few had a heightened capacity to reason? Society, therefore, needed a tool through which that model of moral regulation could be applied, and the family became such a tool.

It marked the start of a relationship between the state and the head of the family that has existed (for many) ever since, in which the state provides all the benefits of membership in return for an expectation that the family will be well managed (based on a hierarchical model). Notably this 'contract' includes the state agreeing not to interfere with how the family is then run. In its early design the 'family' therefore offers a model of the rich, powerful and morally aware man who, through an assessment of 'reason', sat in the *polis* in government over others, and who would come back to his household to run his own mini state. Here, then a moral foundation is built on an accepted belief that adults (in this case men) can provide moral direction as they represent a capacity for moral thought that is hierachically superior to those for whom they are responsible.

This paradigm has strong roots in classical history and places the child at the bottom of a hierarchical model of moral competence, such that they need to be managed. For example, Xenophon in commentary on the Spartan family writes of how the men were not just in charge of their own children but all children:

> in other states each man exercises control over his own children and slaves and property. Lycurgus [Spartan ruler] wanted to find a way that the citizens would profit from one another without doing harm. He therefore gave each man authority over his own children and over the children of others. (Xenophon cited in Pomeroy 1997: 42)

The Spartan model shows the need for governance as pervasive within that society, as men took responsibility to respond to a particular construction of a moral image of the child.

This is also seen in Roman society, where patriarchy defines home as a space of authoritarian management outside the reach of the state (as far as possible). Grand legal powers were given to the head of a Roman family as he undertook a role that could, if conducted successfully, became a personal symbol of power and prestige. It demonstrates the state's clever use of the family as a management tool that would in effect operate itself, without any need for state investment. It was, therefore, in the interests of the *pater* to ensure that his house reflected a sense of virtue and order (Sadler 1994). The power of the *pater* extended to decisions on life and death as 'parental power' (ibid 105) came to be reflected in family ideals such as 'pietas' (dutiful respect), which in reality meant, as recorded by one Roman, 'there are hardly any other men who have over their children a power as we have' (ibid.: 114). The role of the Roman *pater* was to rule over a submissive and obedient household, one that he was encouraged to govern with a 'combination of rein and spur'. This did not always mean physical punishment: 'children ought to be led to honourable practices by means of encouragement and reasoning and most certainly not by blows nor by ill treatment' (ibid.: 143). Whether this advice was followed is not the key point,[2] it was the use of a specific management style which in this case gave fathers considerable power over their household as they took on the role of maintaining a definable order, one that was reinforced by cultural acceptance and expectation that, notably, was formed as a response to a particualar image of the 'moral' child.

Patriarchy is an approach to the family that is founded on certain understandings, a particular conception of children and their capacity to reason. Interestingly, these attitudes to reason can be examined in contrast to other family arrangements. For example, Pomeroy's (1997) review of Roman society, particularly in relation to the late republic, describes an alternative model. Here considering the lower classes, Pomeroy suggests that these families were more closely knit, mothers had more power and there was 'affectionate regard for children' (1997: 9). This brief example offers no conclusive evidence about alternative images of the child per se, but through the lens of reason it certainly invites further consideration of the way in which questions of competence impacted family structure (as reflected here in the role of the mother).

However, it is the sense of reason driving a model of the hierarchical family that has dominated. A recognition of hierarchy in the management of kin relations is provided by Stone (1979) in his look at English society from the 1500s. Stone offers a view of the link between kin relationships and a sense of hierarchy, which I am arguing here is fundamentally linked to understandings of competence or reason. Within the home, the place of the individual was superseded by the desire of the 'unit' as a whole to successfully continue the lineage. As such, 'these lineage and kin relationships provide society with its political framework, and formed the principal bonding of patronage and good lordship on the one hand, and loyalty and deference on the other' 1979: 86.). It is a model that, as Stone notes, links in with a wider political aspiration for the family. From this viewpoint the recognition of succession and continuation were key, and were seen as best achieved through the careful application of a managed model of the home. These desires can be seen as influential in the previous examples from Classical history, and reflect a perspective that was going to inform future societies and their perspective on the home.

Both historical accounts (Stone 1979; Pateman 1988) and more contemporary analysis (Rose 1989) reflect the way in which patriarchy has continued as a theme in the management of the family. Rose comments that the use of the family to regulate children 'had become a key mechanism of social control and ideological support for a patriarchal capitalism that maintained women and children in a state of dependency' (1989: 126). This is reflected in attitudes to women that have only relatively recently been relaxed (Foucault 1977). The extent to which a 'patriarchal capitalism' remains today is perhaps not as definable due to the changing composition of the family, but, although the role of the father might have shifted, the purpose of the family as a site for the management of children has not. Models of management remain topics of discussion. In 2016 British Prime Minister, David Cameron, sparked conversation by his support of the 'tiger mum' (Chua 2011) model of parenting. In relation to strategies for tackling child poverty, Cameron encouraged '"tiger mums" who adopt a disciplinary approach to parenting' (*The Times*, 12/1/2016). This model involves adults establishing a firm timetable within which children's lives are lived, with mums defining and shaping their children's out of school time. In so many ways, it reflects the models of patriarchy that preceded it because assessments about the child define the way in which parents position them within the home. As such, the question of competence (that capacity for making the 'right' decisions) is a significant one that needs to continually be asked as we seek to understand the relationship between children and adults.

5.2   Sharing the Load

A practice that evolved in response to constructed images of the child, driven by dominant attitudes to reason which limited children's competence, was the role of outsiders in helping parents to manage this interregnum between incompetence and competence.

For example, classical Greek and Roman society had a number of adult roles focused on providing oversight of the child during this period of their 'development', from the nurse, whose role included making children 'sensible and not fussy about their food, not afraid of the dark or frightened of being left alone, not inclined to unpleasant awkwardness or whining' (Amos and Laing 1979: 51), through to those who took responsibility for children's education (see next chapter). The use of outsiders to provide support was a model that continues through history. These roles can be analysed in relation to the images of the child that they draw off, images that would have resulted in very particular practices as reason (and virtue in the following chapter) came to be assessed.

Drawing on outsiders is very defined within Roman society (see Ranson and Weaver 1997; Rawson 2003),[3] particularly among the wealthy where the role of the mother appears to have been restricted.[4] For example the *nutrix*, or wet nurse, had a legendary value within Roman society. Romulus and Remus (the founders of Rome) and Aeneas were all said to have had the same wet nurse. The role of the nurse thus became engrained in Roman society. Bradley (1991) illustrates the range of roles that a nurse might have,[5] as well as highlighting their centrality to children's everyday lives.[6] The moral nature of this role and the seriousness with which it was seen, both in terms of its possible impact on the child and, one might argue, wider society as a result, is highlighted very clearly in a decree, issued by Constantine in AD 326, about what should be done if a nurse led a child astray,

> Since the watchfulness of parents is often frustrated by the stories and wicked persuasions of nurses, punishment shall threaten first such nurses whose care is proved to have been detestable and their discourse bribed, and the penalty shall be that the mouth and throat of those who offered incitement to evil shall be closed by pouring in molten lead. (ibid.)

Due to her place in the child's everyday world, the *nutrix* would have been considered to be undertaking a particular role in sustaining social order. It is with reference to 'reason' that this role is shaped because the nurse acts as an extension of the parents to manage, or oversee, the child during this stage of their development.

It is interesting that the use of others was not restricted to women. Men were also employed to provide guidance to children (Bradley 1991). This included roles that have been described in a range of ways, from the simple educator to the pedagogues, who also took on a child minder-type role, but with a greater moral dimension. Importantly, Bradley suggests that these roles were more widespread than might have been expected: 'it should not follow that parents at all social levels constantly used child minders for all of their children, but it is clear that use of child minders was not a practice confined to the upper level of society, as the literary evidence might seen at first to suggest' (1991: 48). As a response to the child's perceived lack of reason, the role of the adult was not only to guide, but also significantly to spend 'time' with the child (which, as argued later, is an important part of a moral learning process). The notion of 'time' as a quality of home is an aspect that children refer to today (Christensen 2002; James 2013). It is, therefore, an important area of both past and current relationships between children and adults, one that can be considered through this lens of competence, as a dimesnion within a wider moral discourse.

The lens of reason offers a source to consider the construction of roles in relation to the home, both in history and today. Historically, it has seen parents relying on other adults, outside of the home through apprenticeships and school, and within the home through nannies, tutors and governesses (McBride 1997).[7] In order to be fully understood, each of these roles must be assessed by considering how it was linked to the competence of the child, the parents' moral goals and ambitions for their children, and how it was to be directed by the parents as they sought to maintain and preserve the social order of their home (Ryan 2013),[8] thus a constructed understanding of the competence of the child becomes a theme in how parents design their role, and carry it out. Indeed, parents are (in many cases unwittingly) called on to make significant decisions about their child's capacity as they align themselves behind certain styles or approaches. As the discussion in this chapter will go on to show, dominant understandings of reason that limit children's competence to their biological age continue to be influential. As such, reference to reason remains a defining feature in structuring the roles played by both adults and children within the home as images are constructed and pursued by reliance on particular practices.

5.3   The Soul of the Child

The framework highlights the extent to which certain forces or parameters come to influence the constructed images of the child, arguably one of the most dominat strains of thought has been theological. Here the discussion will relate to the influence of Christianity on thinking around children and reason. It will show how the weight of these contextual themes, here influenced by the church, come to impact on the interactional settings that children are part of, as an image of the child emerges linked to particular understandings of reason.

In the first instance, the spread of Christianity through Europe challenged the idea that reasoned thought was the province of solely the 'competent man'. Indeed, Christian teaching promoted the notion that the ability to reason was 'universal', that in fact it could not and should not be seen as the preserve of a chosen few. Although many elements of Christian doctrine may be considered to have restricted children's ability to be part of any moral discourse, one should not underestimate the significance of this promotion of the individual to reasoned thinker (MacIntyre 1998). However, this did not result in a pure application of this thesis; reason remained hierarchically bound, and more so as morality became the focus of the 'natural law' theorists.

The breakdown of the Holy Roman Empire saw ideas that had originally been presented by Aristotle being given new energy by Aquinus. Aquinas sought to merge themes from Aristotle with the growing traditions of the church. Within this, 'reason' was to be seen as divinely given:

> human reason (given by God) was a starting point for morality. Reason could offer a logical basis for those moral precepts that were also known through revelation, and which could be supplemented by the specific moral rules presented in the scriptures. (Thompson 2005: 63)

As such Aquinas reasserted that reason was the starting point for moral thought, here within the particular context of a natural and universal ability which each individual is assumed to have. Indeed, Aquinas does not dodge the logical conclusions of his assertions about the individual and their 'personal' capacity to reason. Translations of Aquinas' work use the term 'agent', referring not only to the ability of individuals to act under their own will but also to make decisions that bring an action to completion. As such, Aquinas makes the case for personal responsibility:

> For some things are so produced by God that, being intelligent, they bear a resemblance to Him and reflect His image: wherefore not only are they directed, but they direct themselves to their appointed end by their own actions. (Thompson 2005: 64)

It is as the result of a 'natural' capacity, given in this instance by God, that Aquinas favours the freedom of the individual to act under their own direction. However, those actions and the extent to which they are seen to reflect 'God' are, it is suggested, based on intelligence. This begs the question of how that intelligence is seen to be applied. To what extent are children favoured with such intelligence? It creates what Cockburn describes as an ambiguity about the child in which the early Aristotelian views of children as 'incomplete and incapable' (Cockburn 2013: 41) sit alongside understandings of a 'a saviour, born as a baby, who taught that the kingdom of heaven belonged to those who were little children' (Clarke, cited in Cockburn 2013: 40).

5.3.1 Mediating for the Sins of the Child: The Church

From 600AD Christianity began to take hold in the UK and for the next 1000 years the Catholic church was arguably the most influential factor in shaping children's childhoods (Cunningham 1995). The way in which Christianity took root within Anglo-Saxon England[9] and the implications this had for children and their experiences of home offers a great example of how changing cultural norms (marked here by the move from tribal family patterns to a more patriarchal model (Casey 1939)) can have an impact on the structure of the interactional setting. It provided a foundation that impacted the legal system and, eventually, even the way in which politics came to be done. The rapid growth of the church among the people, but particularly among their leaders, meant that Anglo-Saxon England was quickly deferring to the church at every level of society. It only took 100 years from the arrival of Augustine in

597 for all the leaders to convert to Christianity (Cunningham 1995). The church seems to have taken responsibility quickly for certain key areas of life, not only in terms of guidance but also in judgement, with church courts taking on certain decision-making duties. This is clearly seen in relation to the family, as perspectives on the role of the family were devolved to the church rather than remaining with the state.

An important factor for consideration in the take-up of this new approach must be viewed in relation to the images of the child that the church promoted. Death was a very real part of people's experience. One's mortality, therefore, was constantly being brought into focus and parents were under pressure to take spiritual responsibility for their child. The importance of this should not be underestimated for in simply acknowledging that the child had a spiritual dimension, the value of the child changed which impacted on how children were positioned both within the practical space of home and also within theory and understandings of reason.[10]

This repositioning of the child has been characterised by some as a more personalised approach to the child: '[C]hristian teaching … softened attitudes towards children' (Herlily 1985: 26). What the population were being asked to consider was not the economic value, or necessarily the social value, of children but their spiritual value. The child as a gift of God meant that the 'receiving' parents had a particular role to play in responding to the 'present' that had been given to them. Cunningham sums up this sense of the child being a gift by drawing from the words of an old Anglo-Saxon poem:

> It very often comes to pass by God's might
>> That man and wife bring, by means of birth,
>> A child in the world and provide him with delights,
>> Cheer and cherish him.
> (Cunningham 1995: 23)

For many, parental responsibility had been assessed in terms of the child's economic meaning, such that children could be both a help and a hindrance to the family, with infanticide being one of the outcomes of the latter (Cunningham 1995). However, the church challenged this, so the family, through the birth of children, became a key site with which society made 'morality' of relevance to all.

This comes to be reflected in customs which reinforce a particular image of the child and place it at the heart of society. In emerging Christian Anglo-Saxon England, baptism became an accepted rite and with it a marking of the child's spiritual and, therefore, moral place within society. Such was the importance of baptism that not only were laws in place to make sure that people baptised their children (Cunningham 1995), but also midwives were later recognised as being able to carry out this rite on children they thought might not survive (Hanawalt 1993). Baptism was believed to wash away the sin that had been passed on from Adam, establishing the question of individual morality as the key issue marking a child's entry into the social world. Although, notably, baptism did not mean that the child was free of 'bad' behaviour (see later), what it did do was mark out the body of the child as a site for purification. It identified the individual child as a moral being, with very real implications for those roles within the home.

Baptism also provided an entry point into the 'community',[11] which included bestowing a name upon the child. However, as well as welcoming the child, one cannot move far beyond the rite of baptism as a reaction to a predefined moral nature. The writings of Augustine sum up the stakes he believed were involved, and which made baptism so central. For him, children who were not baptised were not permitted entry into heaven: 'he will be in everlasting hell' (Herlily 1985). For a society in which death was so real, this image must have been very frightening, acting as a driver to engage with the churche's moral teachings and the image of the child it presented . It also marks a journey for the child, that recognises from the start that their life will be one in which they have to come to know what is and is not acceptable.[12] As a result, parents became not just guardians of their children's economic potential in life, but also their spiritual potential in eternity. It marked a real change in the point and purpose of parenting and in the way home life was structured. Managing the child's moral development was now an area where adults could not afford to fail because it would not only bar their children from a place in human communities but also from their place in the everlasting community offered in heaven.

The key factor that emerges through applying this lens of reason is the value that was ascribed to the child. It reflected a tension, considered at the start of this section, between a wider recognition of the child needing to be managed and an acceptance that the child had a level of competence that adults should acknowledge. This is illustrated through the role of children, both boys and girls, within the church itself. In Europe, children at the age of seven years could be invited to enter the church as an 'oblate' receiving a 'master' to supervise them as they took on an official role as either a monk or a nun. Commentators of the time noted how the 'oblate' was granted some sense of being 'special' because they were seen as disconnected from some of the distractions of the adult world and were, perhaps, seen as more capable of managing some of the temptations that could corrupt. As Kuefler notes, 'he does not persist in anger; he does not bear a grudge; he does not delight in the beauty of women; and he expresses what he truly believes' (Kuefler 2003: 825). This placed a value on the child, in this context, as a 'moral' lead, not because they were little adults but because their 'psychological make up …was different from that of adults' (ibid.). This was also reflected in children taking on the role of boy bishops (Cunningham 2006) which, although linked to times of festival, carried a serious meaning as the 'lowly' came to be lifted up, albeit very briefly.

The discussion above creates an interesting tension that demands different considerations of the image of the child in relation to reason, one which continues to be played out in the relationship that children, their parents and the church continue to hold. This is demonstrated by some societies' attitudes towards children being taken over by evil spirits (*Guardian*, 1/3/2012) which need to be beaten out of them, to the other extreme in which children are listened to by adults and respected for their insight (New York Times, 2015).[13]

5.3.2   Mediating for the Sins of the Child: Parents

The contrasts highlighted above were allowed to exist within the pre-Reformation church. However they were quickly closed down as the European church went through a seismic shift. What stands out, as one considers the way in which reason came to be associated with the Reformation, was the increased sense of parents' responsibility, as their role was increasingly defined in terms of shaping the child's spiritual and moral future. For Martin Luther and others, the family became the central cog of the workings of the 'reformed' church and as such the church's teachings and the constructed images of the child it created became a significant factor in shaping the backdrop to children's everyday experiences. What Luther and his followers presented was an understanding that an individual's spiritual journey was not dependent on a human intermediary such as a priest, but was conducted directly with God. The individual, therefore, had to take over the role that had previously been left to the priest – they had to take personal responsibility for their relationship with God. This might not seem a signficant change but it was revolutionary. Moral responsibility and, as a consequence, spiritual well-being became an individual concern.

The Lutherans' interpretation of 'original sin' placed children in a perpetual cycle of sinful action or thought, discovery, admonition, forgiveness and restitution.[14] Notably such sin created a barrier to their spiritual well being and thus it had to be addressed. Previously, as a result of baptism within the Catholic church and one's ongoing relationship with the priest this barrier was managed. Now, however, in the eyes of the reformers, the potential barrier between man and God lay in the hands of man alone. which meant that parents within the home took on a key role in ensuring their child's moral and spiritual well being, as practices were shaped by an image of the child and its associated conception of reason. As a result of this that the Reformation in Europe created an era in which 'no age subscribed more completely to the notion that the hand that rocked the cradle ruled the world' (Bonner 1998). Luther himself stated 'there is no power on earth that is nobler or greater than that of parents' (Bonner 1998: 132). The reason for this is explained by Justus Menius:

> [T]he diligent rearing of children is the greatest service to the world, both in spiritual and temporal affairs, both for the present life and for posterity...just as one turns young calves into strong cows and oxen, rears young colts to be brave stallions, and nurtures small tender shoots into great fruit

breeding trees, so must we bring up our children to be knowing and coura-
geous adults, who serve both land and people and both to prosper. (quoted
in Bonner 1998: 132)

Meniues' analysis highlights how the parental role is concerned with the
moral and spiritual, the day to day and the eternal, is the building block
for family life. It is an approach to parenting that continually lays responsibility upon responsibility, drawing together so many of the themes from
the previous sections. Parenting was a serious business and a zealousness
was encouraged as parents were instructed not to spoil the child: 'the cardinal sin of child rearing in reformation Europe, a common one, according to the moralists, was wilful indulgence of children' (Bonner 1998:
133). The implications of indulging children was that it paved the way
to them becoming 'mercenaries, murderers and criminals' (Conrad Sam,
cited in Bonner 1998: 133). Indeed, sixteenth-century English paediatri-
cians, Phaire and Jones, linked 'coddling' and 'spoiling', with laziness and
crime, with the result that it was seen as the single-most cause for filling
jails and burdening parish charities.

The above examples illustrate how from the 1600's the importance of
the soul of the child took on huge significance for the home and roles
within it. They demonstrate how the composition of moral images of the
child must be explored in relation to a range of contextual parameters, as
here we look to the church in order to trace how its teachings came to be
interpreted within a given time and place. These themes can still be seen
in the image of the child in popular books at the turn of the nineteenth
century. These tales of morality placed children directly within the cycle
(mentioned above) that moved from sin to restitution. For example, in
Mary Sherwood's *The Fairchild Family* (1869), the children's hope lay
firmly in the attention of their parents in dealing appropriately with their
wilful desires. The moral image of the child, as defined with reference
to reason, is such that it creates a means for understanding the zeal with
which parents take on their roles as we are reminded how they are the key
factor in shaping their children's position, both on earth and in heaven.

Simply saying that the church was influential is not enough. By combining this influence with a moral filter additional dimensions emerge
through which it is possible to add some understanding to observable

practices. Although the place of religion has changed significantly in many societies in the past 100 years, it is still an important contextual theme and one that needs to be interrogated further through a moral lens. Indeed, in 2015, the place of religion and its relationship to the family was being presented in stories that related to Islamic extremism (touched on in Chap. 3) internationally (*Calgary Herald*, 1/10/15; *Premium Times*, 30/9/15), as well as in discussions about sex education and corporal punishment. The coverage of Pope Francis' 2016 statement about the family, *Amoris Laetitia* (*Joy of Love*) (Catholic Church 2016), shows that, even though the church might not have the dominance it once did, it still retains a significant voice in framing images of the child.[15] Indeed, faith as a whole must be seen as a dominant factor in influencing the interactional settings in which children live their lives.

5.4   Reason and the Enlightenment

The strength of the church as a factor in influencing constructed understandings of the child and as a consequence, practices, was signficant but this did not stop a challenge to the churches pre-eminence as even in the seventeenth century (at the height of the Reformation) theorists jostled, shoved and pushed one another in a battle to offer a 'definitive' moral view. It marks an approach to reason that was going to offer a foundation for the developmental models that were to be so influential in the 20th Century, as they came to interpret ideas that reflected the importance of a universal understanding of reason.

Thomas Hobbes ([1651] 2008) marks a move from the natural law position (and the views of Aquinas and Aristotle) to what is termed 'social contract theory'. Again with echoes of classical traditions, Hobbes frames a view that requires a level of competence through which the individual can actively enter into an agreement to be part of society. Within this, a certain value is attached to the individual, as one is encouraged to ask who society needs to be in 'contract' with. Cockburn (2013) makes the point that this can be viewed in the context of property. The ability to fulfil such a contract was what marked the citizen. 'Children were written out of this process…children shifted from being active participants towards a special group requiring little more socially than education' (Cockburn 2013: 48). This approach reflects a general trend in which society is ordered by a powerful patriarchy both within the home and within society more widely. As such, the value of the child was increasingly limited, creating a model of division between the competent and reasoned adult and the child. Here, reason comes to be defined by value, establishing images of a moral child in which children (and women) are placed outside of having the formation of mind to make a meaningful contribution.

The sense of meaningful contribution was to be reassessed by Locke (1772). In reclaiming the freedom of the individual, albeit within the boundaries of biology, intelligence was to be linked to experience within a system where all had potential value.

> Children…are not born in this full state of equality, though they are born to it. The parents have a sort of rule and jurisdiction over them when they come into the world, and for some time after, but it is a temporary one. The bonds of subjection are like the swaddling clothes they are wrapt up in and supported by the weakness of their infancy. Age and reason as they grow up loosen them, till at length they drop quite off and leave a man at his own free disposal. (Locke cited in Cockburn 2013: 52)

This process was defined for Locke by the assertion that 'humans become knowledgeable users of reason' (Archard 2004: 2). It is the process of 'becoming' that is key to Locke's thinking. Although it has been suggested that, in keeping with other philosophers, Locke's approach to the child is scattered and unsystematic, it does, as Archard (2004) suggests, offer one of the first efforts to place the child formally within philosophical analysis. This illustrates how children were not (and never had been) a traditional focus for the philosopher, marking a point from which others started to call into question why certain groups had been excluded and how one might be able to inform and be informed better by a greater willingness to engage. It is, therefore, not surprising that Locke's approach to the child is awkward and full of tensions (Archard 2004), although he is able to at least consider the state of ignorance that had so blithely been ascribed to children in the past. In so doing, he reflects on what might be seen as more extensive abilities than had been acknowledged previously and, rather than viewing 'ignorance' as a vacuum, he recognized 'ignorance' that was layered as the result of different and, over time, increasing experiences. From the famous starting point of the child as a 'blank slate' (*tabula rasa*), Locke starts to encourage the need for filling in the gaps as children learn.

> Children, says Locke, are 'travellers newly arrived in a strange country, of which they know nothing'. What makes them strangers in our country is their lack of both knowledge and moral sense. Reason covers both aspects of what must be acquired if they are to become full members of our country. (Archard 2004:3)

This distinction demands that it is simply not good enough to rely on the dispositions that a baby is born with, 'natural tendencies imprinted on the minds of man', because the pursuit of knowledge means that children must learn through experiences. Recognising this and being prepared to engage with it had significant implications for society. Again drawing from the classical tradition, it marked the sense in which the growth to moral knowledge is best achieved within the context of learning. As such, the need for education as a tool for the development of 'reason' is set, providing just one example of the way in which such thinking had an effect on children's lived experiences.

The Enlightenment, not by chance named the 'Age of Reason', produced a re-energising of reason as a tool for shaping practices towards children. This was not only seen within the home, but also, significantly, within education. Although education will be a more direct focus in the next chapter, it is worth reflecting on it here in order to illustrate how conceptions of reason formed part of those images of the child that influenced education. This has implications for the institution of schooling that remain today, and parents' expectations regarding the need for the child to be taught.

> The most obvious features of the Enlightenment are its practical and unimaginative character, its hatred of vague enthusiasm, and misty ideals and ideas, its determination to apply the test of a severely accurate reason to everything and reject outright whatever will not stand the test, and the constant reference in all this, as the court of final appeal, to the one

undoubted fact – the individual himself with his rights, and his rational powers of understanding. (Curtis and Boultwood 1977: 263–264)

Hobbes and Locke have already been mentioned. However I want to reflect a little further on Locke's work and its implications for education, both in the school room and in the home. Locke, as had Plato before, was searching for a role for education that enabled its recipients to achieve a level of competence that would allow them to take up a positive role in social life (Cunningham 1995). However, as with Plato's thinking, the child needed to have the capacity to 'reason' inspired within them. Fletcher writes that Locke presented 'entirely novel ideas of habit formation' (Fletcher 2008: 6), although they seem not considerably different from the ideas of both Plato and Aristotle. However, what Locke did do was ground thinking about education in the context of the child themselves. It was the positioning of the child in Locke's writings that differentiated him, laying the way for Rousseau and others that followed. Unlike his predecessors, Locke (1998) provides an analysis of that journey to reason as the child increasingly (through time) establishes a sense of personal control that brings reason in line with will. This requires the child to recognise the need to submit 'his will to the reason of others'(Fletcher 2008: 6), 'a process whose internalisation was the key to the creation of a successful moral adult'(Fletcher 2008: 6, citing Cunningham). Education, therefore, provided a means for bestowing 'morals' on children as part of preparing them for the adult world. Also, like Plato, Locke promoted the importance of the educator, calling on them to execute their task with 'great sobriety, temperance, tenderness, diligence and discretion'(cited by Fletcher 2008: 7) if they were to be successful. Whether the 'educator' was a parent or teacher Locke left his readers in no doubt of their importance as they were the ones who 'must write on the paper or mould the wax'(cited in Cunningham 1995: 55) – a responsibility that was, as Cunningham suggests, seen to be 'colossal'.

Children's reason needed to be brought out, it needed to be encouraged, and adults could not get away from their responsibilities. Without adults, children had little hope. Whether that is the blank slate of Locke or the innocent child of Rousseau, all children needed support and guidance whilst on the journey to develop reason. One of the significant themes that developed as part of this discourse was a realisation that adults were not as knowledge-able about children as they might have thought they were. Indeed Rousseau starts his work, *Emile*, by saying that 'we know nothing of childhood, and with our mistaken notions, the further we advance, the further we go astray. The wisest writers devote themselves to what a man ought to know without asking what a child is capable of learning'(Rousseau cited in Curtis and Boultwood 1997: 276). The need to understand the child thus became part of that growing responsibility that adults sought to accept as they considered how to respond to this period of moral ignorance, with implications for the images of the child that came to be constructed.

5.4.1 Light and Dark: Tension and Relationship

In light of the changing attitudes explored above, what increasingly emerges is a growing acceptance of a more gentle relationship between children and their parents. It marks the relevance of engaging with these images and their relationship to changing philosophical ideas (Hendrick 1997) as a focus for understanding practices toward the child. Notably, it demonstrates the extent to which different images are at play in society. An example of this can be offered by reflecting on two competing ways of thinking, that were prominant as the eighteenth century became the nineteenth, both of which impacted images of the child and infleunced their experiences of home.[16] One was the evangelical approach to the child, which sat in contrast, to the other, a romanticised view that drew from ideas such as those of Rousseau. The idea of children's innocence during this period will be discussed more in Chapter 6, but what is notable here is that the romanticised image chal-lenged the evangelical view that children were merely vessels of evil. It offered an alterantive image or way of thinking that had many practical implications for how adults approached children's moral development.

> To know good you need to know bad. To the small child, all is the same. It is we adults who introduce notions of morality at too early an age. The natural child does not know the difference between good and bad and cavorts and frolics and cries in happy innocence of these man made con-cepts. (Rousseau cited in Hodgkinson 2010: 21)

The wider romantic movement challenged the church's aggressive attitude. Rather than children's competence being framed in terms of their sin, they viewed the innocent child in relation to their potential. As such this view impacted on methods of parenting with a greater focus being given to persuasion and tenderness, rather than a reliance on the rod. In practice, however, that tension between these two positions continued to be reflected in practice.

A more sentimental role for mothers was still being questioned on the eve of the eighteenth century. An account from Denmark in 1790 depicts parenting among the peasant classes and how such a tendency for affection was still thought to have negative social results.

> For reasons natural to the habits of a peasant, he gives special attention to the physical education of the child; he would attach still less importance to moral education if it were not demanded of him by bourgeois requirements. As far as actually disciplining children, the peasant follows the latest German pedagogy: therefore you only see the old fashioned cane very rarely behind the scenes; there's time enough for harshness, the peasant says, when the child is old enough to understand. In general, in this childish tenderness, the parents resemble all uncivilised peoples, they love their children so much that they do not even hate their faults. Usually these people grow up like wild shrubs, just as are now praised in every book as examples for us to follow. (Guttormasson 2002: 262)

Although, as this extract suggests, there remained a popular sense in which children were best governed through the practice of determined discipline, a change in thinking meant the building of caring relationships was increasingly valued within the home.[17] One example is presented in the writings of Thomas Tryon who advises that 'when your children are of dull capacities and hard to learn reproach them not, nor expose them, but taking them alone, talk to them familiarly, and give them sweet and soft words, show them the advantages of learning, and how much it will tend to their advancements' (cited in Fletcher 2008: 37).

Despite the challenges, what was emerging was a growing sense of partnership, albeit shaped to some extent by class.[18] Fletcher notes how mothers in Victorian England were increasingly taking on a significant role in acting as the primary moral guide ((Fletcher 2008: 49), demonstrating the sense in which an element of compassion can be a positive action in shaping a child's moral and spiritual self, 'overseeing the provision of a sanctuary of well ordered comfort and peace' (Guttormasson 2002). Recognising mothers in this way was a shift in thinking and consequently practice, as mothers engaged more with the everyday task of interacting with their children, reflected by these changing images of the child. The role of fathers was evolving too. There appears to be a slight softening as fathers increasingly became part of the household. This, of course, is going to look very different in different classes but, as we move into the Victorian era, the role of the father changes significantly. This is not to divert the father from his ongoing role as moral overseer, but corporal punishment comes to be mixed more with persuasion and tenderness (Guttormasson 2002).

This section demonstrates further how thinking in relation to the child's moral capacity, and the images that developed as a result, directly impacted on practices within the home. Notably these practices are reflected here in the changing nature of relationships. Recognising the significance of this association between reason and the image of the child, and the way in which it impacts directly on the nature of the relationships that children have with adults, is significant. This theme will be returned to in Chapter 8.

5.5   Ongoing Evolution

Although Locke's ideas viewed children's 'time of ignorance' as not simply a void but increasingly filled with experiences, the divide between knowing and not knowing was still presented as being seperate. The eighteenth century saw writers such as Rousseau try to colour in further this early period of a child's life ([1762] 1911), as seen above, although, it was the writings of Immanuel Kant that would come to dominate our thinking on the child and morality. While Kant did not focus on children his general principles provided a definitive building block in the developmental model of childhood that followed.

Kant viewed moral decision-making as a product of a 'supreme principle' of rationality, which was to be seen as independent of nature and which transcended society and culture, with equal application to all.

Although Kant did not consider himself to be qualified to speak on education, let alone children, one of his responsibilities at the University of Königsberg was to run a series of lectures on the subject. These came together in a treatise called *Über Pädagogik* (*On Pedagogy*). What is notable, is that this spokesperson for universal reason made one very clear exception: children. For children 'education involves nurture, discipline, moral training with a view to the formation of character and instruction' (Curtis and Boultwood 1977: 290). For Kant, 'the young child was little above the animal stage of development' and education was the key to developing 'his humanity' (Curtis and Boultwood, 1977: 291). The role of education, and the place of discipline within it, thus meant that a child 'should be taught to differentiate between right and wrong activities. His sense of morality has not yet developed, but he should be trained to obey and conform to rules' (1977: 294). Children were firmly outside of Kant's universal moral principle, which relied on the individual's capacity to 'reason' (Kant 1949).

5.5.1 A Developmental Model of the Moral Child

It is hard to say why some ideas are taken up and others are not, but in relation to the journey of childhood Kant's work became significant in offering a framework into which children came to be 'fitted'. Perhaps the most influential thinker in this regard was Jean Piaget who sought to apply Kantian notions of reason to the child. Piaget did two things. One was to place children and morality into the hands of the psychologist, such that morality for children was governed by definitions of competence. Second, he offered markers within the life course of the child that were attributed to different level's of competence.

The climate in which Piaget was working has already been mentioned in Chap. 2where we noted how he went against the grain of traditional psychological thought in seeking to understand morality from the point of view of the child. For example, Freud had suggested that morality was governed by unconscious forces over which the individual had little sway, and he regarded the impact of early childhood experiences as similarly definitive in this regard (Sommer 2012). This, in itself, makes

Piaget's work significant and, despite the criticism he later receives, Piaget remains a pioneer for his desire to take the topic of morality outside its traditional preserve of being a study of the 'adult'. By placing children and morality together, Piaget started a debate about children and how we are to see them as participants within the multi-layered discourse of searching for improved outcomes and understandings. This is reinforced by the ongoing themes of respect and co-operation that are evident in Piaget's work (1967).

Despite these positive ambitions, a particular foundation – the desire to further Kant's notion of universal reason – meant that Piaget became interested in explaining morality as a process that happens to children in ways that are both definable and set. This is clearly seen in the different stages of development that Piaget identified.

> The first three take place within a child's first two years and are characterised through the recognition of reflex actions, developing into first motor habits and, later, sensorimoter activities. The fourth stage, between the ages of two and seven years, is linked to intuitive behaviour characterised by egocentricity, although it is only between the ages of seven and twelve that the child begins to use logic in shaping both social and moral interaction. But it is not until the child is twelve that the capacity to think in abstract terms marks the move into the adult world. (Frankel 2012: 16)

In practice, this meant that morality, which in Kantian terms defined good and bad through adherence to a 'common bond of rationality' (Kant 1949: xi), marked children as 'separate' because of an undeveloped competence level that would not allow them to be part of the shared ability to reason. Rules, for example were followed as a response to instruction, driven by 'affection' on the one hand and 'fear' on the other, rather than due to any particular understanding.

Academics readily engaged with this developmental model of childhood characterised by ages and stages. Lawrence Kholberg (1984), a disciple of Piaget, applied similar principles within his work such that, as some have argued, he was able to complete what Piaget started (Hersh et al. 1979). Kholberg, like Piaget, defined stages of moral development. However, his focus hinged around 'moral judgement' and the extent to which the individual became capable of organising a range of different values in framing a response: 'moral judgement is a cognitive process that allows us [the individual] to reflect on our values and order them in a logical hierarchy'(Hersh et al. 1979: 47). Within this he seemed to recognise the value of the social as he considered themes such as 'role-taking' and the extent to which, as their social skills develop, children are more able to place themselves in the shoes of others. Indeed, in Kholberg's six stages, he has a column headed 'social perspective' to mark the progression of the individual's social skills (see Hersh et al. 1979). Stages 1 and 2 of Kholberg's model take a child up to adolescence. Stages 3 and 4 mark the ongoing steps, with 5 and 6 seen as a beyond the reach of most. However, in the context of this study, the way in which those social perspectives are defined is significant. The child below seven years of age is regarded as not being able to consider the point of view of another, such that obedience is simply a response to avoiding punishment. It is not until they are a little older (seven or eight years old) that they start to recognise the two sides of an issue, although the focus is still defined by personal interest. It is not until children become 'adolescents' that they present themselves with reference to others: 'being good is important' because it reflects a desire to act in a way that is expected by others as a means of pursuing 'mutual relationships' (Hersh et al. 1979). Reference to duties, law and one's ability to manage and define morality is reserved for the later stages. Although Kholberg, like Piaget, has faced criticism, his work still marks a significant trend in how we seek to position children and morality today, as we look for a competence to 'reason' with reference to the development of the child. It is these ideas that come to influence children's experience of those key spaces of everyday life.

5.6   Concluding Thoughts

The impact of 'reason' on the constructed images that inform practices towards children is neatly summarised in an article by Geoffrey Short (1999). Writing in relation to schools, he highlights how a perception of reason, driven by thinking, has resulted in children being deemed as 'not ready' to engage with morality. With specific reference to themes of innocence and the notion of 'sequential developmentalism', he argues that children, particularly those under 12 years of age, have been considered as unsuitable for moral education. Although, as we have seen and as we will see in the following chapter, this reliance on ages and stages does not stop adults taking an active role in managing children's moral development, it does make an important statement about how images of the child impact on children's positioning in relation to moral discourses, with implications for practice within different interactional settings such as the home and school.

Reason thus becomes an analytical lens that can help the researcher make sense of the contextual backdrop, as a moral dimension is shown as an important feature to our investigation of childhoods. The image of the child as a biologically 'developing' moral entity, which has dominated this chapter, has two important implications. The first is that moral discourses are voiced by adults. Second, as a consequence of their greater moral capacity, adults decide when and how children should be given entry into those discourses. It is a model that reflects themes of control that reverberate throughout this book, themes which highlight adults, not just in terms of their place as moral dictators but also as gatekeepers because they recognise that at a certain time children must be admitted into the realm of moral understanding. A perspective on the child and their capacity to reason has underpinned, and continues to underpin the contextual backdrop that frames the interactional settings that children find themselves in. As this chapter has shown, this results in particular practices. The question for us today is what our approach to children and 'reason' means for the images that we create and the roles that we and they play in the institutions that we are *all* part of.

Notes

1. These ideas of competence also appear in Egyptian society. The teaching of morality seems to reflect questions around reason: 'a small child was an incomplete person because it lacked knowledge and understanding' (Lichtheim 1997). Not only that but there was a sense in which one's moral character was formed at birth – a person was either good or bad (Lichtheim

1997). Similarly to Ancient Greece, influential Egyptian sources (Papyrus Prisse) suggest that moral guidelines were presented in a hierarchical fashion; for the leader, the average man and the poor man. See also Chap. 6.

2. Indeed, in his review of Roman history, in relation to the late republic, Pomeroy (1997) reflects on lower-class families and how these were more closely knit, mothers had more power and there was 'affectionate regard for children' (1997: 9).

3. Rawson notes the extensive nature of 'others' in children's everyday lives: 'the parent child relationship was, then a core relationship reflected in law, literature and inscriptions. But it was not an exclusive relationship. Most children lived in a network of other relationships' (2003: 262).

4. The limited nature of this role might, for some, have been linked to mothers not wanting to get too attached to their children in a time of high infant mortality. That does not mean they were not emotionally attached to their children, however it does highlight the layers that must be uncovered as one seeks to position parents in relation to their children.

5. In some instances it seems that the nurse would have actually taken the child away from home, reinforcing the sense of detachment from the parents.

6. Bradley recounts Livy's tragic tale of the death of a young Roman woman, Verginia. The details of the story do not matter here, what does matter is the role of the *nutrix* in it. Virginia finds herself 'ambushed' in a public space, and it is the *nutrix* who sounds the alarm and furthermore it is the *nutrix* that is called on to give intimate evidence of Virginia's parentage. It presents the *nutrix* , even for this 'grown up' charge, as having a role of companionship and custody, bound together through strong intimate ties.

The nurse's social role can be defined from two points of view: at the functional level, first, the nurse provided early infant care, including breast feeding, and for older children supervision of a custodial sort, but at a more underlying level secondly, the nurse also acted with parents and other child minders as an instrument of socialisation and became an important element in the child's emotional framework of reference. This is acknowledged across time, in the way nurses were commonly associated with story telling in the commemorative expressions of the inscriptions and perhaps also in the popular saying that grief of a nurse was only second to that of a mother. The nurse consequently was in a real sense part of the child's familial world. (Bradley 1991: 27)

This offers an idyllic view of the loyal nurse, but of course experiences would have differed, with a range of women taking on these roles and the nature of the relationship between nurse and charge being varied. However, although not directly mentioned above, it can also be assumed that a significant part of establishing the emotional frame of reference was guiding and directing the child's 'moral' development.

7. Writing of the upper-middle classes in Victorian England, McBride comments that 'family life in Victorian England would be inconceivable without nannies, nurses and governesses who were more important to some English children that their own parents' (1997: 44).

8. Writing in relation to medieval England, Ryan (2013) makes the case for recognising not only different roles but also how our understanding of these roles can help us in developing a greater understandings of childhood and children's position within society.

9. The culture within England at the time would have been very different from Rome's, and this would have resulted in different experiences for children (Kuefler 2003). The patriarchal 'family'-based approach would have been introduced into a system with moral codes that had been established through tribal patterns (Casey 1989). Notably, the patriarchal model was accepted and quickly adopted. At the centre of this dramatic change was Christianity.

10. This is seen in the expression of loss that had been apparent in earlier cultures being repeated in Anglo-Saxon England (Cunningham 1995). In the words of King Alfred: 'what sight is more intolerable than the death of a child before its father's eyes?' (Cunningham1995: 21).

11. It is interesting to note how this came to contrast with Mennonite and other radical Christian groups, who thought it was wrong to baptise children before they reached an age of responsibility. As such, the baptism became a 'believers' baptism'.

12. In presenting a position that children were only too aware of and wanted to avoid, Volominus wrote that 'if he is allowed to live as he wishes …he will fall into all or many kinds of crime and atrocities' (Herlily 1978). What Voluminous does not mention is the wider sense of spiritual disaster if adults fail.

13. http://www.nytimes.com/2015/06/14/magazine/the-child-preachers-of-brazil.html?_r=0

14. A theme that recurs in later texts, driven by this reformed perspective, written for parents and children that tell tales of this cycle – for example. see Hannah More (1840) and Mary Sherwood's (1869) *Fairchild Family* .

15. Chapter 7 of *Amoris Laetitia* is entitled 'Towards a better education of children' and deals with a number of themes relating to discipline and punishment within the home, sex education and more. Notably, the document directly engages with the importance of sex education for children, challenging schools not to 'trivialise' its importance (Catholic Church 2015).

16. This must also be recognised in relation to changing social and political governance. Donzelot (1980) reflected on the changes following the French revolution and a breakdown in traditional patriarchy, such that a model for family known as a 'tutelary complex', or welfare through advice, emerged as a way in which the state could hold an influence within the home, thus protecting society from future revolution (see McNamee 2016).

17. Melissa Trench in 1768 wrote about the importance of mothers in providing a focus on the immortal soul of their child, and thus earthly happiness.

18. Fletcher offers an insightful view of children's experiences during this period. However, it is very class specific because it focuses mainly on the upper and middle classes. Indeed, the quality of material in relation to the poor is not as strong, raising questions about the differences between children's experiences.

6

Virtue

Doctor Faustus was a good man,
He whipped his scholars now and then,
When he whipped, he made them dance
Out of England into France
Out of France into Spain
And then he whipped them back again.

In Chap. 5, reason was presented in terms of children's competence. Traditional perspectives on reason link it to biological stages over which the adult has no control. 'Virtue' thus became the means through which the adult could engage in the child's moral journey. Of course reason and virtue are closely linked, but here the interpretation of 'virtue' reflects not only the need by adults to define and communicate what is right and what is wrong, but also to establish a set of characteristics that determine social membership. As such 'virtues' can be actively shared and, importantly, taught as society builds up a set of social ambitions for its members, providing the most fertile foundation for the effective development of the 'reasoning' adult.

© The Editor(s) (if applicable) and The Author(s) 2017
S. Frankel, *Negotiating Childhoods*, Studies in Childhood and Youth,
DOI 10.1057/978-1-137-32349-1_6

This chapter focuses on the active nature of imparting 'virtue'. A key theme thus becomes a consideration of the way efforts to share virtues impacts on how practices with children developed. Within this, as the following discussion highlights, adults draw from constructed understandings of the child as an image is created which forms the basis for the practices that will be pursued. It becomes clear that childhood is deeply shaped by attitudes to virtue, and the way in which adults seek to impose or direct children towards those characteristics of membership. At the centre of this is 'education'. In fact, as this chapter shows, education is firmly entwined with the imparting of 'virtues', such that, whether at home or school, adult efforts to 'teach' the child will reflect a stance on virtue. Analysing this helps in framing our understanding of the image of the child that is constructed within interactional settings and the nature of the practices that are set up around it.

Fundamentally, virtue, as a focus within the framework in this book, provides a means through which we can explore the way in which society seeks to communicate right and wrong to the child. It is an investigation that provides continuous opportunities for comparison as differing images of the child result in a variety of practices. However, what is significant is the extent to which defining social ambitions remains overwhelmingly the role of adults. It is an approach that reflects a particular constructed understanding, one that is deeply rooted in classical thinking. It is therefore here that we need to start in order to build up a sense of the legacy that has been, and continues to be, an influence on the contextual backdrop with which the child engages. By considering the place of 'virtue' as a lens to examine these structural themes, one can see how ingrained perspectives on morality in relation to the child are in key social arenas such as home and school.

6.1 Managed Ambitions

Early writings reflect how, for a variety of traditions, a focus on character became the means through which a group of people were able to define themselves. A focus on a person's character – a desire to understand it, to test it and fundamentally to learn from it – reflects themes that are central to early literature. Homer's work (discussed in Chap. 2), for example, should be seen as a social discussion document becaue he provided societies with a basis on which to consider character traits. His heroes are never perfect and as they struggle between what is 'good' and what is 'not' the audience is left to make up their own mind as to whether they are exhibiting the traits of a true hero. Through Homer's work the audience is continually being challenged to consider their loyalties to the characters as they reflect on their behaviours and consequently make assessments about the moral nature of their actions. It is through an examination of 'virtue' that one forms a sense of character (both in the literal and personal form) and in these early works it offered a means through which city states could identify what marked them out, what made them different, and what the defining ambitions were for those within their society.

The desire to present distinctiveness through the characteristics or virtues that a state encouraged becomes a definable point of reference, a theme of belonging between countries and communities that has never gone away. This is visible in the emergence of Athens as a city state. The following extract from *Medea* by Euripides, a son of Athens, highlights the extent to which the Athenians sought to set themselves apart.

> The people of Athens, sons of Erechtheus,
> Have enjoyed their prosperity
> Since ancient times. Children of blessed gods,
> They grew from holy soil unscorched by invasion.
> Among the glories of knowledge their souls are pastured;
> They walk always with grace under the sparkling sky.
> There long ago, they say, was born golden-haired Harmony
> Created by the nine virgin Muses of Pieria.
> (Euripides 1963: 42)

This extract draws out the special traits that were attached to those that lived within Athens, qualities that saw them prosper as they show the ability to defend their territory and grow further in knowledge, creating a state where 'togetherness', amongst other characteristics, was key. The theme of otherness sits alongside more direct challenges to the audience over their attitudes to murder, as Euripides places the drama in the context of a mother planning to kill her children. The image of the children here is interesting because we are asked how these murders should be viewed, and how important it is that the children to be killed are noble, the sons of Jason the famous Argonaut. Throughout, the children are never called by name and as such never really 'be'. It is therefore the loss of their potential as future ambassadors of heroism that becomes defining in their death. As such the image of the child, created here, presents chidren as vessels for the ambitions of society. Indeed it is in recognsing that potential, or in fact the loss of it, that becomes the signficant feature of this play, encapsulating the drama.

This focus on the potential of the child as a vessel for the ambitions of society becomes a defining feature of the constructed images of the child that societies create. Virtue thus becomes an enduring feature of the way in which society thinks about the child, with implications for the way in which the child comes to be positioned and the practices that are developed in response to this image. Indeed, the value of the child to society is framed by virtue as societies recognsie the part children play in ensuring an ordered and sustainable future. As such, the role of adults becomes one of preparation as the child is instructed and taught what those social ambitions are.

6.2   Shaping Education

Education in some shape or form can be presented as a consistent part of childhoods, whether formal or informal, in the home or beyond, with a teacher or another adult. Experiences of education will have varied, with money, gender, class and of course the thinking of the day all playing a part. A common theme, although experienced in a variety of ways, is the extent to which education has sought to communicate 'virtues' to the child. It is the search, therefore, for the way in which virtue is 'understood' (in a given time and place) that can help us to define images of the child. By drawing out the 'moral' dimension we are able to consider more directly the practices that children experience. The relationship between education in its broadest sense and the sharing of virtues is significant, however it is notable that our approach to education, despite the passing of time, remains based on approaches to virtue acquisition that continue to rely on the adult as lead with a focus on teaching and enforcing, rather than learning and reflecting (experiencing).

6.2.1 Training the Child

Plato, writing in *Republic* and *Laws,* helps to illustrate the link between one's vision for society and the role that education needs to play.[1] In his model, 'virtue', as a focus for education, is seen as being of particular value to some groups over others. Defined by their capacity to reason, Plato was particularly interested in those who were going to become the leaders within society, the military classes 'from whom the actual rulers or guardians will be selected'(Curtis and Boultwood 1977: 7), in contrast to ordinary citizens. Education was therefore necessary because it provided training to develop the 'latent talents of the possible rulers'(ibid.: 3). As such, the model was based on social class. For the upper classes who were seen to possess superior 'reason', practices were developed to harness children's sense of right and wrong through a formal engagement with virtue.

As such, the place of virtue within education was to create ways of being that allowed reason to flourish. Reason was not controllable, however virtue aquisition was and it gave adults a practical focus while reason was seen to be developing. For Plato the journey to high functioning reason required adults to take on a role that was far from passive. In the following extract Plato makes the case for education as a process of directed transformation.

> There is a faculty residing in the soul of each person, and an instrument enabling each of us to learn; and that just as we might suppose it to be impossible to turn the eye round from darkness to light without turning the whole body, so must this faculty of this instrument, be wheeled round, in company from the perishing world, until it be enabled to endure the contemplation of the real world and the brightest part thereof, which according to us, is the Form of Good. Hence, this very process of revolution must give rise to an art, teaching in what way the change will most easily and most effectually be brought about. Its object will not be to generate in the person the power of seeing. On the contrary, it assumes the he possesses it, though, he is turned in the wrong direction, and does not look towards the right quarter and its aim is to remedy this defect. (Cited in Curtis and Boultwood 1977: 8–9)

Plato's words reflect the desire to establish a state that is driven by the moral principles of a common desire for 'good'. However, for this to be allowed to happen, those with capacity to reason must be given the opportunity to 'turn' and to recognise that within them lies an ability that will allow them to be part of achieving this moral height. Significantly, Plato states that the change in the individual does not happen automatically, but rather that it follows a process of being 'taught'. As such, Plato points towards the responsibility of adults in society for providing this 'teaching' and, more than that, of developing it as an 'art' so that it can be as effective as possible in creating change.[2]

Recognising the value of investing in what is 'good' promotes the idea of education as a vehicle for society. As Plato suggests, 'education should aim at producing the best type of citizen in both war and peace' (in *Laws*, cited in Curtis and Boultwood 1977: 25). As such, for the first time, education takes on an important formal aspect as one in which the state is encouraged to endorse a programme of learning that is focused directly on the citizens of tomorrow.

> [A]t present when censuring or commending a man's upbringing, we describe one man as educated and another as uneducated (though well educated in his trade). The education we speak of is training from childhood in goodness, which makes a man eagerly desirous of becoming a perfect citizen. (Smale 1998: 59)

The place of education (for those seen fit to benefit from it) is presented by Plato as a powerful tool in maintaining the city state and all that it stands for. However, the task that adults faced was not easy, because if 'goodness' was going to be instilled in their future leaders then redirecting them from the passions of youth needed to be matched with a discipline that allowed students to know and practise those virtues that society set for itself. Plato highlights the forces that society is dealing with:

> of all animals the boy is the most unimaginable, inasmuch as he has the fountain of reason in him, not yet regulated, he is an insidious and sharp witted animal and the most insubordinate of them all. (cited in Pattison: 1978: 3)

This highlights an ongoing theme in the history of education that shows 'education' being used to regulate and direct what were seen as children's natural passions. It is a battle to which biology and habit respond by the 'teaching' of virtues as society seeks to limit the wayward potential of these natural forces. In the minds of Socrates and Plato, this was easier for some to achieve than others. The following extract shows Plato rejecting the Sophist position that rhetoric alone shapes a man's goodness. His explanation reflects the extent to which education came to play a part within a broader balancing of other natural forces.

Now if arguments were in themselves enough to make men good, they would justly, as Theognis says, have won very great rewards, and such rewards should have been provided; but as things are, while they seem to have power to encourage and stimulate the generous-minded among our youth, and to make a character that is well-bred, and a true lover of what is noble, ready to be possessed by virtue, they are not able to encourage the many to nobility and goodness. For these do not by nature obey the sense of shape, but only fear and not abstain from bad acts because of their baseness but through fear of punishment; living by passion they pursue the pleasures appropriate to their character and the means to them, and avoid the opposite pains, and have not even a conception of what is noble and truly pleasant, since they have never tasted it. What arguments would remould such people? It is hard, if not impossible to remove by argument the traits that have long since been incorporated in the character; and perhaps we must be content if, when all the influences by which we are thought to become good are present, we get some tincture of virtue.

Now some think we are made good by nature, others by habituation, others by teaching. Nature's part evidently does not depend on us, but as a result of some divine causes is present in those who are truly fortunate; while argument and teaching, we may suspect, are not powerful with all men, but the soul of the student must first have been cultivated, by means of habits, for noble joy and noble hatred, like earth which is to nourish the seed. For he who lives as passion directs will not hear argument that dissuades him, nor understand it if he does; and how can we persuade one in such a state to change his ways? And in general passion seems to yield not to argument but to force. The character, then must somehow be there already with a kinship to virtue, loving what is noble and hating what is base. (cited in Burnyeat 1980: 75)

If virtue was to be cultivated then education was essential. For some, this meant a chance for their souls to flourish, but only through fighting back those natural passions. As part of this process, punishment became a recognised tool. The model of the educator fighting with these natural forces becomes ingrained, recurring in approaches to education in the centuries that follow. It paints an image of the moral child that we must not ignore or underestimate.[3]

Based on this image, the state was required to recognise the need for and value of education as a tool for offering opportunities for training which had the potential to instil social responsibility in children as they took on the ambitions society proposed and through which it could flourish. This train of thought led to the development of particular practices that impacted on children experiences. This is exemplified in the writings of Xenophon, a contemporary of Plato,[4] who, in observing Persian efforts to 'improve their citizens', notes how the boys are sent to 'school'. Whilst there, they get the chance to engage with 'justice and righteousness', an element of school that is as much a focus as any learning of 'letters'. In this context the boys are given the chance to hear 'cases' and to put into practice the doing of virtue. In describing these cases, Xenophon states that 'there is one charge the judges [the boys] do not hesitate to deal with, a charge which is the source of much hatred among grown men...the charge of ingratitude. The culprit convicted of refusing to repay a debt of kindness when it is full in his power, meets with severe chastisement'(Xenophon 1897: 6–7). The need to make explicit these virtues is key to his account as Xenophon goes on to talk about temperance and self-restraint and the role of 'elders' in guiding their charges day by day. It is an example that reflects a connection between constructed images of the child, framed with reference to virtue, and education-based practices. It is a relationship that has become so ingrained in approaches to children that one is challenged to re-establish its visibility, as we must if we are first to understand contemporary practice and second to challenge it.

6.2.2 Framing Virtue Education

By spending a little more time in the ancient world one can investigate further how deeply rooted a concern for virtue is in relation to a child's education. Particularly in *Ethics* and *Politics*, Aristotle offers some views on education, although perhaps not as succinctly as Plato. Aristotle places similar value on hierarchy. In his discussion of happiness (1999), he points to distinctions between people, placing them into three categories: those that live for gratification, those that are defined by political activity and finally those dedicated to study. The distinction between these 'classes' reflects a very particular sense of applied virtue

> The many the most vulgar, seemingly conceive the good and happiness as pleasure, and hence they also like the life of gratification. Here they appear completely slavish, since the life they decide on is a life for grazing animals. (Thompson 2005: 53)

For some people, therefore, the amount of virtue that they needed to complete the tasks allotted to them in their lives differed from others[5] (Cockburn 2013). Aristotle suggests that this is simply part of the natural order, which defines and shapes the amount of virtue we are required to apply,

> For rule of free over slave, male over female, man over boy, are all different, while parts of the soul are present in each case, the distribution is different. Thus the deliberative faculty in the soul is not present at all in a slave; in a female it is present but ineffective, in a child present but undeveloped. (Cockburn 2013: 32)

The sense of the child as 'lacking' within the context of virtue is a powerful one that has, ever since, remained central to the way in which children experience morality. It reflects a view that virtue was not automatic but, for the male child, was something that had to be worked at. The result is a model wherein adults define and set what is seen to be virtuous and the child is then 'encouraged' to achieve this.

For Aristotle, education continued to be 'essential for the well being of the state', providing the means by which society could interact effectively. In expanding on Plato, Aristotle looks further at the distinction between applying virtue for different groups within society in their pursuit of the good life and following what is seen to be the right rule. Here he separates goodness of intellect and goodness of character. The *few* can obtain and demonstrate goodness of intellect and the full demonstration of reason, but *all* can attain goodness of character. He breaks this down further through the notion of shame which is 'the semi-virtue of the learner' (Burnyeat 1980: 78). Aristotle saw young people in general as being driven by a search for pleasure, something that 'has grown with us from infancy which is why it is difficult to rub off this feeling which is dyed as it is into our life'(Burnyeat 1980: 86). As a result a young person gives into those natural forces, is compelled by 'the feelings of the moment and for that reason makes mistakes. He wants to do the noble things but sometimes does things that are disgraceful, ignoble and then he feels ashamed of his conduct'(ibid.). In order to traverse this time in their lives effectively, young people needed to have those tendencies curbed through training, with punishment or the fear of it being a helpful tool. Aristotle notes that young people need to be provided with training through which to learn which are the right habits, the right behaviours within society.

> We become good builders by building and good harp players by playing the harp. In the same way it is by doing just acts that we become just, by doing temperate acts that we become temperate, and by doing brave deeds that we become brave. (cited in Curtis and Boultwood 1977: 39)

The need to train and educate is made clear by Aristotle through the illustration that one could just as easily pursue a life of 'bad character'. To protect against this, society created roles, such as that of the *paidagoges*. This role was given to a member of a Greek nobleman's household and involved directly taking responsibility 'for teaching the boy good manners' (Amos and Lang 1979: 161). The strong moral dimension to the role (with crossover to themes of reason) is highlighted by Bradley in his review of the Roman play *Bacchides*, in which Lydus, the pedagogue, is described as 'more than a simple servant entrusted with children's earlier academic training. The shaping of a child's character from boyhood to manhood has been and still remains the dominant feature of Lydus's relationship with Pistoclerus' (1991: 52). The pedagogues would follow their charges around at home, school and in public spaces as they undertook their role of ensuring character development by placing themselves alongside the individual and helping them interpret right and wrong (see also Dixon 1992).

This has been an overly brief analysis, but one which has highlighted the relationship between education and the application of moral instruction seen through the lens of 'virtue'. The use of virtue as a lens draws out those examples in which children are positively engaged in certain activities, but it also highlights the elitist way in which these practices came to be applied. This does not mean that virtue as a filter for understanding is only relevant to a few, but rather that the way in which virtue came to be related to other children has had (and still has) an impact on the practices that are developed. Without engaging with these building blocks it is impossible for us to understand fully the way children have come to be positioned in relation to both formal and informal education, then, in between and now.

6.3   Christian Virtue

The connection between Christian thinking on virtues[6] and its application to children's lives (here seen primarily in relation to education) first observed in the church's role as the sponsor of education. Chap. 5 looked at the important part that the church played in shaping roles within the home. Here, the developing discussion of virtue adds to this, furthering an awareness of the context that both parents and other adults were operating in. However, education can also be considered in a more formal sense and, as the tide of Roman rule fell back (here in the context of the British Isles), formal education went through two changes. The first was that the state educators employed in the towns,[7] could no longer be financed. New support came from the church, with monastic communities, for example, taking on the role of 'educators'. The second change was that native languages increasingly became part of the process of learning (Orme 2006). As education, therefore, passed out of state control and became the province of the church there were a number of ideological and philosophical shifts, with implications for the structuring of morality such that 'the influence of Christianity towards children and the Christian clergymen's praise or condemnation of certain practices affected the theoretical status of children in Anglo Saxon England perhaps more than any other single factor' (Kuefler 2003: 824). The stance of the church in the fifth and sixth centuries was strongly shaped by the voices of Pope Gregory and Augustine, views that continued to have an impact for some time. At the centre of Augustine's argument was the notion that the acquisition of knowledge was the result of an inner realisation. In practical terms, this meant that the process of education was focused on a realisation that came from the inside out and not the outside in. In some senses, this position challenged the value and need of formal education by saying that one's relationship with God became key, and that building up a body of facts was not as important as establishing a life of devotion. However, this life of devotion could be nurtured and, therefore, the role of the church in promoting education came to be dominated by the setting of customs and attitudes as directed from the pulpit, as well as by relying on specific programmes of teaching that allowed the chosen students to pursue a higher level of moral understanding and awareness (themes that were discussed in the previous chapter).

6.3.1 Educating the Flock

Although schooling was not to remain the sole preserve of the church,[8] its capacity to influence children's lives was set for the next 1000 years. Society was, through the church, encouraged to recognise the need to focus on the inner dimension of the individual where that sense of character was a key element in shaping who the child was to become. As such, the church created a 'curriculum of virtue' which was laid down and pursued in both formal and less formal ways in society, with a significant impact on children's experiences. This is perhaps most clearly seen in relation to the changes within the church in the sixteenth century.

As seen in the last chapter, the Reformation in the European church saw a redoubling of efforts to deal with the weakness of human nature that was so readily ascribed to the child. Education (in its different forms) was a key component in tackling this by-product of the human condition. The key to effective virtue education was the role of adult as enforcer. If the child was to develop their ability to reason, it was necessary that someone defined what was seen to be right and wrong. It is a discussion that reiterates how 'virtue' as a lens for analysis must form part of the contextual backdrop being suggested in this book as part of understanding adult practices used to assert and reinforce a moral direction within society.

For example, in Scotland in 1561, John Knox and others put together a treatise known as *The Book of Discipline* (Smout 1969). In it they presented a model of society that clearly positioned the school as the third tier in a hierarchy that started with 'state' and 'church'. It reflected a social drive on discipline that was to be 'supplemented by a national scheme for education, for while discipline serves merely to correct the adult after the offence, education by touching the soul of the child may altogether avoid the sin' (cited in Smout 1969: 68). However, the process of 'education' did not include all children, and so the home continued to be a site for children's moral learning,

> Those parents who take an interest in their children's education are more worthy of respect that those who just bring them into the world. They give them not only life but a good and holy life. This is why those parents are right to send their children at the tenderest age to the market of true wisdom where they will become the architects of their own fortune, the ornaments of their native land, their family and their friends. (Aries 1962: 413)

This development means that the drive for moral education could not be considered in the context of schools alone, but within the wider society as well. So, in yet another reapplication of the previously mentioned themes around human nature, adults within society had a responsibility for ensuring that children were moulded (indeed broken) to the will of society, such that they grew up with the virtues of the Reformation at the centre of their character. A lack of perceived reason meant that children were simply not ready to engage with society in the same way as adults, they were therefore a risk, both to themselves and to others, such that adults had a responsibility to do something about it. Aries considers this with an apt illustrative analogy:

> Henceforth it was recognized that the child was not ready for life and that he had to be subjected to a special treatment, a sort of quarantine, before he was allowed to join the world of adults. (1962: 412)

The idea of quarantining the child offers a strong image of how children were positioned in society. Not only were they to be kept separate but, whilst that was happening, it offered the chance for society to instil in the child those virtues that it recognised as being important.

6.4   Enforcing Virtue Education

6.4.1   In the Home

Despite those voices that called for the natural goodness of the child to be embraced[9] and to provide the focus for virtue education, this was seen to sit at odds with a traditional notion of sin, in which the child was born with an innate evil. Practice, as introduced in the last chapter, therefore demanded that this evil be dealt with, and the child's body was the focus. Children's minds could not be relied on because their ability to reason was not formed, but the body offered a focus for a model of instruction that allowed what was, primarily 'wrong', to be communicated. The focus on the body is very significant. It highlights an approach to 'virtue' education that drew from a particular image of the child and constructed understandings of the relationship to the body. This must be seen in the further context of the way in which other bodies were seen. Notably, it was not simply the child's body that was of questionable moral status, but also that of the mother. There was a real nervousness around women's bodies particularly in relation to child bearing and rearing that was assocaited with the transmission of corruptness to the child which baptism sought to clense. As one twelfth-century writer reflected:

> It is asked, why are children not nourished by menstrual blood, as it is asserted by certain people? Answer. Menstrual blood is corrupt [and] ought to generate corrupt and fluid humours. Therefore children are not nourished by menstrual blood because it is corrupt, since if they were nourished from thence they would be quickly corrupted. (Madehose 1996: 3)

This attitude had potential implications for breast feeding and more generally for the role of mothers and indeed nurses. As is suggested here, 'distrust of women's bodies as a source of menstrual nourishment and concern over nursing women's habits were linked to moral worries about women's actions and their consequences for children' (1996: 15). It illustrates just how deeply ingrained was the relationship between the child, the body and morality, hence the need for steps to be in place within the family (and wider society) for this 'evil' to be directed out of the child's being. The attitude to women (which was to continue in different forms for many years) reinforced and heightened the role of the father as overseer of the moral journey through effective education, with implications for the family and society as a whole (McLaughlin 1974; Ozment 1983).

This resulted in fathers in particular being encouraged to learn about the moral frailness of the child and how *they* needed to combat it. This can be seen in the growth of advice for parents, which can be assumed to have followed a good deal of spoken instruction formally presented within church. An example of this is the work of John of Wales who, in preparing some model sermons, identifies parents as a target for his wisdom. His writing drew from Roman and Greek literature as he pursued thinking on children, showing the ongoing link with those more defined philosophical themes around virtue. John is clear that children are there to be 'trained', to 'love their parents, obey them, honour them and help them if they fall into poverty' (Cunningham 1995: 30). This is a process of education that if successful will help children to be prepared to be moral (and therefore spiritually grounded) adults. The central ingredient to instilling this moral curriculum was discipline. For John, discipline was key: 'severity in discipline is to be commended, but it must not be to excess, and it should be accompanied by moderate praise when it is earned' (Cunningham 1995: 30).

A particular discourse around discipline now emerges. The word 'discipline', with its roots in Latin and the connection to 'teaching', finds itself in Middle English with a far more aggressive interpretation. Discipline becomes associated with the scourging of the body, an interpretation that is played out in the practice of children's everyday lives. Bonner's (1998) review of pre-Reformation and post-Reformation England explores the age at which children were seen as ready to begin the process of being 'disciplined'. It marks out 'discipline' as a definable practice that children go through at a definable stage in the life course. As such, being 'disciplined' becomes part of one's journey to adulthood, and a necessary step to taking hold of the moral mantle of society. Bonner reflects on how this process, which was left to the father, would have begun for a child at the age of around six or seven years and continued until around twelve years for girls and fourteen years for boys. As such, it marks an important aspect of the curriculum of virtue, in which the place of 'discipline', and its connection with strict and direct punishment, was central as a vehicle through which the child could be taught. Indeed, advice on appropriate discipline was easy to come by, the striking nature of this being the level of force that was both suggested and encouraged[10] (de Mause 1974; see also Frankel 2012).

The focus on children's bodies as a means for directing a virtuous 'education' (and as a response to a perceived capacity to reason) continued with an ongoing reliance on corporal punishment[11] in order 'to achieve by fear the obedience a child would not give freely out of love or a sense of duty' (Bonner 1998: 147). Parents were 'compelled' through extensive instruction and guidance from the church to use this method as part of their parenting, it is no wonder that this apporach became pervasive.[12] Parents were condemned if they were perceived to be sparing the child. One telling example sees Menno Simons mocking the parent who is too lenient or who is quick to take the child's side as 'one motivated more by fear of the child than by love' (Bonner 1998: 147). Hitting one's child, therefore, became the true sign of demonstrating one's love rather than anything more malicious. It was a zealousness for the eternal health of the child by correction through the temporal body of the child that drove this approach. The child's role was to defer to their parents, to be obedient and return their parents 'love' and 'care' (ibid.: 151). It was a formula that came to be repeated in countless texts wirtten for the 'family' (see Frankel 2012 for more).

The link between the body and punishment continues today (it is discussed further in Chap. 9). It reflects the importance of understanding context in shaping the moral image of the child if we are to make sense of related practice in the home. Indeed, current debates highlight the extent to which parents still desire, in many countries, an ability to rely on force as a means of 'engaging' children in a moral discourse.[13] To suggest that legislation alone will remove this way of dealing with children does not recognise how deeply held these views are and how, if society is truly to move forward, these contextual themes need to be untangled and explained rather than ignored and rejected. In short, it demands that we seek to understand the 'context' as we try to make sense of adult–child relationships within the home, recognising the extent to which parents are driven by moral attitudes (or forces) that are deeply held and determinedly expressed.

6.4.2   In School

The need for 'violence' as a tool for educating the child as part of this curriculum of virtue was not just the responsibility of the parent. The following discussion explores the way in which institutions developed a service that was directly focused on providing what was seen to be the best 'virtue' education. It was a commercial enterprise in which different brands of 'virtue' were on sale to those who had the funds, such that parents could export their responsibilities to some extent and look for professional input from 'schools'. Although themes of violence were very real in other forms of schooling, the British public school stands out as an exemplar of the place of violence in the curriculum of virtue.

Fletcher (2008) reflects that being taught Latin was one of the rites of passage within the English public school; an experince that children had to go through. Another rite of passage was violence. What is so surprising about this, is that there was a genuine desire for children to experince violence, which was seen as an important part of the curriculum of virtue within school. It was a recognised and sought-after part (from the perspective of the adult) of a child's moral journey. In examining the English public school, Fletcher suggests that it was, indeed, these rights of passage that became the unique selling point of such schools in the nineteenth century, as the professional and middle classes joined the aristocracy in using them to produce a particular type of boy.

> ['Boys"] who would rule England in Parish, country and nation and who would rule the Empire besides, these schools became the front of English patriarchy. They were men's foremost instrument for the maintenance of class and masculine hegemony. Their importance in the story of boyhood experience between 1600 and 1914 is therefore incalculable. (Fletcher 2008: 196)

The public school was used by society, therefore, to create a conveyor belt of boys who had certain characteristics that were seen as the essence of an Englishman. These desired life attributes were not simply the ambition of teachers but encouraged by parents and others throughout society, as boys were, as Fletcher suggests, educated in 'endurance' and 'self reliance' through majoring in school on the Classics and violence.

Violence was not only an adult–to-child phenomenon, it was also a core aspect of child-to-child interactions. A grounding in this world of hardship and conflict was seen as preparing boys for the challenges of their place in the world following school. Indeed, as one commentator says, the desire to use violence as part of forming the character of the child became more than just indifference, it became from the 1850's a 'product of adult calculation' (see Fletcher 2008: 197). Fletcher draws on an article in a publication of the time to sum up this attitude towards the child and the need for violence within their education.

> Boys, like nations, can only attain to the genuine stout and self reliance which is true manliness by battling for themselves against their difficulties and forming their own characters by the light of their own blunders and troubles… the object of public school is to introduce a boy early to the world, that he may be trained in due time for the struggle that lies before him. (ibid.: 198)

It is notable that Fletcher reflects on the role of Thomas Arnold (the head teacher at Rugby School between 1828 and 1842). His policies were seen as revolutionary because he mounted a battle against the evil which he saw in the boys' attitudes towards each other and the culture in which 'the watchword was survival of the strongest'(2008: 199).

In this culture boys could be humiliated and victimised in any number of ways, from servitude as a 'fag' complying with the whim of older boys to being 'roasted' by being held close to a fire for a few minutes. Fletcher reflects on the different value systems that existed amongst the boys as they created a perpetual cycle of initiation and defined hierarchy based on strength. It was the unauthorised violence of this 'unlicensed anarchy' that so affected Arnold and, as a result, left him wanting to create a more 'moral, more caring and cleverer' environment.

His boys would learn self denial, self mastery and self-restraint; their characters would be moulded as 'regular and amiable, abstaining from evil and for evil in its lower and grosser forms having a real abhorrence'. What should be looked for at Rugby, Arnold told his prefects, was, in the first place, 'religious and moral principles', in the second place 'gentlemanly conduct' and in the third 'intellectual ability'. (Fletcher 2008: 20)

However, all that Arnold really did was to move the violence that had been the preserve of the boys and legitimise it by making it increasingly the role of the adult. As a result, flogging and caning by teachers became seen as an increasingly necessary tool for dealing with teenage boys. This institutional violence was extreme, exceeding in some cases what would be seen as acceptable if it had been adjudged by the criminal courts. It became a part of the tradition of school, recognised and endorsed by all within society (and not just in England but on the Continent (de Mause 1974)). The impact of engaging with this particular contextual backdrop is interesting because children were seeking to negotiate social life, and thus develop a sense of identity, on the basis that being able to handle such violence was seen as commendable. It thus reflected practices and, perhaps more importantly, ways of experiencing those practices that carried particular meanings in relation to what was acceptable. It highlights how recognising the moral dimension to the way in which childhoods come to be constructed provides an insight that can help to frame understanding that has relevance not just for yesterday but also for today. Fletcher, in reflecting on these practices, comments that they were 'a sorry preparation for future relationships'(Fletcher 2008: 207). These are the lessons that we need to learn from a consideration of history. Although this is not the place to examine the extent to which these practices actually influenced children's relationships, the connection is significant. There is a clear link between the practices of the institutions within which childhoods are experienced and the individual's efforts to create and shape meanings as a response. It is in a desire to understand that relationship and its implications for the individual, within a more dynamic definition of socialisation, that we should be increasingly concerned.

Before leaving this section, it is important to reflect on the experience of girls at the same time. Although girls (here with a focus on the 'sisters' of the boys who would be attending the schools discussed above) did not face violence in quite the same way as boys, their bodies were still the targets for physical manipulation as part of reaching the virtues society had defined. In their case, the ambition 'set' for girls was to conform to a particular sense of female beauty. For girls, Fletcher suggests, the key word was 'improvement', which meant a focus on the 'moral and the spiritual' (2008: 220). Part of this approach was shaped by the thought that the mind of the girl was different from that of a boy. It presented an alternative assessment of reason, so the techniques used to instil virtues in girls reflected a more subtle sort of moulding. As with boys, parents wanted girls to have the best moral education in terms of taking on a defined role in adult life. Girls were, therefore, to be trained in virtues of 'good manners and learning to play gentlewomen and good housewives' (Fletcher 2008: 259). As one commentator of the time noted: 'one good mother is worth a thousand school masters'(Samuel Smiles quoted in Cockburn 2013: 96). It is a historical illustration of how gender (and class) impacted the way in which adults viewed children and morality, with different images of the child clearly resulting in different practices.

6.5   A Curriculum of Virtue for All

The model for receiving a more formally delivered brand of this virtue-based curriculum was, as explored above, limited to those who had money. It was a way of training the child that could be bought into. But, with the rise of industrialisation and the increased visibility of children in towns, formal schooling took on a more important role as a tool for transferring or at least supporting society's efforts and imparting its moral code on children. As discussed in Chap. 5, there was a particular relationship between the state and the family that resulted in the state keeping its distance. This meant that the state was not necessarily able to control what was going on in the home. School, however, offered a much more direct vehicle through which the state could be involved in shaping its perception of the moral child, instilling virtues and protecting society from the threat posed by the child. It was a significant development which was to fundamentally change the contextual backdrop framing children's experiences.

Cockburn (2013) considers this through the setting up of 'ragged schools' which offered towns a means of dealing with working-class children. The growing visibility of children caused by the industrial revolution made this need ever more real. A consequence of this was a growing nervousness about the under classes, with questions about how they were to be instructed in grasping those understandings of right and wrong that were needed for a stable society (Kamur 1978). In 1867 education secretary Robert Lowe stated that:

> the lower classes ought to be educated to discharge the duties cast upon them. They should be educated that they appreciate and defer to a higher cultivation when they meet it, and the higher classes ought to be educated in a very different manner, in order that they exhibit to the lower classes that higher education to which, if they were shown to them, they would bow down and defer (Cockburn 2013: 94–95)

For some therefore, compulsory schooling provided a means to address the perceived threat from the under classes at a time of significant change. As such, school offered a model for unity and stability, albeit built on control, that, through a rigid curriculum, could ensure all children be shaped into citizens of the Empire (see Cockburn 2013). The reference to nationalism as a driving theme reflects the extent to which countries were recognising how their 'curriculum of virtue' could be used to distinguish themselves from the 'competition', in terms of both colonial ambitions and, significantly, military passions.

Formal schooling was, therefore, an important tool of the state. Hendrick reflects that this application of school as a means of structuring and defining the child's everyday life created a 'new construction of childhood' (1997: 46). He develops this as follows.

> It [compulsory schooling] threw aside the child's 'knowledge' derived from parents, community, peer group and personal experience. Instead it demanded a state of ignorance. Secondly, it required upon pain of punishment, usually physical, a form of behaviour, accompanied by a set of related attributes, which reinforced the child's dependence and vulnerability and, in terms of deference towards established authorities, its social class. Thirdly, the ability of children to work for wages was no longer viewed

from the perspective of their exploitation by adults, but rather from that of their own moral weakness: wage-earning children were not 'proper' children and, therefore had to be made 'innocent' of such adult behaviour, and the school was the institutional means of achieving this end. Fourthly, in claiming the legal and moral right to inflict punishment upon children, the school reinforced the idea of the child as a being in need of a particular form of discipline for, although children had always been assaulted in their capacity as employees, wage labour had obscured what was coming to be regarded as an essential feature of the new condition. Fifthly, it further institutionalised the separation of children from society, confirming upon them a separate identity: their proper place was in the classroom. Finally the school emphasised the value of children as investments in future parenthood, economic competitiveness, and a stable democratic order. (1998: 46)

This is a model for doing school that came as no 'bolt out of the blue'. Rather, the themes that shaped mass schooling continued to rely on the curriculum of virtue that had been seen in previous generations. What was different was that now there was scope to ensure that *all* children were drawn into this process of moral education (see Cunningham 1995), defined and overseen by the state.

Part of our constructed image of the child, which emerges when considering virtue, is the idea of school as a place to deal with children's moral instruction, and this continued throughout the twentieth century. Although many examples could be used to illustrate this, the state-sanctioned policies towards aboriginal children in Canada ('sixties scoop') and Australia ('stolen generations') stand out (Nagwegahbow 2015; ABC Online, 8/9/2015). In these, the model of schooling was driven by colonial arrogance that the approach that had been relied on to create a perceived sense of 'greatness' on the basis of a particular 'curriculum of virtue' was the only way to ensure a successful society. Significantly, the model reflects a set of measures that were to have calamitous implications for native peoples, effects that continue to be felt by today's generations. Such policies are no longer formalised, but that does not stop discrimination on the grounds of race, class and gender being part of school practice, nor has it stopped school being seen as a place for ongoing surveillance with, for example, ever - lower ages being suggested for children starting school (*Guardian*, 4/11/13).

6.6   Educating the Future Citizen

This chapter has argued that by applying virtue as a filter to an investigation of our understanding of children and morality, it is possible to engage with a 'curriculum of virtue', that reflects adult practices for 'teaching' children right and wrong and instructing them in the knowledge they require to be citizens. It is significant that these themes persist today, reflecting those that were drawn from the partial historical account in previous sections. The final section of this chapter explores the continuing debate about the influence of a curriculum of virtue in children's lives in relation to not just school but also home and the neighbourhood.

Arthur (2010) asserts that 'the formation of character could be said to be the aim all general education has historically set out to achieve' (Arthur 2010: 11). If that is the case, what is the role of education within schools today, and how is the child positioned in relation to it? The model of the curriculum of virtue that we have been considering establishes an image of the child that is distinguished by its need to be 'taught'. It reflects a view of the child in which themes of the child as a project, passivity and lack are all prominent. To what extent do those themes continue to pervade the way in which we consider children and their engagement with a developing understanding of right and wrong?

In the first half of the nineteenth century, men such as Robert Owen (working in Scotland) flew the flag for the role of education as a transformer of character. Indeed, as the century developed, character became a 'form of social and moral capital' (Arthur 2010) that sparked character development as a focus for later organisations, such as the Scouts and Guides. In the school system, character thus became increasingly defined. The Board of Education's 1906 Handbook stated that 'the purpose of public elementary school is to form and strengthen character', which included, industry, self control, duty, respect, good manners, fair play and loyalty. There was a dip in interest during the mid-twentieth century as psychology 'became the dominant discipline in moral and character education' (Arthur 2010: 37), but by the 1980s values were making a comeback (Arthur et al. 2009).

A 2010 report by Demos in the UK reflected on the central role of 'active character development' in the education system, marking the place of a contemporary curriculum of virtue. It is a model that can be contrasted with similar practices in other countries, where education is seen as a focus for the sharing of social ambitions (as defined by the state). This might, as in the UK, see virtues driven through particular aspects of the curriculum – for example, in the Citizenship Curriculum in England (Department for Education 2013a)[15] - or as in Canada as part of an underlying school ethos –as seen in the Ontario Catholic School Board's graduate expectations (2011). However, despite these documents, an unwritten role in teaching is to impart appropriate standards of behaviour as teachers recognise and pursue a sense of moral purpose (Pollard 2014). This theme is built into the structure of schooling with its long list of rules and strategies, as children are encouraged to care for each other, to respect people and property and to develop positive relationships as they learn to collaborate.[16] The challenge, however, is that defining the look of a character-based programme of learning varies significantly. Indeed, one chapter in Arthur's edited collection highlights the range of value-based learning that takes place in school (Arthur 2010), with one school being recorded as having 20 value-based words.[17] One of the challenges for schools, therefore, is to define character-based learning. The very fact that these values have to be defined raises questions: Whose responsibility is that? How much does identifying the ambitions for positive behaviour involve the children themselves? These sit alongside questions about teachers' confidence in developing learning in this area and on the long-term effectiveness of project-based interventions for character formation (Harrison 2010). Where to place this aspect of children's education is the focus of an ongoing debate by policy-makers. Should it be a distinct curriculum activity or should it form part of the overall ethos of the school (see House of Lords debates on PSHE (Hansard 2014))? Indeed the 2013 National Curriculum in England is notable for its lack of focus on morals or values – these themes are not even mentioned (Department for Education 2013b). It leaves schools with an awareness that they should be engaging with virtue (in its broadest sense), but there is a lack of practical clarity on what it means to fulfil this requirement (HM Government 2015).

As such, for many, virtue education is an informal aspect of the teacher's role, supported by the optional use of outside programmes such as Steven Covey's Habits of Power and the international Philosophy for Children movement (IAPC 2016). Although they investigate elements of character with children, they remain adult-directed programmes which generally see the children responding to a set of virtues that are defined by adults. This focus seems to be at the centre of the Department for Education's desire to invest in character education in England,[18] and develop further programmes.[19] It reflects the ongoing image of the child as, a project, passive and lacking and as such highlights the role of the government of the day in directing virtue education as schools are used to transmit what they consdier the virtues of society should be (James and James 2004).

6.7   Concluding Thoughts

This chapter has highlighted that the images of the child that are con-structed within the interactional spaces in which children operate can have a significant impact on adult-defined practices and, therefore, the child's everyday experiences. What stands out in these sections is the extent to which key institutions of childhood, such as home and school, need to be examined in terms of the moral image that they hold of the child, as part of seeking to understand the practices that emerge. What is clearly reflected above is that adults' efforts to pursue a curriculum of virtue have had significant implications for the nature of the backdrop with which children interact.

Notably a curriculum of virtue with a particular focus on an aggressive form of discipline continues to be reflected in different ways in homes and schools. For example, corporal punishment in state schools in the UK was only banned in 1987, and not until the turn of the millennium in private schools. Indeed, even today teachers look back to the time of corporal punishment for a way of dealing with the perceived behavioural problems that they now face (Guardian 2012). In the home, globally, corporal punishment is only banned in 48 countries (OHCHR 2016 – see discussion in Chap. 9). Outside of the home and school, the focus on punishment and its connection to a curriculum of virtue must also be noted. The justice system is the obvious example and will be a focus in Chap. 7.

It is notable that this curriculum of virtue is common to all children and is experienced in the different spaces within which they find themselves. This has implications for the way in which children come to be positioned in relation to education and how they are defined as learners. As a result, 'learning' is presented in a very particular way, such that adults, as fonts of knowledge, take their wisdom and force it onto the child. The image of the child is thus constructed around the notion of the need for children to be 'taught to be' if, in their future role as adults, they are going to be able to sustain the moral order of society.

As such, the approach taken by adults towards the curriculum of virtue and the images of the child that come to be constructed have direct implications for the substance of adult efforts to impart moral knowledge reflecting a dimension that cannot be ignored as we seek to construct any image of the child.

Notes

1. The Torah in Judaism, for example, reflects a society's efforts to define a set of rules, which would then have been shared. Of course what the Torah reflects is the need to impart knowledge of God's laws, which as a society this particular community of people saw as the framework for living a 'valued' way of life, one that enabled interaction and personal fulfilment. It presents a direct invitation to include children within a moral discourse and appears to be a pronouncement to all, rather than a limited few (Barton 2003). Smale (1998) reflects on the 613 laws 'mostly regarding moral issues' and how, by 12 years of age, a boy became a 'son of the law' (1998: 130).

2. Plato argues for a programme of study in this quest for 'reason', and the implied moral connotations that this holds, as part of nurturing the child's soul (Curtis and Boultwood, 1977). This included using music and gymnastics, the former in order to engage children's emotions and the latter offering opportunities for children to take control of their bodies through physical exertion. This aim formed part of a Platonic plan for children to develop a knowledge of what is 'good'. Notably it reflects a socially orientated model of moral learning, in that reason is directly linked to the individual and their ability to manage feelings and emotions.

As children (boys) got older, so they were invited to take on rhetoric and subsequently to engage increasingly with politics. Although restricting the child to a model of development, this early approach did at least seek to support some children's learning with direct reference to social life. The need to deal with children's lack of reason meant that an engagement with 'virtue' was to become a cornerstone of education. It raises questions that can be asked throughout history and which offer a number of challenges to our contemporary efforts, which often rely more on 'expected' than on 'encouraged' conceptions of reason, defined by an academic rather than the social curriculum.

3. R.G. Collingwood (2013), a twentieth-century philosopher and proponent of home schooling, in referring to the foundation for the professional educator following Plato's views defining teaching by space, a prescribed curriculum and the person who is eventually produced, described it as nothing short of 'the biggest crime'. His opinion reflects not only onto the ongoing prevalence of Plato's work but on how it sits alongside more progressive thinking around the child.

4. Plato and Xenophon were both born 50 years before Aristotle, wh was born in 384BCE. However, both lived long lives that overlapped with Aristotle's.

5. Cockburn notes how a separate word (*arête*) was applied to slaves, one that reflected a lesser capacity for moral action: 'the moral virtue of slaves is only minimally required to perform the tasks of the master' (2013: 32).

6. Aquinas (1225–1274), drawing from Aristotle, combines early secular views on virtue with the teachings of the church. As such, in presenting an understanding of 'natural law' or a presentation of 'ethical truth', he suggests four cardinal virtues: prudence, justice, fortitude and temperance (Aquinas, 1880 [part of his *Summa Theologica*]). Of course, from a Christian perspective, the Bible offers theological virtues, but Aquinas presented these cardinal virtues, as he reflected on a sense of purpose in life and that other pillar of ethical thinking, reason. Although later movements in the church sought to separate themselves from Aquinas, in particular the protestant revolution, the work of Aquinas shows the extent to which the provision of aspirational human goals could be set, disseminated and to some extent monitored and reviewed.

7. A consequence of the value of education (and its relationship with 'virtue') had been the further formalisation of teaching as a profession. Municipalities within the Roman Empire were meant to have on their

staff a supply of professional teachers on which they could draw to educate their citizens. Within this, the role of the educator was increasingly growing in value. Trade was a factor because languages, writing and maths were important for furthering business, but education still retained its role for developing the character of the child (Orme 2006).

8. Orme (2006) reflects on how, with the rebirth of the towns around the thirteenth century in England, formal schooling moved away from the church with its professional teachers and formal classrooms. The focus was more on academic attainment linked to commercial goals, than on character development, which perhaps was seen as adequately provided for elsewhere.

9. Pelagius, a fourth-century contemporary of Augustine, risked the wrath of the Catholic church by challenging this image. He argued that each child was made in the image of God with a natural goodness and, as a result, any later sin was the result of the temptations of human life (Newell 1987).

10. De Mause reports how parents were taught how to hit their young children correctly, making sure that they learnt to find the 'golden mean' between enough punishment and knowing when to stop so that the child might not 'die' (1974: 42).

11. See Kuefler, 2003 for more detail.

12. This is illustrated by an extract from a letter written by Henry IV of France to Madame de Montglot who had care of the three-year-old Dauphin,: 'I have a complaint to make: you do not have to send me word that you have whipped my son. I wish and command you to whip him every time that he is obstinate and misbehaves, knowing well for myself that there is nothing in the world which will be better for him than that' (cited in Hunt, 1969: 135).

13. Although more than 100 countries ban corporal punishment in schools only 31 ban it at home (CNN 2011).

14. In reflecting on education in Roman society, Quintillian comments on the use of violence:

As for corporal punishment, though it is recognised practice ... I am completely opposed to it, first because it is disgusting, fit only for slaves and undoubtedly an insult ... in the next place, because a pupil whose mind so ill befits a free man's son as not to be corrected by reproof, will remain obdurate even in the face of blows – like the vilest of slaves. And finally because there will be no need of such chastisement if there is always somebody present to diligently supervise the pupil's studies ... If you coerce the child while he is young by means of blows, what will you do when he is a young man who cannot be compelled through fear and has many more important things to learn (Institutio Book 1, c. 2. Quoted in Curtis & Boultwood, 1977:60).

15. The Citizenship Curriculum (Department of Education, 2013), which opens with the sentence: 'A high-quality citizenship education helps to provide pupils with knowledge, skills and understanding to prepare them to play a full and active part in society', is only statutory for key stage 3 and above (that is, secondary school children).

16. Also associated with the professional standards laid out for teachers – Pollard, 2014: 7.

17. See discussions in the UK to define British values (Guardian, 9/6/2014).

18. Note the work of the Jubilee Centre at the University of Birmingham. This project to further character-based learning in England is part-funded by the Department for Education. Also note work the Cambridge Primary Review (2009).

19. The work of the Jubilee Centre, Birmingham University reflects this focus on character learning. This has been supported by significant funding from the Department for Education – https://www.gov.uk/government/news/character-education-apply-for-2015-grant-funding.

7

Social Harmony

Tom Tom the pipers son
Stole a pig and away he ran
The pig was eat and Tom was beat
and Tom when roaring down the street

The third filter that can add to our understaning of those moral themes that influence our construction of childhoods relates to a desire to see children comply with adult perceptions of harmony. With close links to reason and virtue, social harmony provides an additional layer through which to consider the way in which society seeks to protect a perceived ideal as moral norms or virtues come to be accepted and revered. It, therefore, becomes important that the ideal is maintained and that society recognises and responds to any group that seeks to threaten this equilibrium. This chapter, with particular reference to the neighbourhood, looks at the extent to which maintaining the status quo comes to inform images of the child, with direct implications for the way in which practices come to be created and used.

© The Editor(s) (if applicable) and The Author(s) 2017
S. Frankel, *Negotiating Childhoods*, Studies in Childhood and Youth,
DOI 10.1057/978-1-137-32349-1_7

The previous two chapters have drawn from some historical sources to reflect on the importance of reason and virtue as filters that can be considered as part of constructions of childhood. In this chapter, history continues to feature as we build up the sense of legacy that sits behind these moral filters. It is an investigation that reflects themes of citizenship (see Cockburn 2013 for more) and the extent to which the individual is recognised as having a status within society. Just like morality, views around citizenship considered through a historical context play an important part in structuring the way in which children are engaged with today. This chapter will show that the moral elements that inform images of the child are beset by ambiguities because the child is controlled with one hand and protected with the other. The following discussions highlight how these images reflect an adult desire to maintain supremacy within the neighbourhood, since adults mark their territory through practices that ensure children's place in moral discourses is either as a target for constraint or as an object of concern.

7.1   Order: A Product of Society

An important feature of society is the sense in which we search for ways to live together effectively. Morality thus offers a core purpose for any social group. It offers a means through which it is possible to make sense of actions by identifying what is acceptable and what is not acceptable, what actions are right and what actions are wrong. Morality, therefore, has an intrinsic place in providing a means through which social harmony can be established.[1] Rules are created through which the ability of that group to live together is not just made possible, but improved. Indeed, if one looks at the development of societies, one can see the importance from the earliest time of rules through which to make sense of human behaviour (Douglas 1966). For example, Douglas' work invites a consideration of the extent to which established and less-established social groupings all draw from the same processes, formalised in different ways, through which they seek to make sense of social action in the hope of creating and shaping an order that allows the society to operate effectively. Perceptions of belonging and the maintenance of peace, therefore, become woven into the fabric of society, whether within culture, through formal laws or in the institutionalised nature of the setting. It is, therefore, with reference to context, through this lens of social harmony, that we can consider an element of the way in which childhoods come to be constructed, as we respond to those notable features of control and constraint that pervade contemporary and historical practices towards children.

A sense of harmony as a focus for how we think about morality is present in the earliest writings. Plato took on the notion of justice as he reflected on the severity of the conflict that had consumed Athens and its neighbours. Within it, he sought to draw up a blueprint for moving forward and for re-engaging with one another. Fundamentally, it was a plan by which people could get along. This is reflected in Plato's definition of the human quest for 'good' in *Republic* (1988). It is onto this that Aristotle's *Nicomachean Ethics* (1999) introduces the notion of *eudaimonia* (happiness). The concept of the happy individual is a further reflection on an ability to co-operate with one another, acknowledging that together we find a means through which to get along. Aristotle, in comparison to Plato, places the ability to reach a sense of goodness firmly in the hands of the individual. The search for a shared goodness as the product of moral inquiry is of course reflected in the work of later philosophers too. The utilitarians, such as Bentham (1879) and Mill (1910), offer a further sense of morality in terms of its ability to find a model that recognises the good of all.

What is 'good' is another question. Although many have set out to define and shape a sense of the common good as a means for reflecting on perceptions of happiness, it is clear that this is framed in very adult-centric terms (Bacon and Frankel 2013). The ongoing desire to find the 'best' way of living together, positioned alongside the notions of reason and virtue presented in Chaps. 5 and 6, starts to help us make more sense of adults' need to keep control over children (James and James 2004). It presents a set of discourses in which children were seen as lacking the ability for moral thought but also (for those that had greater expectations of a future capacity to reason) in need of training that would mould them to fulfil the ambitions that society had for them. In both these regards, children were cast as actors in a play for which they were unable to learn their lines or to form a sense of what the play was about. The only way for the children to play their parts was for them to submit to the ongoing supervision and direction of adults, without which chaos would ensue.

This analogy reflects children's potential to destabilise the world of adults as a consequence of their lack of reason, which might or might not be being managed by a 'curriculum of virtue'. This perhaps has been summed up in more recent history through the notion of panics (Pearson 1983). The theme of panic will be considered later, but it reflects a sense in which adults continue to pull the strings which, as a result, frames the context for children's experiences, one in which a desire to achieve an adult understanding of the common good is of the highest importance. Notably, it is an understanding that is maintained through constructed images that reflect the dominance of the theme of the threat that children pose to social harmony.

7.1.1   A Space for Judgement

The neighbourhood is a very different setting from home and school. The link between the individual, regulation (formal or informal) and an enforcer is complicated in a way that it is not in the other spaces. Indeed, it can at times be hard to define the rules and whose job it is to maintain them. Previous chapters, have touched on some of society's ways of dealing with this complexity. For example, the role of the father in Classical times meant that his remit would have extended to his family's behaviour outside of his four walls. Other agents, such as the *paidagoges*, provided an adult overseer to keep an eye on children as they journeyed outside of the home. This sense of working within the wider bounds of the community is reflected in the well-used African proverb: 'It take a whole village to raise a child'. That sense of community relates to comments in Chap. 5 about all men within Spartan society taking a role in a child's moral journey. These models of regulation would have varied, but all reflect an implied purpose of at most controlling and at least directing the child.

The need for direction is reflected not just in the Classical era but also in other societies. In Ancient Egypt, the role of the adult was triggered by a perception of children's limited competence 'a small child was an incomplete person because they lacked knowledge and understanding'

(Lichtheim 1997: 16), which as a result required society to find ways to ensure that this 'lack' would not effect the functioning of society. In this close relationship between reason, virtue and social harmony one can see the extent to which these elements combine in shaping images of the child. This is highlighted in writings known as the 'Instructions' of Ptahhotep from the *Papyrus Prisse*. In them, good and evil are associated with virtues which were specifically laid out and focused on behaviours to ensure a sense of harmony such as justice and loyalty, not quarrelling or being greedy. The focus is clearly very relational in nature and offers a framework from which society could work. A similar focus on harmony can be explored in those spoken and then written texts that made up the Judaic Torah (offering a foundation that is recognised in all of the monotheistic faiths (Barton 2003). Here, stories dealt directly with the way in which certain behaviours can disrupt harmony with lessons for both adults and children (Smale 1998). The sense of 'law' represented by the Torah created a formalisation of the image of the moral child. Of course, this was simply the start of the moral image of the child and its place within the legal system.

The above examples all stress that moral regulation comes from a focus on establishing social order. As societies grew, so did the need to manage the harmony of society. Goebel's (1976) analysis of the origins of criminal law reflects this desire to protect the harmony of society, rooting it in notions of 'peace'. Breaching that peace, therefore, needed to be marked (as it was in the societies mentioned above), because the breach announced the decision of an individual to step outside of the group and thereby suspend, or even relinquish, their membership. This makes good theoretical sense, but of course acts against others are not always easily defined, you are not always going to catch a perpetrator red handed. For example, acts of theft required an evolved system, one in which it was possible to act on the basis of 'suspicion', which in turn required the need to build up evidence. Dealing with evidence and suspicion meant that eventually a decision was needed, a judgement call, as an individual or group of individuals took responsibility for deciding 'guilt'. This process was heightened by the fact that those judges would have the power to respond to this act against the community by imposing, on behalf of its members, a punishment. Thus the law stood to identify those who had violated public peace or good order, to punish them and as a result to ensure the protection of all (Calhoun 1927). This moved 'crime' from being a self-help issue to one in which there was considerable regulation as society responded to the 'pollution' (Calhoun 1927: 26) caused by such behaviour and acted to wash it away.

As suggested above, the theoretical implications of such a process required someone or some people to identify what those 'crimes' were, whether they had been committed and what the appropriate response should be. It has been noted elsewhere that certain groups were seen as having a higher capacity to reason. Clearly, the perception of moral reasoning meant that those who were so endowed would become the creators of the 'law' and with it the setting of the virtues to which the society aspired. It is a model, therefore, that is inherently power-driven, with some notable implications. The primary implication is that, from the start, the law promoted the views of one group over others. Aristotle identifies this theme as he comments on the hierarchy of the law and the fact that it gives certain 'men despotic power over their neighbours' (Tamanaha 2001: 67). The theme of power is certainly a focus for Douglas as she draws out the extent to which the law becomes a social filter to 'force one another into good citizenship' (Douglas 1966: 3). So what does this mean for children?

Children's perceived lack of reason immediately placed them outside any of the processes for setting and defining social rules. As a result, the neighbourhood (both in the past and now) comes to be defined by a particular group who are fundamentally more powerful than children. This group of adults has the formal ability to define behaviour within this space, the power to make judgements on infringements and to inflict punishment as a consequence. This system of power implies and indeed offers a means for controlling social threats. The lack of representation that children have within this model of 'justice' becomes a theme that remains today.

7.2   The Ominous Child

The law and assessments of social harmony have, therefore, a close relationship. Children's position in relation to the law can be considered both with reference to managing the threat that they represent and the extent to which the law draws from certain understandings of reason in order to justify its position. I have considered the idea of children as a threat elsewhere (Frankel 2012). What becomes compelling in this investigation is the extent to which the notion of threat has surrounded children from the earliest of writings. As such, it becomes too simplistic to define children only in terms of evil or innocence. Instead, a further category needs to recognise the representation of threat that has cut across generations, one that is not necessarily about the actual threat but more about the potential for threat. This can be characterised in a representation of the child as 'ominous'. The ominous child is heavily defined by age. What is significant is the way in which age becomes a marker by which adults are able to manage the potential threat from children as it comes to take on meaning within constructed images of the child. Although this can be highlighted in a number of areas, the law offers a good illustration of the use of age as a means of framing images that reflect the 'ominous child'.

7.2.1 Age

This section will be developed with reference to English Law. I recognise that the model will look different in other jurisdictions, but what is important is asking the questions, and not necessarily in the similarity of the findings. In respect of Roman law, children's place can be summarised by notions of 'intent' (and how this related to crimes against the person or property), 'consent' (and its relationship to children's ability to, for example, enter into contracts and receive inheritance) and control. Although the Roman system recognised that some children, particularly those from wealthy families, might find themselves in need of the law to deal with, primarily, financial issues, the law ensured control through the 'catch all' of *patria potestas*. In short, this provided heads of households with whatever power they needed in order to keep order within their 'homes'.

The link between images of the child and the practices that result can be seen through the evolving way in which children were brought under the criminal law. In England, it was not the criminal law, but rather common law, that set out to define the child and to manage the threat that they were seen to pose. Thus, common law established an age at which the child was seen as being responsible for their 'criminal' behaviour. The age that was set was seven years old (Leng et al. 1998). Below this age, children were not seen as capable of committing a crime; above it they could, in theory, be dealt with in exactly the same way as an adult. However, even though the law, as it developed in England, maintained seven years as the moment of moral awakening, it was felt that children needed extra protection. Thus, from the time of Edward III, children in England were tried under the principle of *doli incapax* (Cavidino 1997). *Doli incapax* required those judging a child to ask whether the child knew the act was wrong, thereby establishing some sense of wilful intention, and also recognition of whether the act was 'seriously' wrong. In practice, during the fourteenth century, this meant that children who were under 12 years of age 'could expect charges against them to be dropped because they had not reached a presumed age of reason' (Hanawalt 1979: 43). The history of *doli incapax*, and its eventual removal by the Crime and Disorder Act 1998, reflects the way in which age became a gateway into the system, one that provided adults with options in terms of using the law to engage with the threat that children posed, but which sat alongside, sometimes in tension with, the need to acknowledge children's competence and their 'developing' moral understanding.

In 1998 the extra protection that had been provided for children by *doli incapax* for 700 years was removed (Bandalli 1998). In presenting the case for its removal the government of the day argued that it was a 'doctrine that defies common sense, most young people between the ages of ten and thirteen are clearly capable of knowing the difference between right and wrong' (cited in Cavidino 1997: 165). The abolition of *doli incapax* and the setting of the age of criminal responsibility at ten years[2] have resulted in the UN asking repeated questions in their reviews of how the UK is fulfilling its responsibility under the United Nations Convention on the Rights of the Child. The abolition of *doli incapax* is a measure that grew out of social fears following the murder of James Bulger (Carlen and Morgan 1999), considered later in this chapter, reflecting a policy designed directly in response to efforts to maintain social harmony. To say that the images that emerged left the child vulnerable is an understatement, not to mention that it also shows a lack of understanding about the way in which children engage with morality. It is a stance that can only be understood in terms of an ongoing desire to ensure that children are fully controlled and constrained (James and James 2004).[3]

The use of age must therefore be considered in terms of its role in managing the potential threat that children pose. Obviously, thinking in relation to reason provided a useful tool in shaping these approaches. However, what is significant is that different ages came to apply in different contexts. The lens of reason does not necessarily help in answering this question. If we were pursuing Kant's case for the universal application of reason, then setting age limits for certain defined behaviours in the law should be easy because they would all be the same. Piaget provided a clear age at which children were seen to be able to engage in reasoned thought, but the ages used in the legal system do not fully represent this. In fact, they are incredibly different around the world. The lens of social harmony provides a useful tool in trying to analyse such differences and to add further to the way in which we come to see how moral images of the child are constructed.

The discussion about social harmony can be explored in relation to two opposing images of the moral child which sit at the heart of the legal system in England and Wales (see Frankel 2012 for more). On the one hand, the criminal law takes an approach that is based around individual accountability and high levels of knowledge about right and wrong. In contrast, the civil law sees children in terms of their lack of competence and limited capacity to take personal responsibility. The approach within the criminal law appears to invite the younger child into a moral discourse, but one that becomes defined by access to knowledge. It means that, rather than responsibility being linked to experience, it is tied to the quantity and quality of a child's knowledge. For, within the realms of the criminal court the child is seen as having complete knowledge of the law ('ignorance or a mistake of law is irrelevant as the citizen is presumed to know the law of the land' (Allen 1987: 87). This position is reinforced by the fact that the process of English criminal law is focused on legal guilt – was the crime committed? – rather than a moral guilt – why?[4]

This approach can be summed up by an illustration from a case I have considered elsewhere (Frankel 2012). It is an example that not only draws on themes of reason, but one that can only be interpreted through a further reflection on social harmony. In the case of Stephen Malcolm

(1984), a 15-year-old was found guilty of recklessly endangering life by throwing Molotov cocktails at the wall of a house. The case relied on previous case law in relation to recklessness which held that whether an act was reckless should be based on the standards of a reasonable bystander. The reasonable bystanders were the members of the jury. To be on a jury one must be at least 18 years old, three years older than Stephen Malcolm. Not only would the jury be considering the actions from the cold light of the courtroom, but also they were not allowed to take into account Stephen's age. Instead, the actions were to be considered from the perspective of the reasonable bystander. In denying the appeal, one of the 'justices' involved reflected:

> We would have preferred that the judge [in that original trial] should at least have been entitled in law to have left to the jury the question, would a boy of the defendant's age have appreciated that to have thrown petrol bombs very close to the windows in a dwelling was a danger to the life of the occupants (Stephen Malcolm R (1984) 79 Cr App R 341)

Judgements like this must be considered in light of their capacity to manage a social threat. Although the original case that limited the consideration of recklessness to the 'reasonable bystander' was overturned in 2004, it reflects the attitude of a system which is institutionally orientated towards control. The determination to manage the threat stands out when one compares what happens in the criminal courts with what happens in the civil courts. In the case of Mullins v. Richards, for example, a fight between two 15-year-old girls, in which one was injured by a breaking ruler, was assessed, not on adult standards of whether the risk should have been foreseen, but on whether these two 15-year-old girls might have foreseen this risk.

These two cases concern children of the same age. One reflects a desire to maintain control, the other protection. What is significant are the different images of the child that emerge from the same system. These images carry with them very different assessments of reason, with different implications for the way in which practices need to respond to those children in assessing the wider threat of these situations. It is these contrasting images of the child that is the key focus here, and the resulting question about the extent to which adult agendas, including maintaining a sense of social order, are reflected in policies.

The extent of this contrast can be seen clearly in the way age is used to define when certain behaviours are accepted.

10	Be held responsible for a crime in England, Wales and Northern Ireland
16	Consent to sexual intercourse
	Buy a lottery ticket
	Buy aerosol paint
18	Vote in elections
	Buy alcohol
	Buy a knife or razor blade
	Bet in a betting shop
	Get a tattoo
21	Entitled to adult rate of national minimum wage

(See Muncie 2015: 225)

It seems perverse that one system uses age in such a variety of ways. Why is it that within the same system a child could be criminally responsible for a sexual offence years before being seen as competent to commit to a sexual relationship? Casting the filter of 'social harmony' over these issues offers a tool for analysis that allows this contrast (alongside considerations of reason) to be examined. As such, both areas of law emerge as tools for control. One ensures adult intervention, with a recourse to punishment for those that present a threat; the other seeks to remove opportunities for that threat to be presented in the first place. It certainly reflects wider discourses around moral competence, one that is well highlighted in relation to the age at which one should be able to vote.

In relation to voting age, discourses reflect the sense of uncertainty that might result from offering the vote to those below the age of 18. The strength of international feeling in relation to this issue was highlighted by the consideration that South Africans gave to including children in the first democratic elections following Apartheid. An idea had been to lower the voting age to 14 years in recognition of the role that young people had played in bringing about political change (particularly seen in relation to education). The politically competent child was an image that the rest of the world were not prepared for, as it placed the child outside of internationally accepted thinking on the role of the child in society. Such pressure, which resulted in South Africa not following through with these radical plans (Pendlebury et al. 2014), refelcted adult concerns for the stability of society if children were given the vote and allowed to have their say. Questions of how opening the vote up to children might impact on adult ambitions (or assessments of maintaining a status quo) can be seen in decisions to involve children aged 16 and 17 years old in voting for the Scottish Referendum and (in an announcement made on the same day) to bar those of the same age from voting in the UK referendum on EU membership (*Independent*, 18/6/2015).

When the child finds themselves in adult 'owned' settings where they have the potential to bring about change, the image that accompanies them often reflects a need to limit opportunities for agency, and diminishes the value of the child's voice. Another notable legal contrast is the extent to which, when the focus is on protection and thus the child poses no wider threat to society, the voice of the child is more readily heard. As one seminal case noted, 'a minor's capacity to make his or her own decisions depends upon the minor having sufficient understanding and intelligence to make the decisions and not to be determined by reference to any fixed age limit' (Gillick v. West Norfolk HA, 1986 1 FLR 250). This case offered a starting point for engaging with children, but notably in a context in which the child presented no wider threat to society. (Ultimately, it reflects situations in which adults have the final say as they act in the perceived 'best interests' of the child.) This argument can be reflected in the way in which children are positioned in relation to their rights, as well as those aspects of the legal system where they are more readily 'heard' (Birnbaum 2009).

In practice, therefore, one ends up with a range of images of the child that are reflected within the law. These images come to be framed by questions of care and control as assessments are made in relation to the wider threat that children pose to society.

> On the one hand, then there is the denial of children as rational responsible persons able to receive information, participate in frank and open discussions

and come to well reasoned and appropriately informed decisions about their interpersonal relationships (family, friends, sexual), about school and developing sexuality. On the other hand there is the imposition, using the full force of law, of the highest level of rationality and responsibility on children and young people that seriously offend. The paradox is that the same sources appear to propose that childhood represents a period of diminished adult responsibility governing certain actions while being a period of equally responsibility governing others (Scraton 1997: 182)

Notably images of the child within the law vary between countries.[5] This offers a rich field for analysis as researcher ask questions about social harmony (and the other moral filters) offering contrasting pictures of childhoods within different contexts. An interesting factor in exploring these images is the extent to which a rights agenda is having an impact (Muncie 2015). Despite the United Nations Convention on the Rights of the Child being almost universal, its application in different countries is significantly different. Considering moral filters offers a way to make sense of the clash between domestic law and international convention as countries consider how they will position children, reflecting on different images that are framed with reference to, amongst other criteria, a consideration of social harmony.

As this section has discussed, age is a defining feature in shaping the way in which children are provided with opportunities within all spaces, but particularly in relation to the their place in the community. Here, the recognisiton of age has been reflected in themes of competence but also in assesments of the threat that children pose to society more widely. In building up a sense of that threat, age is an important criterion, as it impacts on the way in which images come to be constructed and practices come to be defined.

7.2.2   A Visible Target

Another characteristic of 'ominous' images of the child is visibility. The changing dynamics within post-Reformation England provide a clear illustration of the extent to which a particular moral image of the child became a driver for policy, impacting directly on the public space that children inhabited. Cunningham (2006) demonstrates the extent to which legislation was connected with the growing concern about children and the need for the state to be seen to control them.

Cunningham reports that, during the 1520s, there was a large increase in population. Children under 15 years comprised one-third of the population and, as a result, children were not only becoming more visible, they were also becoming a practical economic challenge, which meant that the middle and upper classes were compelled to react. Society had already found ways to respond to this threat by passing laws which, for example, included the right for men younger than 24 years and women younger than 20 years to be taken from their families if they were found to be wandering alone. Not only that, but an apprentice who escaped from their master could be put in chains and used 'as his slave' (Cunningham 2006: 93). Although this measure was only short lived, such legislation reflects the changing attitude towards children and how 'in these laws and policies rank social fear seems to be the dominant motif. Children are dangerous' (Cunningham 2006: 95). It was this well advocated need to bring order and at the same time to offer a perception of 'care' that came to be defined in law, framed by an aggressive image towards the child. This culminated in the 1597 (1601) Act for Relief of the Poor in which children who were vagrants, destitute or not fulfilling their role as apprentices could be sent to the colonies. In 1627 some 1400–1500 children found themselves sent to Virginia. Such was the strength of this legislation that the Privy Council had the power to 'imprison, punish and dispose any of those children, upon disorder by them committed...' (2006: 98). Such policies reflect the fear of the threat that children posed, as the image of the child altered with the changing demographics, informing policy and impacting children's experiences.

All this was taking place against a wider backdrop of the fear of violence. Stone notes how 'casual violence from strangers was also seen as a daily threat, brutal unprovoked assaults by gangs of idle youths... were frequent occurrences in London streets' (1979: 94). Indeed, these idle youths came from 'respectable families' and were seen to be part of defined gangs, such as the 'Mohawks'. Such characterisations simply added to the wider sense of fear about young people that is reflected in literature such as Shakespeare's *A Winters's Tale*:

I would there were no age between ten and three and twenty,
or that young wicked sleep the rest;
for there is nothing in the between but getting wenches with children,
wronging the anciently, stealing and fighting
(Shakespeare 1986: 1257)

This fear was not restricted to London's streets but is presented by Stone as being a wider problem between factions of young people.

> The violence of everyday life seems to have been accompanied by much mutual suspicion and a low general level of emotional interaction and commitment. Alienation and distrust of one's fellow man are the predominant features of the Elizabethan and early Stuart view of human character. (1979: 95)

This position was reflected in legislation as lawmakers sought to deal with the problem by criminalising as much as they could, creating crimes out of low-level behaviour such as lewd and disorderly conduct through to sabbath breaking and profanity (Hunt 1978). The law was positioned, in relation to certain groups, as a tool that society could use to respond to particular social fears.

An important feature in this chapter is the link between the law reacting to the concerns of the powerful within society and the moral image that is connected to it. The following example shows just how deep-rooted was the interconnection between the media, the people and the legislators – a theme that appears later in relation to children. The Black Act of 1723 was created to deal with a need by those in power to reasert their authority, in front of a backdrop of a growing (and therefore increasingly visible) population. The 'Act of Terror' saw the reintroduction of hanging for 'crimes' that had not been seen as capital offences for more than 200 years. The behaviour that concerned the politicians (drawn from a narrow social group) and the press was poaching. The 'Blacks' became framed as a 'threat to authority, property and order' and as a result they were a 'real danger to peaceable men' (E.P. Thompson 1975: 195). In reality, poaching presented a small problem for a small number of people but, because the group affected had such large power, the consequence was the construction of a particular image that saw the underrepresented poor the target for this increasing number of capital offences[6] . Although not directly dealing with children this illustration highlights the growing power of the combined forces of press, popular opinion and politics. It marked a powerful triumvirate that would soon include the child as a focus of its attentions.

As we move into the nineteenth century the fears about children and crime became increasingly explicit (Taylor 1998). This was reflected in the increasing profile of official statistics with a corresponding increase in legislation.For example, more behaviours were criminalised through acts such as 1824 Vagrant Act and the 1827 Malicious Trespass Act and their focus on petty crime. The introduction of the police force during this time meant that the neighbourhood now had a 'point' man to direct its efforts in dealing with the threats that society faced. This meant that, in practice, it was not only possible to enforce the legislation more easily, but also to capture and convict increasing numbers of children (Taylor 1998). The more frequent appearances of children in the dock impacted on the perceptions of the magistrates, who defined children as 'depraved' and, as a result, there were suggestions that the child 'could be criminal at any age' (1998: 66). The number of crimes went up, which was leaving children increasingly vulnerable as more and more of these crimes were being turned into capital offences (for example, shoplifting and theft). Although a glance at the Newgate Calendar (a popular publication in England that reported on crimes) revealed that children under 16 years rarely seemed to be hanged for anything other than murder, the potential of the black cap should not be underestimated as a sign to the public at large (Rayner 1926).

The pervasive ominousness of the child is so clearly reflected in Pearson's (1983) book *Hooligan*, which highlights the attitudes around 'threat' and the extent to which they are closely linked to the older child through the representation of the 'hooligan'. Notably, in characterising the Victorian home, Pearson draws on sources that repeat those themes of pollution and, as he terms it, 'moral contagion' (Pearson 1983: 158) that were mentioned earlier. The metaphors of the day, he suggests, convey 'the oozing tide of poisonous violence and wretchedness that might burst from its subterranean home and sweep away the social order if not checked' (Pearson 1983: 158). Such language, whiich is very colourful and unreserved in its characteriation of the threats, added to a climate in which drastic action, such as transportation, was used to respond to worries that. 'London has got too full of children' (Pinchbeck and Hewitt 1969: 552). This rich contextual analysis highlights a number of themes that could be used in furthering our wider desire to understand the structural context, and shows not only the threat, but also the ongoing sense that the only way to respond to it was to separate the criminal child from the non-criminal child. A quote from the day refers to the child involved in crime as knowing 'much and a great deal too much of what is called life...He is self-reliant...he submits to no control [he is] a little stunted man' (cited in Pearson 1983: 167). The criminal child thus was put in the category of giving sufficient reason that the law could demand an account for their behaviour and punish them if found guilty. It shows that, despite the protection offered by aspects of the law such as *doli incapax*, the criminal law was not prevented from targeting children, which in turn maitained a level of public concern.

7.3   Managing the Ominous Child

The visibility of the child presented a threat but the nature of this threat and how it should be managed became of increasing interest in the nineteenth century. Here, the notion of innocence, introduced in the last chapter, comes to influence the constructed images of the child. Notably, social harmony remains a defining theme as society deals with issues such as poverty, with the aim of breaking a cycle and offering children a chance to engage with an ideal that will further the effective running of society as a whole. It is a journey that paves the way for the discussion on children's rights, but it is deeply rooted in an ongoing need for children to be managed. By reflecting on social harmony, one can more effectively create a foundation to engage with children's rights and to ask important questions about the image of the child that these rights reflect, with very real implications for the way in which adults come to engage with them.

7.3.1 Innocent?

Part of managing the threat that children posed was a growing recognition of the need to ensure that children were adequately protected from the harsh realities of the world and provided with basic needs. At the dawn of the Victorian era, acknowledgement was given to the extent to which society as a whole needed to take some responsibility for the conditions that people lived in. By doing so, the problems that society feared could, to some extent, be contained. The harsh and determined effort described above, therefore, came to be seen increasingly alongside themes of protection and provision, and a desire to manage social harmony through adult-directed 'care' framed by what was in the 'best interests' of the child. For Mary Carpenter, during the mid nineteenth century, this meant that the young offender was to be seen as somoene who had lost their childhood. The right response of the adult, therefore, was that this offender 'gradually be restored to the true position of childhood...he must...be placed in a family' (cited in Cunningham 1995: 148). It highlights the sense amongst the middle and upper classes of 'rescuer' which, within a set of circumstances that they could manage, made intervention in children's lives focused by a notion of the ideal childhood something that was not only perceived as right but also a desirable thing to do.

However, if the child was to be seen as worthy of rescue, what did that mean for the way in which their ability to reason was considered and how their actions were judged with reference to social harmony. Whether this is in the poems of Wordsworth or novels such as Barrie's *Peter Pan* ([1906]1989), images of the child emerged that reflected in different ways Rousseau's ideas of innocence (Chap. 6). Cunningham draws from William Blake's *Songs of Innocence* to show the changing attitude towards the child that stemmed from Rousseau's work. The opening poem simply sums up the tenor of these writings, both in terms of their reflections on the child's competence but also, notably, on how these relate to a wider sense of harmony.

Piping down the valleys wild,
Piping songs of pleasant glee,
On a cloud I saw a child,
And he laughing said to me:

'Pipe a song about a Lamb!'
So I piped with merry cheer.
'Piper, pipe that song again.'
So I piped: he wept to hear.
'Drop thy pipe, thy happy pipe;
Sing thy songs of happy cheer!'
So I sung the same again,
While he wept with joy to hear.
'Piper, sit thee down and write
In a book that all may read.'
So he vanished from my sight:
And I plucked a hollow reed,
And I made a rural pen,
And I stained the water clear,
And I wrote my happy songs
Every child may joy to hear.
(Blake [1789] 1971)

Harmony, surrounding the innocence of the child, is reflected throughout the verse, painting a picture that suggests that, if innocence is embraced, happiness and joy will result. This portrayal of innocence alongside a sense of harmony is reflected widely in the literature of the time (for example, *Water Babies* (Kingsley 1900)), notably offering an image that contrasts with the evangelical assessment of the child touched on in Chap. 5. To some extent, these perspectives reflect a desire to lift the child out of the reality of everyday childhood so that innocence is protected and preserved.

> [I]n an age when it became increasingly difficult to grow up, to find valid bearings in an adult world, the temptation seems to have been for certain authors to take the line of least emotional resistance, to regress, literally, into a world of fantasy and nostalgia. (Coveney 1957: xi)

Some opted for fictional approaches that protected innocence in the hope that if this 'could be preserved into adulthood, [it] might help redeem the adult world' (Cunningham 1995: 77–78). Others such as Dickens used innocence as a way of creating contrasts to offer a particular social commentary by which the drama of his work drew out a 'moral interest' that had meaning beyond the pages of his books (Coveney 1957: xii). In *Oliver Twist*, Dickens directly engages with different moral images of the child as he contrasts the 'innocent' Oliver, with the 'ominous' Artful Dodger. The Artful Dodger is characterised as 'snub-nosed, flat-browed, common-faced boy... as dirty a juvenile as one would wish to see; but he had about him all the airs and manners of a man' (cited in Pearson 1983: 167). For him, knowing replaces innocence, and the tranquil song of nature is replaced by the smog and dirt of an inner city. The Artful Dodger characterises the threat from the child. In contrast, Oliver's innocence leads him into a life of happily ever after's, a life in which the themes of harmony are not dissimilar to Blake's reflections above.

Notably, if one looks back on some of the themes from Chaps. 5 and 6 – whether they be the focus on violence in school or indeed the ongoing drive to see children disciplined within the home (Sherwood 1869) – one can see that different images co-existed, each influencing to different extents the way in which the moral child came to be constructed. It is a competition that Cunningham (1995) suggests is won by the 'threat' that the child poses rather than by their 'innocence', although it was reflected in nineteenth- and twentieth-century practices under the umbrella of the child in need of 'rescue'. Cunningham (1995) dedicates a whole chapter to the movement of 'rescuing' the child, with headings such as 'child labour', 'street children', 'cruelty to children' (themes that continue to be relevant).[7] Works of the time that challenged this image of the child are highlighted by Cunningham's reference to the writings of Jonas Hanway, whose titles in themselves underline a certain emphasis: *An Earnest Appeal for Mercy to the Children of the Poor* (1766) or *A Sentimental History of Chimney Sweepers* (1785). In both works, Hanway appealed to his readership to recognise the hardships that these children were facing, reflecting the children as 'objects of our mercy and tenderest kindness' (cited in Cunningham 2006: 141). It is just such an assessment that paved the way for all the efforts that followed, whether from Barnardos, the NSPCC or later Save the Children to name but a few. Despite the banner of rescue, it must be recognised that ultimately these aims reflect a sense in which leaving the problem would only cause challenges to society at a later stage. The children, therefore, summed up by their vulnerability and the ominous threat that they posed, provided society with a project. Such children needed the support of adults if they were to become an asset to society. This is highlighted most clearly in Baden Powell's efforts to set up the scouting movement. In an assessment of the situation in the early 1900s Baden Powell considered:

> We have at the present time in Great Britain 2 million boys, of whom a quarter to a half a million are under good influence outside their school walls…the remainder are drifting towards 'hooliganism' or bad citizenship for want of hands to guide them…just for the want of a guiding hand or two…cannot we find these guiding hands amongst us? (cited in Pearson 1983: 108)

This was the challenge for society as it sought to position the threat that children posed alongside a desire to provide them with a 'guiding hand'. The problem was that the perception of the necessary guidance was driven by an assumption that reflected a distancing between the child, the regulation and the enforcer. Ambiguity abounds, as different images are relied on at different times to deal with different issues. To punish or protect? That was and still is the question. The need to control, however, remains consistent.

7.3.2   Children's Rights

It is the theme of control that has to be taken forward into a moral consideration of children's rights. Recognising the context out of which rights emerged provides a significant factor in furthering our understanding of the discourses that are reflected within a rights agenda, and the extent to which images of the child continue to be restricted by considerations of competence and threat. The focus on rescuing the child (for UK see Cunningham 1995; for Canada see Bell 2007) raised the profile of the way in which states engage with children. This was brought sharply into focus by the dramatic events at the start of the twentieth century in which an increasing sense of globalisation extended to a 'colonisation of attitudes' towards what childhood should be (see Savyasaachi and Butler 2014). One export of western society during this period was a growing sense of what were, and should be, universally accepted levels of protection, provision and participation for children.

The rights agenda has a strong 'moral' thread running through it. A major question is how these rights are to be applied. Are rights there to ensure that children are not treated badly and they get the protection they deserve? Or are rights about ensuring that all children receive a recognised level of social support and that they are provided for? Or is the purpose of rights driven by a desire to give children a voice so that they can be part of shaping and defining their communities? Of course it is not necessarily a choice, but drawing out the distinction is helpful. Are rights about protection, provision or participation? To what extent is our answer to that question shaped by our thinking about the moral construction of the child?

Initiated by the 'rescue' movements considered earlier, children's rights became an increasingly recognisable theme in the twentieth century. This approach to children was keenly promoted as a new opportunity to question the images of the child that had restricted the contribution of children to society. But did it? The 1924 Geneva Declaration on the Rights of the Child presented the international community for the first time with a set of ambitions for the children of the world. These ambitions, that were made up of five points, sought to ensure that children's needs were met and that they be given a foundation in life that allowed them to develop their 'talents to the service of fellow men' (League of Nations 1924). The Declaration seemed to recognise that children were to be protected but also given a chance to participate and get involved. The international community did not pursue a more formal international agreement, although principles from the Declaration were interpreted through the work of Eglantine Jebb, one of its authors and the founder of the charity, Save the Children. However, although perhaps not moving as far as the Declaration had proposed, a debate had begun, one in which children's rights were increasingly on the radar.

Following the Second World War, the journey to engage with children's rights became associated with the positioning of children as citizens. Commentaries on the notion of citizenship and how this combines with children's rights often draw from a common starting point, the work of T.H. Marshall (1950). Marshall presented a discussion that linked citizenship to rights. For him, there were three types of rights: civil, political and social (Faulks 1998). Access to these rights thus reflected an individual's status as a citizen. However, in respect of children, Marshall's focus was on the citizen of the future: 'it should be regarded, not as the right of the child citizen to go to school, but the right of the adult citizen to have been educated' (Marshall [1950]1995: 16). This approach leaves an image of the child as someone who is not to be trusted (Cockburn 1998) because they are positioned outside a working definition of rights (see Bacon and Frankel 2013 for more).

The sense in which rights are something chosen by adults as being appropriate for their definition of childhood is a strong theme in the 1989 United Nations Convention on the Rights of the Child. Although making a very positive statement, this, the most internationally signed UN declaration,[8] was a document by adults for adults. Archard (2004) offers additional comment to this effect, suggesting that, although children's rights are directed at children, they must be managed through the gatekeeping of adults. In Archard's view, rights may well have a 'moral' element but, due to children's limited capacity, their ability to fully engage with those rights is restricted. The result is that children are seen to 'lack certain cognitive abilities – for example to process information in an ordered fashion, to form consistent and stable beliefs, and to appreciate the significance of options and their consequences' (2004: 11). It is a perspective that highlights how the way we come to engage with children's rights is a reflection of the moral image of the child that we hold

A constructed image of the child thus has direct implications for the way in which the state (at one level) seeks to manage moral questions. It is this assessment of the child in the broader terms of reason, virtue and social harmony that comes to inform the way in which the state engages with managing the child. It is, therefore, too simplistic to rely on a rights agenda, for the way in which rights comes to be applied will be shaped by the images of the child that come to be constructed. This can be seen in the variety of ways in which different provinces in Canada have sought to establish advocates' offices for children (White 2014). Each of these offices can be considered in light of the image of the child that they hold and the extent to which that shapes the way in which these offices engage with children, and consequently informs some very different practices.

At its best, some have argued that an acceptance of rights 'pulls together' some of these inconsistencies of policies towards children (Fortin 2009).

However, in practice, the rights agenda simply emphasises, in a different context, the extent to which those in power are left to frame an agenda for children's 'engagement' (Bainham 2005; Fortin 2009) and thus maintain control. The lack of children who know about the Convention (James and James 2004), simply furthers the case that the rights model is simply another tool for controlling children (Rose, 125). The ongoing prominence of 'welfare'-based rights in practice means that adults remain the ones who control children's access (see Wyness 2012). Adults define what rights are worthy of investigation, they make the decisions about whether the right has been met and they dispense the relevant solution. Children are kept outside of this process. Even in relation to those articles within the convention associated with participation such as Article 12 (commonly linked to children as decision-makers) are constrained by wording that restricts children's engagement in light of assesments over their age and competence. Indeed, the text supporting Article 12 only states that the child has the right to a 'view', not to make decisions (Frankel et al. 2015). As such, the Convention can and has been read simply as a tool to maintain the status quo within which the child is an object of concern rather than an active player in the social world around them. It reinforces a moral image of the child that is in need of adult direction and concern – in short, the child remains in want of control.

7.4   Moral Panics

Much of this chapter has been built around the theme of threat. Of course Stanley Cohen's *Folk Devils and Moral Panics* offered an opportunity to consider the way in which that threat was structured and some of the implications that this has. Cohen is clear that calling something a panic does not mean that this 'something does not exist' (2002: viii). It is the existence of a 'threat' that has been a feature in the discussion of the past, reflected and maintained not just in culture and attitudes but also in institutional practice, as well as in governmental discourse and action. The media, Cohen suggests, are key players in the public's knowledge about 'deviance and social problems' (2002: xxiii) because they take a significant role in identifying and defining what is going to be seen as a panic, and creating the context for the story that is about to be told. As part of constructing images of the child, within this discourse of panic, themes around children and social harmony play a significant part. This can be illustrated in a number of clothing-related stories. These include reports of children being outlawed for wearing hoodies because of their perceived association with antisocial behaviour (*Guardian* 2005), contrasting with demands for retailers to remove certain items of clothing from sale because they were seen as sexualising the child's body (BBC 18/2/2010). The latter reflects the discomforting threat to the harmony of society provoked by stories around children and sex. None of this is new, and simply highlights the way in which a moral images of the child can end up giving meaning to what children wear (Hebdige 1979) or what they listen to (Redhead in Muncie 2005: 155).

Cohen talks of the extent to which 'societies [are] subject, every now and then, to periods of moral panic' (2002: 1). These panics are fuelled by the media with a range of outcomes. Some just disappear, while others go on to shape policy. One example of the latter is the murder of James Bulger.

> [In 1993], James Bulger was a month short of his third birthday when two killers lured him away from his mother in a busy shopping mall, dragged him to a lonely railway embankment and murdered him. It was an unspeakably cruel death. The thought of anyone being cruel enough to inflict such a fate on an innocent little child defies comprehension. Astonishingly, the killers in this case were both just ten years old. (Thomas, cited in Jenks 1996: 118)

The case saw an explosive reaction from the press, the public and politicians. The images of the child that were constructed from this very particular context had significant implications for the practices that came to affect children. This can be seen at a local level from the *Guardian* newspaper's account of the arrest of a suspect. It describes children hanging out of trees as they watch '[a] 12-year old…lifted in a Liverpool CID Starsky and Hutch raid – police cars on the pavement while 200 neighbours bayed for the 12 year old's blood' (*Guardian* 20 February 1993). This child was later released without charge. This example raises important questions about the extent to which the theme of threat can become defining in shaping images of the child, with extraordinary implications for practice as these fears over children came to be played out not just at a local level, but at a national level too.

The extreme coverage that the press gave to this story[9] saw some commentators suggest that it moved the reaction from a moral panic to a total panic (Bell 1999). The aggressive way in which children were perceived by the press and subsequently within their neighbourhoods became an important focus for legislation. As we discussed above, it saw the effective reduction of the age of criminal responsibility (without the additional protection of *doli incapax*). However, it also laid the foundation for a very particular way of framing children that was characterised by an image of the 'antisocial child' (see Frankel 2012: 66).[10]

It took the criminalisation of the child through the law to a level that has not been seen before, with child curfews, DNA profiling, child safety orders and of course the antisocial behaviour order or ASBO. The result was 'Asbomania' (Squires 2008), and with it came an ongoing cycle of increased social fear and the use of extreme and unprecedented measure in order to deal with this constructed moral image. More recently in England, the language has changed and antisocial behaviour is a less-used political term. Indeed, the wording of the 2014 Antisocial Behaviour, Crime and Policing Act includes, through the removal of ASBOs, a desire to reduce the number of children who are criminalised. The raft of replacement policies, although using different language, reflect the ongoing power of the state to control the child through the criminal law (Hollingsworth 2012). It would, therefore, be wrong to suggest that the perception of threat has been eliminated or changed (Bailey 2011). A 2008 YouGov poll demonstrated just how close to the surface those fears are. It recorded that:

43% of adults believed "something must be done to protect us from children"

35% agreed with the proposition that "nowadays it feels like the streets are infested with children"

45% said people "refer to children as feral because they behave that way"

49% disagreed with the statement that "children who get into trouble are often misunderstood and in need of professional help"

These figures reflect, if not that total threat of children actually destabilising society, then certainly that they are represented by their 'ominous' potential to unsettle an adult imagined harmony.

A defining theme of 'moral panics' is the their reach and the extent to which they seep into society. The link to certain broadcast media sees that notion of threat transmitted, impacting on the wider context from which the structures of each interactional setting draw in framing an image of the child. Further examples of the impact of panic and its association with themes around harmony can be seen in stories relating to poverty (street children), teenage pregnancy (Corsaro 2005; Rosier 2011) and a range of concerns about the place of personalised web-linked devices in children's lives, as worries about social media and gaming come to sit alongside those of TV, film and music (Wyness 2012). Postman (1983) heralded these changes some time back as announcing the disappearance of childhood because children were accessing material they were not ready for, with the result that it was taking away their innocence. Those themes form part of the 'panic' that continues to surround this area because these sources (whether games, films or music) are considered to be a destabilising factor, not just for children but notably for society more widely. This was brought into particular focus in relation to online games through a spate of shootings in the United States, Germany and Finland (Drotner 2011), with demands for answers as to whether such games really are 'murder simulators'. It is an argument that continues to be built around a traditional perspective of the socialisation model, one in which the child simply draws from the source and regurgitates what they have seen. It is a position that sits outside of the notion of children actively processing content (Buckingham 1993). However, the passive child is a far easier target to manage and the situation is one in which cause and effect are more simply connected. The dynamic nature of the internet, however, means that, although a child may be cut off from the source of this concern in one space, they can access it in others.

The mobile nature of the virtual neighbourhood (Drotner 2011) reflects another area of concern relating to children's vulnerability. Above, the fear was for the way in which children are influenced negatively by virtual space as an 'offender'. However, the other pressing area of panic is the extent to which the web offers up children as victims. This presents fears about the 'paedophile', who engages with children in chat rooms, to the fellow teenager, who bullies through the use of sexting. It has resulted in a struggle to position the innocent child. The Canadian province of Ontario has introduced a wide ranging sex education programme (mentioned in Chapter 3) to highlight this problem and to make children more aware (Ministry of Education 2015). However, the 'explicit' nature of the course has resulted in many expressing concerns (*The Globe and Mail* 1/10/15). It raises the very real question of how children can be equipped to deal with maintaining the integrity of their bodies within a system that applies more entrenched images of the child (see Kirtzinger 1997). Applying the moral filter to this question would not only allow the researcher to consider the notion of reason and virtue, but also to ask questions about why the Province is so keen to enforce this measure. As well as inviting thoughts on the extent to which this programme could be seen as progressive by recognising children's competence, it also invites a more cynical assesment in which the responsibility to conform is passed to the individual. As such it is now, due to appropriate education, the responsibility of the individual to act in accordance with the social ambitions set out by the state. The state has thus diverted the focus of responsibility, so that rather than the state being the target for blame, they can enforce control by being the one who points the finger. The application of a moral filter, with a focus on social harmony would have relevance to many areas such as considering children's relationship with the police (Brunson and Miller 2006; APPGC 2014), through to children's status as victims (Victim Support 2014).

7.5   Concluding Thoughts

A final theme is the extent to which the desire for society to manage the threat posed by children relates to a sense of citizenship that society ascribes to the child. This will be considered further in Chap. 9, but the essence of this argument, drawing on our earlier discussion of rights, is that children's citizenship is accepted as long as adults are able to control it. This was considered in relation to the age of voting and how the theme of threat becomes a factor in framing the extent to which society should tolerate the voice of children. Writing an analysis of the way in which children responded to the Iraq War in 2003, Cunningham and Lavalette (2004) reflect that the English education curriculum had only recently developed to give formal citizenship education to all secondary school children. Within these lessons, children were taught about the value of civic engagement and the democratic process and, as discontent about the UK's role in Iraq grew, so school pupils sought to add their voice to the protest. Then, when schools refused to allow pupils to join marches, children went 'on strike'. Rather than complimenting the effectiveness of their teaching, the schools, amidst wider pressure, actually did the opposite. Faced with the threat of students campaigning, and challenging the authority of not only the school but also the state, some schools punished those children who had chosen to voice their concerns over this policy. This reflects most clearly the extent to which children can be seen and heard, but only on adults' terms and on subjects that are 'suitable' (see Chap. 5). The child's place as citizen is within the confines of an adult-prescribed model that is orientated by a desire to manage any perceived threat that children pose.

Concerns about the threats that children pose to society are pervasive and constant, and as a result constructed images cannot be understood without reference to social harmony.

Notes

1. This is reflected to some extent in wider nature through the social groupings of animals (Høgh-Olsen 2010), a connection that has provided the link to models of learning such as those supported by psychologist, Albert Bandura.
2. England and Wales have one of the lowest ages for criminal responsibility in the world (Muncie 2015). Although Scotland has a lower age, it does have better protection, and Muncie notes the only other legislatures to go below 10 are certain states in the United States, where some have an age as young as six.
3. This has some crossover with Foucault's (1988) work on madness in which he links a perceived lack of reason in madness to 'childhood'. 'Madness is childhood. Everything at the Retreat is organised so that the insane are

transformed into minors. They are regarded as children who have an overabundance of strength and make dangerous use of it. They must be given immediate punishments and rewards; whatever is remote has no effect on them' (1988: 262).

4. The English model contrasts with Children's Hearings in Scotland, which take a more welfare-based approach and in which the question of 'why' is a more marked part of the process.

5. A similar case to that of the murder of James Bulger, discussed in this chapter, in Norway, shows the contrast between countries. Here the child involved was treated very differently to the two young Bulger killers not only marking the differences between the Norwegian and British Press in relation to youth crime (Franklin and Petley 1996), but also in the formal administration of youth justice (Muncie 2015).

6. The number of capital offences rose from 50 to 200 between the mid-eighteenth century and the nineteenth.

7. Contemporary additions to this list might also be the 'child soldier' and the 'trafficked child'.

8. Only the United States of America has not signed.

9. Only two newspapers did not have this story as front-page news. One paper actually included an eight-page supplement.

10. Notably, this was not a one-off. More recent headlines in the British press have continued to show an unforgiving attitude towards young people: 'British youths are the most unpleasant and violent in the world' (*Daily Mail* 10/8/2011).

Step 4

Recognising Agency in Action

Chapter 2 started by introducing a short vignette of an interaction between two of my children. A list of questions followed, questions that reflected the dominant images of children and morality as shaped by reason, virtue and social harmony. When I shared what I had written with my son, he got very upset. He rightly pointed out that this account misrepresented him because it painted a picture of him that did not recognise the fullness of the interaction with his sister. However, it was a concern for how others might think of him that worried him the most. He did not want people to think of him as a boy who shouted at his younger sister, in fact he wanted me to make it clear that he is a 'runner'. What was so telling about the conversation I had with my son was his desire to re-establish control over his identity in this situation. Indeed, it brought into stark focus the way children are generally positioned in relation to moral discourses, which are characterised by the extent to which the child is muted and their moral identity is shaped for them by adults.

The previous chapters have highlighted some of the dominant themes that allow adults to so comprehensively take control of the image of the child, such that it comes to instruct attitudes and options, policy and practice. The aim of the following chapter is to set these adult-constructed ways of thinking against the accounts of children themselves, as we now concentrate on the second part of the framework.

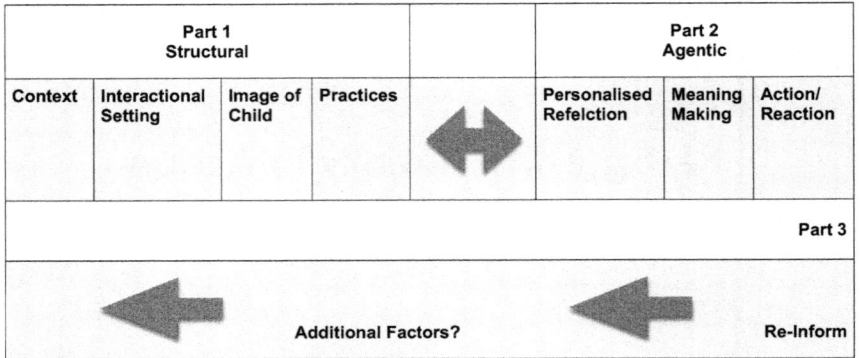

Fig. 1   The framework

This chapter will seek to position the child more in relation to the definition of agency that was shared in Chap. 4. This definition suggested that agency was the *contextually mediated capacity of the individual to make meanings that inform their actions, that are relationally situated and morally constituted and which are framed within a range of elements that make up children's personal lives.* The focus of the coming section is, therefore, to engage with the active way in which children interact with an interactional setting, forming meanings as they manage a sense of self in relation to others. Through this process, children are constantly negotiating morality by wrestling with what is and what is not acceptable. It is the desire to draw out the subtleties that sit behind children's moral engagement that is the aim of the following section as it demonstrates the extent to which morality is central to both the structural and agentic ways in which children manage their everyday lives.

8

Negotiating the Everyday

Building on the themes in Chap. 4, this chapter explores the relevance of the framework to the way in which children engage with morality in their everyday lives. It offers an opportunity to re-establish the relevance of the bi-directional arrow (see Fig. 2.2 from Chapter 2) that links the structural dimension of interaction with the individual themselves. As such, the structural backdrop comes to be an interactive frame of reference for exploring meaning-making as the individual engages with it through the personal elements of self introduced in Chap. 4. This chapter will draw on those themes of agency, giving particular consideration to those personal elements, as it seeks to consider, with reference to children's voices, the application of 'morality' within their everyday lives. *Children, Morality and Society* (Frankel 2012) was directly focused on exploring children's engagement with morality. This chapter touches on some of that research as it seeks to extend the case for a moral dimension to children's agency, as presented by the framework. By acknowledging

© The Editor(s) (if applicable) and The Author(s) 2017
S. Frankel, *Negotiating Childhoods*, Studies in Childhood and Youth,
DOI 10.1057/978-1-137-32349-1_8

children's agency, and the extent to which it reflects a moral perspective, one can then explore children's engagement with the interactional settings in which they find themselves as they respond to adult-defined images and associated practices.

This chapter considers the way in which children respond to a contextual backdrop as they interact with it to shape meanings as part of negotiating the social world around them. In order to do so, and to highlight the contrast with the three previous chapters, it uses those filters of reason, virtue and social harmony alongside a more active understanding of children's agency. Notably, these images reflect a different view of the child, a view that is demonstrated by the importance of recognising the integrity of children's personal lives, their social role as learners and their potential as collaborators.

8.1   Reason: Engaging with Emotions

Tensions between adult practices and child accepted approaches (as highlighted in the opening extract) reflects a consequence of the way in which thinking around reason is given applciation. In seeking to negotiate everyday life, children have to respond to an ongoing battle for ownership of their emotions. By highlighting this battle, one is able to reflect on both the impact of assumed understandings of the child and the more active way in which children do engage with morality as part of their everyday lives.

8.1.1   Home

One of the significant implications of the 'traditional' model of parenting has been the extent to which it has sought to maintain control of children's emotions. This has meant that children's emotions have not been seen as valid and have been an element of the child which, due to their underdeveloped state, carries little importance other than a way of engendering a sense of reward and punishment. The following extracts highlight two contrasting approaches that reflect very different images of the child, with implications for practice. The way in which the setting is structured directly limits the opportunities for agentic engagement, with consequences for how incidents within these spaces come to be negotiated. Both families lived in the same community, although they represent the creation of home as two very different interactional settings.

The first extract describes a child, his mother and, principally, his father.

Harry   *Once my brother was being really annoying he wouldn't go to bed, he wouldn't brush his teeth and um my mum got so annoyed she slapped him round the face but he had a cough so he was crying really loud, then my dad came in and said what's all this noise went over to my brother and he was wearing a collar like this and lifted him up like that right to his face and said go and brush your teeth right now and get into bed. So he went to brush his teeth, put his pyjamas on, went to bed and said can I have some water and they're really annoyed, water now, then my dad says fine I'll give you some water so he gives him the glass of water, and he says want some water and then he smacks, he throws it all in his face, just because he didn't want to go to bed.*

The second extract is a mother talking about rules within her home.

Mrs G   *There's not hardly any discipline because um this sounds so sort of, but I don't have to tell them off, you know. I have to tell them off for bickering or you know for punching one another, I do have to stop that but in terms of getting things wrong other than between themselves I can't. And even then I can't totally discipline them because I see it as practise for the rest of the world, so if they can't practice, being a bit emotional with one another then… they've got to practice somewhere. So on the whole there isn't a lot of sanctions going on round here but Danielle gets it wrong occasionally with friends. I just talk it through and say I was a little bit disappointed because next time you can try this one, you know. I tell them off for running round the house on roller-skates but on the whole I don't.*

At the heart of the difference between these accounts of home lies two opposing images of the moral child (with reference to reason, virtue and social harmony). A central feature of this difference is the way in which the home as a setting was framed as a space in which the children's emotions were recognised and, perhaps more importantly, taken into account in shaping adult action. Harry reflects on his dad's behaviour in the following way,

> Harry   *I don't think my dad should have been that angry because it was a Friday night and we weren't doing anything the next day, so I think, and it wasn't that late it was about half past eight, so I think we should have been able to stay up a bit longer, and its because we've got babies and toddlers living next door, we weren't being that loud either, we were just laughing loudly. Sometimes we weren't laughing that loud.*

Harry paints a picture of high spirits on a Friday night. Harry and his brother were having fun, they were laughing but their dad's response did not recognise any of these factors. Harry had taken into account the fact that their home was near younger children who might be trying to sleep but, despite that, questioned whether his actions were really inappropriate. His dad's explosive response does not give Harry any room to present his emotions, both in terms of how the boys were feeling before the incident and the feelings he was left with following his dad's actions. Notably, Harry demonstrates that, far from his father's actions establishing a black and white line that defines right and wrong, Harry is left entangled in shards of grey, as he, as a social agent, is left tyring to process and make sense of this interaction.

As Harry's response shows, the journey of socialisation cannot be drawn in a straight line from structure to action. It challenges an important theme of the legacy-based image of the moral child which saw adult authority create a structure that defined the child's moral understanding. Will Harry behave in the same way on another Friday night? Maybe not, but importantly such a decision must be seen in a far more complex way than as a simple response to the punishment that was 'meted' out. This sits in contrast to the way in which the interactional setting is set up in the second example. Here a space is created within which there is the potential for the children to more directly re-inform the interactional setting because their emotions are acknowledged and they work with the adult in shaping the space together. In terms of the framework, these examples highlight the extent to which a perception of the moral image of the child can increase or reduce opportunities for practice.

Reflecting further on the discussion of the personal elements that individual's bring to interactions and Smart's work, looked at in Chap. 4, one can see that there is a growing need for researchers to tune into 'emotions' as a focus of enquiry. One approach, not discussed previously, to showing how emotions carry meaning uses 'narrative constructions of our personal biographies [by which] we formulate self identities embedded in social networks' (2007: 83). These narratives portray and give meaning to particular relationships and provide the back story on which the emotions sit. For example, Harry processed the interaction with his father with reference to a much wider back story. He drew from this as he tried to explain his father's reaction in relation to his emotions. This is connected with themes such as secrecy and conflict and the additional layers of meaning that are associated with them. For example, Smart talks about conflict in terms of how intimacy 'can be toxic and even destructive of the self' (2007: 155). The relationship between the meaning associated with conflict and its impact on the self is particularly important. It creates a dynamic within which the researcher is challenged to understand interaction in a context that not only recognises the structural factors, but also what the individual brings to those settings as personal 'elements' (whether they be experience, perceptions of power, interpretations of capital or belonging and so on).

To root the process of meaning-making not only to the setting but also to the individual invites some interesting reflections on themes such as 'love'. Love as a discourse can be analysed through the moral filters considered in this book. First, children have been passiviely positioned in relation to love, in a similar way to to 'morality', 'to love' has been seen as outside of a child's ability to 'reason' (their emotional competence). Second, 'love' can be considered as a vehicle adults use through which the acceptability of behaviours come to be communicated. A concept of love plays a significant part within the home, and has a very real implication for moral meaning-making: 'parent child relationships are shaped and sustained through a unique and enduring love' (Guldberg 2009: 146).

The challenge, of course, is how do we come to deconstruct 'love' and explore it as a social force within a dialogue of structure and agency that moves it away from a model of application in which the adult is the bestower and the child merely the beneficiary? We first need to link 'love' to a range of emotions, and then to consider how these emotions influence action.

Faurehold (2010) studied both of these factors in research on children's experiences of disability within the home. Despite the many occasions that their sense of self came to be questioned or challenged, the children would draw from the nature of their relationship with (in these cases) their mother as a means for finding a way of navigating a way through different experiences. A major coping strategy was that a 'mother's love outweighed the humiliation' (Faurehold 2010: 66). Not only does 'love' show the children weighing up competing sets of emotions (the way others make them feel compared to the way their mums make them feel), it also highlights that the realisation of their feelings for their mother is a more influential factor in shaping their sense of self than anything else. Love thus provides an important element that the individual uses in seeking to make meanings in response to the world around them (Layard and Dunn 2009). Applied within a structure–agency dialogue, love can be examined as a feature of an individual's meaning making within particular interactional settings, rather than being dismissed as a sentiment that is outside the scope of a study of children. It moves us on from a perspective in which reason is centred around adult feelings towards the child to one in which the child also has feelings that are not only valid but are central to the socialisation process.

As shown above, a consideration of emotions is complex and tied up in a variety of layers. If we are to move away from a model of home that suppresses children's emotions, then it is important that we begin to recognise the active way in which children are managing emotions and how these are linked to making meanings. The way in which the interactional setting of home is structured clearly has an impact on the child's ability to practise their agency. For example, in a discussion of power, R.D. Laing (1969) (see also Fingerson 2005 – Chap. 3) highlights that, family relationships which reinforce power can have an impact on children's sense of self because such power can be a real barrier to the effective and full expression of emotions. The management of emotions that the 'context' creates, thus, has implications for actions and the meanings that are attached to them. As Smart suggests, some children deal with negative experiences by trying to block them out; an action which can only be understood by the researcher if placed into the wider framework that this book is presenting. In short, 'we cannot grasp how people behave in relation to one another unless we are attentive to emotions' (Smart 2007: 58). Emotions, and the extent to which they demand an engagement with many of the themes considered in Chap. 4, are fundamental if we are to understand how moral meaning comes to be attached to actions. Home has provided a useful focus to start to explore these elements of self through the vehicle of emotions, although, of course, the relevance of this discussion carries across interactional settings and informs moral meaning-making in the variety of arenas in which children live their lives.

8.1.2   School

The discussion above introduces a range of terms that can inform a dilaogue around those 'elements' that the individual brings to meaning making. These terms, such as emotion, narrative and conflict, complement the discussion started in Chap. 4 and offer vehicles through which to explore the 'self'. This section picks up on the notion of body and belonging as it explores the active way in which the child responds to the social world, with implications for how they come to engage with morality.

One of the realities for children is that school (indeed, any setting) demands that they look at their sense of self within a particular mirror. The mirror within which they see themselves is defined by their perception of the interactional setting. It will impact different children in different ways (see Chap. 4 for more). The following example sees Ed looking in just such a mirror as he recognises his 'tallness' and, when associating it with the setting of school, gives it a particular meaning, with implications for the way he thinks about that space.

Ed	*When I was in my reception they all use to call me Lanky, all the people in year 6, and I got really annoyed so I told my mum and they got told off and they stopped.*
SF	*How did it make you feel?*
Ed	*I didn't want to go to school, every time my mum said, go on its time to go to school I said I don't want to go.*

Not only does his 'tallness' make Ed not want to go to school but he labels himself as an 'outsider', a meaning that is context-specific and only created as a response to his perception of this setting. Indeed, when at school, a perception of oneself within that space also has significant impact on the way in which the individual comes to process moral meanings. For example, one implication of seeing yourself as 'different' was that the children would either work harder to establish membership, or try to disappear into the background. This is reflected in Nic's comments as she considered what she would do if she was being pushed:

> *I don't know really, I think if it was really hurting me and I was about to cry I probably would tell Miss but then if it wasn't that hard I think it's only a push, because I was shy. Because if you tell the bully might come back and hurt you because you told on them.*

As a result of being shy and not wanting to stand out further, Nic thought that her best course of action might simply be to attach a moral meaning to this action, such that she 'accepted it' and, as a result, she could simply remain in the background. Similar responses are reflected in other research (Aye Maung 1995) highlighting how children's sense of self shapes the meanings that children attach to their emotions, here played out in connection to themes of power (see Chap. 4)

It is also important to reflect on the fact that referring to emotions also provides children with some guidance on how they judge others' actions, as well as how to shape their own behaviour. Amy provides a useful illustration of this as she talks about the power of 'names' and the extent to which they can be hurtful. It is by referring to a sense of how she might feel that she offers an opinion on the use of such names.

Amy   *Sticks and stones really, really do hurt but names —like, say if I went up to Cas and said I don't like you because you have got different coloured hair to me or different coloured skin, say I went up to any coloured person and said I don't like you because you're not my colour you're not like me, so I'm not going to play with you. If I was that person I would be really, really upset. I'd think I wish I was that colour now because it really does hurt.*

This example takes on additional meaning when emotions are put in the context of themes such as body and belonging within the context of this interactional setting. It is particularly troubling that a 2015 report highlighted the big impact that bullying (continues) to play in children's experiences of school (The Children's Society 2015). It suggests an institution that has still not found a way to engage effectively with themes of belonging, whether from the point of view of the bullied or indeed the bully, as schools maintain a reliance on particular images of the child.

However, this does not have to be the case. Research is showing that schools which do embrace children's capacity to be engaged and active social agents report implications, not just in terms of relationships, but also in their academic results[1] (Public Health England 2014). This is illustrated in Rietveld's (2005) research on how children with Down's Syndrome could be effectively integrated into the mainstream classroom. At the centre of this is the need for the child to perceive themselves as included, which directly demands reference to emotions. It means reflecting on the way in which the child cross-references their perception of the setting with how they see themselves fitting in. Rietveld (2005) suggests that inclusion happens through opportunities that make the child feel that they are taking an active part in social roles such as friendship: 'experiencing the full range of roles is facilitative as it allows the child access to greater opportunities and learning conducive to a quality lifestyle, which is denied to those who are excluded' (2005: 130). Significantly, this worked best when adults intervened to manage the setting, such as finding the right teacher to provide these opportunities and identifying a group of peers who would be most open to engaging with this classmate. The aim was to create a context that allowed the child to be integrated and to give them the chance to feel they belonged, based on their sense of self within the space. Other research has also reflected the negative way in which a feeling of exclusion can impact on the child. However, by establishing 'common bonds', a sense of difference can be broken down as the individuals within a group begin to share a sense of belonging (Devine and Kelly 2006). Of course, our ability to respond to our emotions can only be activated if we acknowledge them in the first place and, as part of establishing new images that reflect that competence, that means increasing the vocabulary of children to engage with this essential moral dimension of everyday life as they are continually managing similarity and difference within the context of body and belonging. The following chapter returns to the implications for schools in moving beyond a staged interpretation of reason and recognising an increasingly competent image of the child.

8.1.3 Neighbourhood

Our emotions linked to those personal elements of self must also be seen as a central ingredient in shaping how we value action. The following section, therefore, highlights children's strategic flexibility in managing interactional settings, moving the child a long way from the limited perspectives of reason described in earlier chapters.

Children's friendships offer a useful place to consider how the emotions attached to these relationships become influential in meaning-making as children respond to interactions in settings within their neighbourhood. The steps that children would take to maintain a perceived mutuality with those around them reflected strategic choices that influenced how they came to define right and wrong. Here Jack reflects on being dared to ring a door bell and then run away.

Jack	*Only once.*
SF	*Why did you do it?*
Jack	*Because it was a dare,*
Cara	*Was it Claire's door? Jack you always knock on Claire's door.* (Laughs)
SF	*Did you think it was wrong?*
Jack	*Yeah*

Cara   *So why did you knock on the door?*
Jack   *Because it was a dare.*
SF   *So why do you do a dare, if it was wrong?*
Jack   *Because I think it's quite comical*
        (Clara laughs and Jack then acts it out)
SF   *If you know it's wrong do you do it because it's quite funny?*
Jack   *Yeah*

For Jack, his action was driven by meanings linked to his desire to achieve capital as part of his ambition to secure his place within a group of friends, one that takes on extra meaning due to the setting in which it took place. Jack's 'thing' was being funny, an attribute he used to even up a perceived difference caused by his autism. Throughout, Jack's emotions, here framed by capital, power and fun, are a significant factor as he seeks to position himself on an equal basis to his friends. Although Jack recognised the act was wrong, the strategic decision he made as part of establishing a place amongst this group meant that in this case ringing the doorbell was seen as an acceptable thing to do.

The sense that an action can be right for one person and then wrong for another is discussed in Zimbardo's account of life in the Bronx. It highlights the complexity of the way in which we perceive morality in the wider space of the neighbourhood, such that capital itself takes on a variety of values that can alter significantly between users of the same space. That capital (value given to actions), however, cannot be understood without considering the way in which the individual perceives the wider structural context. For example, it is only the individual's recognition that wider society might frown on an action that then provides them with opportunities for subversion and resistance.[2] These values come to be set through relationships: 'social ties...create independent systems of obligation and restraint that impose significant costs for translating criminal propensities into action' (Helpern 2005: 115). As such, it places the individual, as considered in relation to the elements of self that they bring to interaction, at the centre of a process of meaning-making that is directly framed with reference to the wider context in which the interaction is taking place.

The connection between capital and behavior, and its link to moral decision-making, is a theme in Winlow and Hall's (2006) look at young people and the night-time economy. They make direct reference to the extent to which the cultural climate means that it is hard for young people to make moral decisions (2006: 21). As a consequence, identity becomes an important marker in seeking to position oneself, such that extremes of behaviour are seen not only as a sign of capital but also as a bond of friendship. Violence and alcohol just become part of the 'show' (2006: 96) as young people seek to present themselves in terms of their ability to have a laugh. It is a way of acting that is driven by 'self-interest' and the desire to achieve a certain emotional fulfilment, irrespective of how this might impact on the feelings of others (Centre for Social Justice 2014).

The application of the desire to position oneself in relation to others through personal actions that reflect a sense of capital was also highlighted with younger children. This is played out in the extract below, in which Toby focuses on the fun that a certain action could achieve while he is with his friends. He was asked whether throwing a stone through a window would be wrong.

Toby   *At the time when I was close to my friends I would probably not know that it was wrong, because I was probably just having fun with them, you're having a laugh and then you start doing it until something bad happens when you realise its wrong.*

Alex   *But why don't you stop yourself.*

Toby   *I think I would try to but then suddenly they're all like come on Toby (imitating an encouraging and friendly tone).*

Whilst Toby was with his friends, this action carried some value that was linked to emotions of fun and 'having a laugh'. These emotions are linked to meanings that are reflected within the specific context of this interactional setting. The connection between emotions, memories[3] and those wider themes of power and capital are all present, playing a part in Toby's moral choices. Far from Toby displaying a limited capacity to reason, he is demonstrating the complexities of the different factors that he has weighed up in forming meanings in the moment, which he acknowledges might be flawed. This view represents an image of the child that is very different from those adult-assumed perspectives that were considered in earlier chapters. Here, rather than the child being a specimen to be worked on, children are actively engaged with morality as part of dealing with the management of day-to-day life.

8.2   Virtues: The Learner

One of the assumptions in the earlier chapters was that effective virtue education was driven by adult-defined targets and communicated through adult-defined regimes (which often relied on punishment). Here socialisation was presented as a model in which being 'taught' was key to the process of preparation that was required to create the moral being. It is important to contrast this approach with a sense in which children are active learners and, although they rely at times on adult guidance, essentially 'only children themselves can "make sense", understand and learn' (Pollard 1994: 22). In following Pollard's call for us to recognise children's agency, although for him within the context of the classroom, this section offers a more personalised reflection on virtues as children seek to establish a set of moral meanings that will help them more effectively navigate their social world. The legacy-based image of the moral child promoted a one-directional view of socialisation in which the link between reason and knowledge assimilation (as opposed to learning) was clear. However, if we accept emotions and the range of identity-based elements that sit around it, then the trajectory of the journey between an adult understanding of right and wrong and how it is shared with the child must take into account a range of layers if we are to gain insight into how (and how not) values can be effectively shared.

8.2.1   Home

The nature of the relationships that children have with their parents offers a useful starting place to consider the acquisition of virtues. This was a particular focus in *Children, Morality and Society* (Frankel 2012), which saw children recognising the importance of adults as moral guides and interpreters in furthering their understanding of what was acceptable. Significantly, this recognition came through a realisation that their personal understanding of right and wrong was not just the result of 'something that happened' (a product of a biological interpretation of reason), but rather was the result of a process of learning. This means that conversations and explanations – 'it's having it explained to me, why you should or shouldn't do it' – were very important. Such explanations worked best when they formed part of a positive relationship which included a recognition of a personal 'biography' (an awareness of the child's life narrative), as touched on earlier. This reflected a sense in which children appreciated opportunities within the structural model of a home where they could value their parents (see also Jensen and Mckee 2003) as guides and interpreters, recognising the relevance of the knowledge that their parents had about them. As one group of children said:

Gerry	No, parents understand you
SF	Parents understand?
Gerry	Yeah parents do understand because they know you and parents know like their children
SF	Who agrees with that? Rob
Rob	Yeah
SF	Ryan
Ryan	Yeah
Alex	They know how you feel because they have been with you a lot longer than…
Rob	…teachers

This was just one conversation that highlighted the importance of a guide in the process of understanding right and wrong. However, it also suggests that the guide is far more effective if they are someone with whom the child has a positive relationship and, as a result, 'understands them'. Here the coming together of emotions and positive relationships such that the child feels they are 'known' should not be underestimated. It is far more than simply a knowledge of what the child has previously been told, but rather a deeper recognition of how guidance is tailored to the particular nature of that individual, reiterating earlier themes of narrative. As a result, it demands that the 'guide' is acknowledging, as much as possible, the personal elements that the individual brings to decision-making.

These themes are investigated in research on punishment because there is an increasing call that the 'punishment' should not only fit the crime, but more importantly, the individual (McDiarmid 2013). This research reinforces the idea that children want to be guided as they seek to make sense of actions within the context of a relationship of mutuality, and not dictated to in one that continues to reinforce a sense of power. The use of corporal punishment, for example, immediately re-positions the adult vis-à-vis the child in such a way that power becomes the defining feature of the interaction, leaving children with feelings of revenge, embarrassment, anger and fear (Saunders and Goddard 2010). Interestingly, one child in Children, Morality and Society who mentioned being smacked, reflected that for him, in the context of specific behaviour, he understood why his parents acted towards him in this way. The emotions that were linked to this interaction thus took on meanings that for this child supported his developing knowledge of right and wrong. This is not an argument to say that corporal punishment is not all bad, but rather one that reinforces the sense in which sanctions must be seen within a process of learning, one that acknowledges the importance of adults as guides, appreciates the value of relationships and sees how an understanding of the individual is key (see Twum-Danso Imoh 2013).

Through such interactions between children and adults, which are contextually situated and performed on and by social agents drawing from those elements of self, families are able to convey moral messages. In doing so, they provide children with a 'moral lexicon' and a 'vocabulary of values' (Smart 2007: 101). The messages must, however, be seen within the broader narrative of common experiences within the home that see the individual 'reflecting' and 'interpreting' in framing an ongoing resource for meaning-making. Significantly, in the home, this moral map can be cast without an explicit list of rules. Instead, these meanings develop as the individual seeks to position themselves within the particular interactional setting of home.

A model of virtue acquisition in which the child frames individual meanings within a particular context is a theme in James' (2013) assessment of values. He presents values as things that are not imposed on children, but as things they not only choose but self-construct. The child's active recognition in engaging with themes of everyday morality is highly compelling. It is effectively illustrated in James' (2013) interview with a child who had chosen to be vegetarian. It is interesting to consider the context that gave this child the space to make a (moral) choice about whether eating meat was acceptable or not. His mum and dad also don't eat meat, so one might assume as a natural progression that their son, Tim, would not eat meat either. However, this case study suggests that it means something so much more to Tim than simply following a pattern set by his parents. In fact, his choice about the acceptability of meat becomes a central component of his identity: 'his not eating meat is accompanied by other dietary restrictions that are in many ways unusual for a 12 year old boy. 'Timothy doesn't like chips, he doesn't *really have things like Sunny Delight or, erm, sweets or anything really.* This is something that he himself acknowledges must sound a *bit odd*' (2013: 63). This case study offers a useful example of how the moral dimension may come to have wider meaning as it is performed through a variety of other techniques that allow Tim to define himself by his position in relation to food. It is the process of interaction through which Tim is able to explore his identity that stands out. He reflects a view of socialisation in which he has been able to 'learn' a position for himself, as he manages his sense of identity in relation to these issues.

A 'curriculum of virtue', here, looks different from that in Chap. 6 as emotions become key to moral learning. Previosuly the child's feelings were seen as the 'fall out' from adult efforts to 'teach' the child through a focus on their 'behaviour', here those same emotions become central as children learn to make sense of these in furthering their understadning. By drawing out those emotions and giving them a place within the child's wider sense of self in the context of the interactional settings they find themsevles in the child can then be part of establishing a sense of 'virtue' that has personal application and relevance, which they can then draw off in their dealings with others.

8.2.2 School

If positive relationships are key to a 'curriculum of virtue' that fully supports children's developing understanding of right and wrong, where does that leave those interactional settings in which personal relationships are not quite as strong? School (for many) can be characterised as a space that is defined by an authoritarian, adult-driven, rule-laden approach to managing the child. Chapter 6 provided some examples of this. One of the significant implications is the extent to which that approach impacts on the relationships that children are then able to have with teachers, and particularly the consequences this has for the moral learning process (see Thornberg 2008). Notably the *Good Childhood Report 2015* highlighted that a particular problem affecting children's enjoyment of school was their poor relationships with teachers[4] (The Children's Society 2015).

Children, Morality and Society (2012) saw children question their teachers' moral character as a result of arbitrary acts such as being told to stop talking: '*makes you feel like he's evil*', one girl said. Part of this is based on the children's perception that adult actions were rarely carried out with reference to the feelings of the children in their class. As such, the children found themselves holding emotions that they could do little with, apart from link them to their perception of their teacher. In the following extract, which raises some interesting themes around fairness, the children highlight how, despite their feelings, their options within this setting are very limited.

Mia   *The other day we had these cards that we had to make ourselves and some of them didn't work properly and he just chucked them in the bin, but we spent time on making them.*

SF *How did it make you feel?*

Louis   *Upset*

Mia   *Annoyed,*

Andy   *Because we've spent ages on them*

Mia   *We've spent our time and you think what's the point of doing it if you're just going to chuck it in the bin, there is just no point. And he would shout at you if you didn't bring it in but then he just chucked it in the bin.*

SF *So how do you deal with it, do you just accept it or what?*

Andy   *We have to accept it because if we shout at them we will go to Miss Phillips [the head teacher] and she will probably suspend us if we shout at her.*

Here the institutional expectation is that the child will accept the teacher's action and, although they do, it reinforces a process in which their feelings are not acknowledged. A key question is how this impacts on learning opportunities within the classroom. Some thoughts on this are reflected in research on schools' use of corporal punishment in South Africa. The key divide between such schools was the nature of the relationship that the teachers were able to build with their class. In cases of corporal punishment, the relationship was fundamentally damaged by this overt act of power, resulting in feelings of 'injustice' and problems with the 'efficiency' of the classroom (Paget and Fronchi 2008: 162). Schools that used alternatives to corporal punishment were said to provide a 'catalyst for more efficient educational relationships' (ibid.). In a similar way to home, therefore, relationships that acknowledge a child's sense of self (and related emotions) are key to children's learning.

For schools, the challenge is to establish such relationships as they seek to engage more effectively with this process of moral learning. An indication of a possible solution is provided in the following extract from a conversation with two boys who had found themselves (on a number of occasions) experiencing their school's use of sanctions.

Josh   *Well they never exactly explain it because they haven't got a lot of time.*

Nat   *They tend to think …*

Josh   *get on with it…*

Nat   *I've got to get on with this lesson, so I'll just send them to the hall for five minutes.*

Josh   *I think we shouldn't get sent to the hall because then we're missing out on the lesson…I think what we should have, we should have like a co-teacher that teaches you about right and wrong and when the teacher sends you out to the hall the co-teacher goes and explains everything to you and why it is wrong.*

SF *So you think in each class there should be two teachers?*

Josh   *Yeah*

SF *One teacher who does the explaining?*

Josh   *Yeah and one just teaches you normal lessons.*

It is a conversation that highlights *time* as a key part of building relationships, as well as pointing to one of the structural challenges faced by schools. The result is that the effectiveness of the learning process, particularly in terms of moral awareness, is restricted. Such is the importance of this to the children that they suggest a second adult should be available to take on the role of guide.

Indeed this can be done. Here the same boys reflect on their head teacher and how, by stepping outside of the traditional structure, she provides a way for children to look past a dominant perspective of power to one in which the authority of the adult is re-perceived as a genuine interest in them as an individual, with expected implications for the effectiveness of this adult as a moral guide.

Nat   *I think Miss Phillips [the head teacher] is quite good at sorting out problems. Because I did a trade the other day with my friend, my sort of friend Robert and all of a sudden he said he wanted to trade back and I didn't want to and so Miss couldn't sort it out so we went to Miss Phillips. Miss Phillips always has the sensible way to sort out the fair way. She listened to both sides of the story and she made us trade back but now Robert's not allowed to bring his cards in so I got an unfair part and Robert got an unfair part.*

Josh   *Nathan remember when you were like really, really, really like annoying me and intimidating me in the playground last year*

Nat   *Yeah, I had to run away from you*

Josh   *I ran and I jumped and you cut your knee so badly*

Nat   *It was funny*

Josh   *And we went to Miss Phillips and she just sat us down and said what's the problem, she listened to both sides of the story, exactly the same as that, and she gave us both a fair thing that we stay away from each other. But now we've made up.*

Miss Phillips does not need to rescind her role as head teacher to get alongside Nat and Josh. Instead, she can establish a sense of mutual respect as she manages the setting so that it allows reference to some of Nat and Josh's 'personal elements' as they recognise the structural components and limitations of this space. The result is that, by allowing the boys a chance to work through some of these 'elements' as framed within interaction, they are able to reach a 'fair' conclusion.

Reflecting on home and school here indicates some of the themes that are linked to the process of learning that is an important feature of a more active image of the moral child. It is a process that, as defined above, is driven by the recognition of an adult as a guide who has a positive relationship with the child. This is supported by the need for interactions to recognise a personal understanding of the child, one that comes through 'spending time'.[5] However, in an environment where schools are increasingly driven by performance rather than any recognition of the processes of learning (James 2013), the stark question is whether most schools are effective as spaces for children to experience this form of 'virtue' education. It is a question that Dweck (2006) succinctly sums up in this contrast between performance and process by asking 'is success about learning or proving that you're smart?'. A focus on learning demands more than just a concentration on the academic, but rather a recognition of social skills as tools for now and the future (Frankel and Fowler 2015). It is an approach to learning that is personalised, challenging the traditional image of the moral child and the way in which this has defined the structure of school itself. Rather than those elements of personal life such as emotions being outside of the school's attention, they become the focus (Frankel and Fowler 2016). A 'curriculum of virtue', therefore, must reflect that complexity and must place the individual at the heart of a 'structure' for doing school if learning, both academic and social, is to be maximised.

8.2.3   Neighbourhood

Interactional settings can provide opportunities for efficient moral learning when practices allow room for the individual to be recognised. Key to this is the nature of the child's perceived relationship with those who share the interactional setting. By its very nature, the neighbourhood is a space that often exists for children outside of the direct relationships that are such a part of home and school (Wooden 1995). The neighbourhood, therefore, becomes a very interesting space in which to consider moral learning because it is a setting in which there are a range of preconceived ideas about what children should know about that space and, hence, how they should behave. This becomes marked by the difference between adult expectations of children's knowledge and the reality. For adults, relying on a legacy of reason linked to the criminal law, creates an image of the child who, whilst in the neighbourhood, is deemed to have a clear and defined sense of right and wrong. The extract below shows that children's understanding is perhaps not as neatly linked to socially defined expectations as society might hope because children, at times, work together to create meanings. Here a group of girls were discussing kidnap, which was the subject of a play that they were performing.

SF	*Why is something like this (kidnap – the theme of their play) likely to happen outside school and home?*
Jane	*Because there are rules in school and home.*
Amy	*Yeah but there's rules out of school.*
Jane	*They're laws not rules*
Amy	*Yeah well I call them rules.*
SF	*Why are they rules not laws, don't laws come into home and school?*
Anna	*No because thingy [government] don't make them up do they.*
SF	*Where do the government make the laws for?*
Anna	*Outside*
	(Noisy discussion)
SF	*Rules and laws are different, why?*
Liz	*Its not against the law for babies to chew wires but it's certainly against the rules.*
Sarah	*There rules as in do this, do listen ...*
Amy	*Cos we have the St Stephens Code of Conduct, don't listen, don't interrupt, I mean do listen, don't interrupt, do work hard, don't waste time (helped by other), do be kind, don't hurt people's feelings, do be honest.*
Jane	*So basically that's like our laws.*
Any	*Do be gentle*
SF	*That's like the laws of your school?*
Liz	*That's our rules, rules not laws*
	(The others agree)

Amy	*The reason why rules and laws are like the same because really if you're in your house or school you can like (pause) go up to someone and blow their head off and go bang.*
SF	*You're not going to do that at home is that what you're saying?*
Amy	*Yeah*
SF	*Why are you not going to do that at home?*
Anna	*Because it's stupid*
Sarah	*But it's not stupid out in the town though? … These are going to be rules for outside as well.*

This a conversation raises some really important themes around the processes of moral learning. The neighbourhood is clearly a space in which children are able to test out their own understandings as they employ 'rules and codes of conduct'. However, significantly, it is also a space in which their understanding of those formal markers of right and wrong, the criminal law, is limited. A consequence is that part of the gap in knowledge becomes filled with assumptions in relation to that space. These assumptions include framing understandings on wider contextual sources such as television. It was certainly significant that, in those areas where children needed to fill in the blanks as a result of a lack of experience, media in its broadest terms offered a guide. For example, as the children developed dramas that they set in the 'neighbourhood', a strong militaristic theme emerged in relation to the characters they created. This included the perception that the 'characters' would carry weapons. When I asked about what 'realistically a group of 17 year olds might have', the response was:

Joe	*They would have a weapon*
Tom	*Knuckle dusters*
Joe	*A gun*
Tom	*It would have to be hidden*
SF	*A hidden gun?*
Joe	*A hand gun*
Tom	*In, like their waistcoat*

The complexity of their assessment of the stranger here characterised as a teenager, must not simply be viewed as a response to what they might have seen on television. However, it must be seen as part of a far more complex process in which they are producing meanings through a combination of elements by which they manage similarity and difference, and power alongside stereotypes and experience linked to those personal elements of self.

The neighbourhood, therefore, emerges as a space where there are significant questions about the way in which the process of learning is acknowledged and practiced, and what this means for a wider 'curriculum of virtue'. For example, in the discussion above, it highlights how the neighbourhood offers spaces in which children find themselves shaping, defining and giving judgement on the acceptability of certain behaviours, as assessed through their constructed understanding of what is right and wrong. Here, then, children rather than adults are responsible for shaping the nature of the structure as it comes to affect this interactional setting. This might be seen in the framing of the interactional settings at a skateboard park or freestyle ski hill, where children become the architects of the structue that comes to apply within these arenas. To consider the nature of 'virtue' acquisition outside of adult-defined institutions, is an important area for further investigation, here the framework offers a means to begin to consider such spaces and the way in which interactions within them come to assume meanings.

8.3   From Control to Collaboration: Social Harmony

A significant part of the model considered in the previous chapters was the theme of threat that has pervaded constructed images of childhood. This section seeks to re-engage with this, but rather than focusing on children's role as a destabilising presence in society, it considers the efforts children go to to establish and maintain a sense of harmony as part of negotiating their everyday lives.

8.3.1   Home

Solberg's well referenced work on negotiation (1997) marks an important starting point because she explored home, not as a place of dictates, but of varied opinions that can come together as children and adult find a shared path. It was a sense of working together that was a theme in the comments of the 'Mum' at the start of this chapter, as she shared an image of the child that allowed opportunties for her children to be involved in moral discourse. For her, moral learning was best encouraged by releasing her children from traditional constraints that might hold them back, and instead to invite them to take on the role of partners within the home. A similar theme is drawn out by Frost's (2011) assessment of Butler et al.'s (2005) research, which begins by highlighting children's active role in meaning-making within the home: 'they found that decision making was usually informal – there were few explicit or formal rules' (Butler et al. 2005: 2). Significantly, in making explicit the democratic nature of the decision-making process, Frost signals the 'moral' dimension connected to this decision-making through extracts from the research that relate to trust, fairness and 'having a say'. Throughout, the research highlights the strategic way in which children respond to the structure of the home as they make meanings. This study concludes that research within families should:

- [consider the] complexity of the family processes, family histories and the particular ways that families have of going about their everyday business;
- respect the authority of parents, the confidence that many children have in their parents and the capacity of children to engage meaningfully and purposefully in determining the conduct of family life;
- respect children's inclination towards participatory forms of engagement in family life and be sensitive to children who are in the process of developing their capacity for autonomy and independence;
- respect and respond to children's claims to fairness and equitable treatment. (Butler et al., cited in Frost 2011: 86)

These conclusions highlight the extent to which children can be active members of the social space that is the home, if parents are encouraged to recognise children's capacity to draw from the interactional setting and to make meanings as a response to it. The research invites further consideration of why children will follow rules that are not explicit or managed through the constant use of arbitrary punishment. In the following extract, two girls consider their thoughts of what is right in light of promoting a sense of social harmony within the home. As such the views they present reflect a process that shows how they have reflected on their sense of self in light of particualr relationships.

SF	*So what makes something right, how would you know?*
Lisa	*It would kind of make her [mum] feel happy and you don't forget her and you think about her.*
SF	*And is it important to make her feel happy?*
Amy	*Yeah 'cos she's the one that gave birth to you so*
SF	*What do you reckon Amy?*
Amy	*To start off with she gave birth to you, she is like your very first friend.*
SF	*So is it important to make them feel good?*
Lisa	*Yeah my mum. My dad I don't know him and I don't really care about him.*
Amy	*She knows you better than anyone else, and she gives you pocket money during the week.*

In framing moral meanings, the girls show a sense of commitment and duty, linked directly to emotions rooted in relationships. It reflects themes around family bonds that were expressed in Finch and Mason's (1993) important work showing the centrality of relationships and its link to a sense of responsibility, obligation and duty within the home. This approach offers a way of thinking about 'harmony' within the home that is jointly constructed as all members of the family work together to establish it.[6] It reinforces the power of relationships which, Smart suggests, 'captures a way of thinking and motivations', as it works from the basis that people exist in 'intentional, thoughtful networks, which they actively sustain, maintain and allow to atrophy' (1993: 48). The need to understand the layers within these relationships provides some interesting and important contributions to thinking about how 'order' is created (see Bacon 2010),[7] which has relevance not just within the home but also beyond.

The ideas explored above suggest that placing children into an interactional setting in which elements of agency are recognised and engaged with does result in more opportunities for children to use their skills to be part of constructing practices that reflect a shared sense of moral meaning. This approach, and significantly the active image of the child that it demands, allows a common set of values to be created in the home, one in which the rules are collaboratively made and, therefore, carry joint meaning which is focused on a sense of order in which all of the group feel valued. This is not an idealistic imagining of home, but rather one that moves away from a traditional image of the moral child and recognises children's sense of agency, and, as a result, draws on a view of the child which is dynamic and active. It is an image that, if applied, changes the way in which practices within home are set and, perhaps more importantly, alters the opportunities for the child to engage in this process of socialisation as they seek to create a sense of moral order by balancing a notion of self with the structural realities in which they find themselves.

8.3.2 School

Previous discussion has primarily focused on school as a space in which order is imposed through adult regulation rather than collaboration. Collaboration of course does take place in schools all the time as children work together to create shared moral meanings that reflect their interactions with others (also considered in Chap. 9). Pollard's early work provides indications of the way in which children collaborate with their peers, with implications for the meaning they gave to their interactions. This is reflected in the way children are linked to taking on particular roles. In an ethnographic investigation of life in school, Pollard (1985) identified three categories: the goodies, the jokers, and gangs. Each of these groups Pollard considers in relation to the way in which they challenge the 'moral' space around them (1979). The 'goodies' always conform, but this has implications for the way in which they are perceived by the student body as a whole. The 'jokers' will conform, but they will also challenge and push at the boundaries of what Pollard calls 'routine deviance'. This group is well-liked, they are able to assess the social situation to such an extent that they can have a laugh with their teachers but are able to react to mood changes and know when to stop. The 'gangs' will not only get involved in 'routine deviance' but members will also get involved in individual acts of 'disorder' as part of defining and shaping their reputation as 'rough and tough'. The study is an intriguing insight into the different ways in which children come to present themselves as they reflect on the various 'elements' in framing a sense of identity and creating meanings of acceptability within school. Just having three categories perhaps does not recognise the dynamic nature of the variety of roles that children play in school, but it certainly offers evidence of the extent to which children create a sense of collaborative 'order', notably with different meanings of acceptability, within the same setting (see also Corsaro 1985).

The process of collaborative meaning-making, with a reflection on moral meanings, is highlighted by the way in which children grant consent.

Becky	*You have to hurt someone if you're playing squash [a playground game]*
Eli	*Or murder slapsies when they can't move and you go and whack them*
SF	*Oh, and is that alright?*
Eli	*Yes*
Becky	*Yes*
SF	*Why?*
Becky	*Because if they know the game then they know what's going to happen, if they're going to be slapped really hard and they wouldn't play it if they didn't know the game so (little laugh) I didn't know the game and got hit.*

How children give consent marks a useful way in which children share order. At the centre of this process is further connection to a sense of identity because children manage the granting of consent with reference to how they position themselves in relation to others. A key question is about 'power' and the extent to which 'consent' reflects a perception of a mutual relationship. It is an important theme within school, whether on the playground, the sports field or indeed in the classroom. Where the perception of 'power' comes to be imposed, rather than agreed (as with consent), the ability to establish a shared set of goals is less effective. Such that without a sense of mutual engagement any joint effort to pursue a 'common good' will at best be partial. Despite the efforts of schools to offer students opportunities to participate (McGinley and Grieve 2010), significant questions remain about whether those settings truly offer children chances to be part of establishing a shared vision for a 'common good'. Indeed, is this an ambition for schools at all (see discussion on Yamishita and Davies, 2010, in the next chaper).? By looking at schools through the framework within this book, one is able to consider in more detail the extent to which institutions such as schools are creating structures that provide the opportunities for the individual to feel as if they are effectively collaborating. It is a discourse that reflects the ongoing tension between embracing the capacity of the child and creating relevant opportuntities against the perceived ceding of control required of adults to allow participation, and the subsequent risk it might have to the maintaince of the status quo. As schools continue to face the need to respond to challenges such as behavioural issues in the classroom (Ofsted, 2014), so we should be looking more to understand how shared goals and common ambitions inform effective learning. However, as suggested above, it is an approach that has to engage with the child through the lens of structure and agency.

8.3.3 Neighbourhood

School is marked as a space that has in the past (and in many cases continues today) to limit opportunities that would allow the social agent to be invovled in co-creating a shared sense of harmony. The neighbourhood adds additional layers to this as on the one hand it is an arena of extreme supervision, whilst on the other it offers children the chance to escape adult control. Seeing seetings within the neighbourhood (in its broadest sense), therefore as somewhere children go to be free means that the idea of 'threat' (so commonlly attached to children in this space) is not for them driven by a desire to cause trouble but rather in terms of how they manage the risks that they might face with a desire to have fun and to reinforce or promote their place within their peer group.

Although in *Children, Morality and Society* the children reported on the value of the space that the neighbourhood provided, their responses did raise questions about how images of the child come to be applied, with implications for how the children came to negotiate these spaces. A 2007 UNICEF report found that children in the UK scored lowest in their response to the question 'Do you find your peers kind and helpful', with only half saying yes. Peers are likely to be a factor in children's engagement with the neighbourhood, but a lack of trust has implications for the way in which children manage the ambiguity of this space. The sense of 'threat' that surrounded children's assessment of other, generally older, children ('teenagers' – see the earlier discussion in this chapter) was a strong theme in *Children, Morality and Society*. As such, it reflects the sense in which children's engagement with the neighbourhood is marked by how they come to interpret the threat posed by other children as they seek to find a way in which they can establish their own presence in this space.

This reinforces the sense of a moral learning journey that is marked by complications created by new experiences. In the home and school such experiences could effectively be understood through explanation and communication with certain adults. So what about children's relationship with adults in the neighbourhood, and to what extent do these provide avenues for moral learning and effective negotiation of these arenas? For example, how do children relate to the police, and what impact does this have on the way in which they then seek to manage this space? This relationship has not always been easy (Frankel 2009) and it continues to position the police as the enforcers of an adult agenda that seeks to maintain its control over children. Examples such as a 13-year-old boy being 'arrested, DNA'd, fingerprinted, charged', resulting in a criminal record, for stealing 49p-worth of sweets highlights the tensions in this relationship (Aynesley-Green 2007). The difficulties of this relationship were highlighted more recently by the All Party Parliamentary Group for Children in a report that was aptly titled 'It's all about trust: building good relationships between children and the police' (2014). The report highlighted poor communication and a lack of mutual respect (2014: 5), as well as reflecting on the importance of professional development for police forces and the recognition of children's rights. What is missing from this list is the need for children to be more involved in the way in which they and the police work together to shape those community spaces. This requires a change in the way children perceive the police, and in the way the police see the child, as the role for both moves from potential threat to community partner.

The implications of this in relation to both peers and the police contextualise comments, discussed in *Children, Morality and Society*, about children feeling that out in the neighbourhood they are on their own. Indeed, only three groups of adults emerged as people they might possibly turn to: lifeguards, neighbours and the police (although only in relation to very specific circumstances). When it came to meaning-making, children recognised that they did not necessarily have the guide that they might find at home or school. These findings are echoed in Spilsbury's (2002) research with children in Cleveland, Ohio. The study showed how, within a violent community, children chose strategies that saw them turn to 'safe' people when in need of support. These adults included mums with children, old people and police officers. However, it also noted that these children would avoid people with tattoos, smokers and people with gruff voices. The research confirmed the moral judgements children made about strangers in *Children, Morality and Society*, highlighting key themes that identified difference, and which were notably linked to aspects of a threat to their person (as considered through their sense of self). As such, children's sense of right and wrong was governed by an awareness of the fact that this space was different – actions that would be clearly defined at home or school might take on different meanings in the neighbourhood.

Mike	*Hurting people is wrong but sometimes you have to do it*
SF	*Why would you have to do it?*
Mike	*If someone was in a fight and there were no grown ups around or no-one you could tell you'd have to go and stop it or kind of hit someone to get them off of the other person.*

What Mike's assessment so starkly highlights is the perception that, when there is not the luxury of knowing that an adult might take up the 'fight' for you, action is very much dependent on the individual. Meaning-making, therefore, needs to reflect this assessment as the child employs actions that are shaped by a defence of their personal integrity and sense of identity. It is through the concept of habits that Mathews (2002) seeks to explain how children draw up rules in relation to the neighbourhood as they seek to manage the risks by themselves and create a sense of 'street literacy' (2002: 108). This work also highlights the gender differences between the perceptions and subsequent meanings that boys and girls create to manage being out on the 'streets'.

Although a feature of the neighbourhood is that it is a public space, so much of the thinking in relation to it has reflected the way in which groups come to 'privatise' parts of the space as they give it a particular meaning. It is not a significant leap to place the internet and the use of social media into a similar category. Like more traditional neighbourhood spaces, it is a setting that is marked by adult worries and efforts at regulation. However, in reality, it has become an environment in which children are having to rely on their own personal code of conduct. The divide between how adults seek to define the neighbourhood and the way in which children practise within it is significant. It reflects how children collaborate with one another in order to create meanings, although these meanings may be different from those that adults hold. The result is that order out on the street (or in these other virtual domains) is not necessarily the result of commonly (across society) shared thinking and collaborative engagement. It can be, but in many of the day-to-day settings in which children live their lives, 'order' is narrowly created because rules are shaped within particular groups. It is a way of thinking that highlights the importance of the image of the child within settings because this understanding frames the nature of possible opportunities. A more active acknowledgement of children in terms of their competence and ability to be part of constructing shared social ambitions should establish them as collaborators in defining a common vision of community harmony, with implications for the way in which such spaces come to be experienced by all (Jans 2004).

8.4   Conclusion

Increasingly, research is reflecting the impact that collaborating with children can have (for example Tisdall et al, 2014). This chapter has presented a case for more active images of the child, ones that, if acknowledged, demand that children are given chances to participate in discourses that are directly relevant to their daily interactions as part of an ongoing process of learning. This does not mean paying lip service to children, by including them in a school council for example. Rather it means being prepared to acknowledge children's capacity to be part of discourses that deal with the complexities of social life and that both implicitly and explicitly deal with 'morality' (the acceptability of behaviours). This chapter has shown that children are actively practising morality as part of the everyday. Questions over the acceptibility of actions form a continuous part of how they seek to navigate the social world around them. To suggest that children are without the competence to engage in moral discourses is not true. In fact, children demonstrate significant skill in deploying moral awareness to manage their interactions. That does not mean that children do not need adults. However, rather than separating the being (the knowledgeable adult) and the becoming (the developing child), it is more realistic to recognise that all are becomings (Bacon and Frankel 2013) and that, through collaboration, a process of socialisation can be effectively created that sees a greater focus on a 'common' good and a shared sense of social order. Embracing the child as a participant in social discourses provides the focus for the final chapter.

Notes

1. This has been reflected in reports such as 'The link between pupil health and wellbeing and attainment' (Public Health England 2014) as well as 'The impact of non-cognitive skills for young people' (Gutman and Schoon 2013).
2. Criminological literature around 'edgework' also offers an interesting spatial element to this discussion. Lyng's (1990) work, for example, highlights the way in which the individual draws meaning directly from the space itself in defining and shaping their actions as they seek to 'take on' the space – testing out the limits. Muncie, drawing from the work of Lyng, reflects that edgework provides an illusion of control in an alluring space of 'experiential anarchy in which the individual moves beyond the realm of established social patterns to the very fringes of ordered society' (Muncie 2015: 219).
3. Torstenson (2007) looks at the way children recall and use memories of significant happenings from early life in shaping understandings of the world. The research suggests how experiences play a key part in shaping individual memories, linked to significant relationships.
4. In regard to pupils' relationships with teachers, this report placed England 14 out of 15 countries.

5. In Ontario, Canada, schools have introduced a secondary member of staff in their kindergarten classes. This member of staff is seen to be on par with the teacher and has specific responsibility for children's development. Driven by a psychological understanding of the child, this member of staff brings a staged approach to the classroom with potential for relationships to be built.

6. Smart builds on this theme as she looks at the notion of embeddedness which, she suggests, reflects 'the tenacity of these [family] bonds and links, sometimes even to the extent that family members and close kin or friends can feel as if they were part of one' (2007: 45).

7. Bacon's (2010) work on twins is full of examples of children, looking at how they participate in meaning-making as a response to their interactional setting, decisions that are firmly tied into a wider sense of a developing identity, in her exploration of themes such as belonging and togetherness. The importance of the process of participation is that allowing children to practise their agency has an impact on the extent to which they are able to explore their sense of personhood.

Step 5

Re-positioning Children Within Structure

1.1 Shaping Structure

This book has been about introducing a framework for integrating a moral dimension into the way in which we investigate childhoods.

The framework highlights the relevance of structure and agency as factors through which an understanding of childhoods can be presented. It draws from an idea, considered in Chap. 2, that illustrates the relationship between structure and agency in terms of a fabric, with some threads reflecting the social forces that inform structure and others being the personal elements that the individual brings to interaction (James 2010). However, what is not so clear from this conceptual characterisation of structure and agency is the extent to which children themselves can be part of informing that structure. In order to challenge dominant discourses on morality, the next step must be to recognise children's capacity to shape structure. Part 3 of the framework considers that an ability to inform structure is a logical progression to a set of processes that have seen the individual engage with the wider context, make meanings that lead to actions and reactions. The extent to which children are able to inform structure, and particularly for this input to have implications for practices, is largely dictated by the opportunities that adults provide. It means that certain opportunities within key institutions have the potential to reconfigure the membrane that surrounds certain

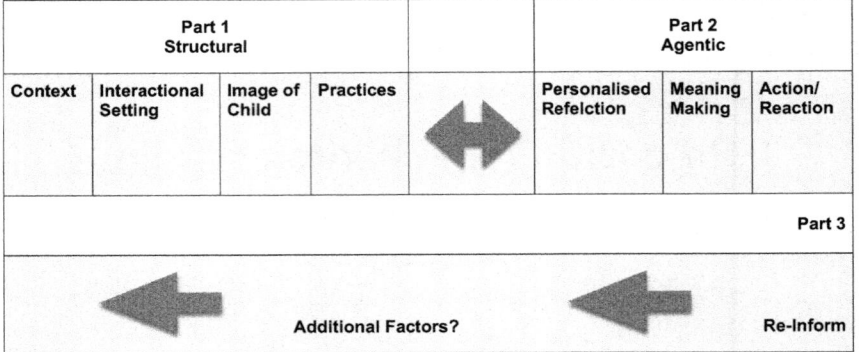

Fig. 1   The framework

interactional settings (see Chap. 3). Rather than seeing structural institutions as being populated by adults, children also become part of shaping the way in which an image and subsequent practices come to be constructed. It reflects a model of co-participation, one that can only begin with a mutual recognition of children as social agents.

1.2   Re-informing

As part of a process of agency, the framework suggests that the individual is involved in a constant and ongoing reconsideration of the contextual backdrop that frames interaction. These considerations will take account of meanings represented through actions and reactions as the individual builds up a sense of their place within a setting, as well as responding to any additional factors such as new people. As such, whatever the action or reaction that stems from meaning-making, this will, to some extent, reinform the process as a whole. It will see the individual 'reflect' again on the interactional setting in light of the meaning that they have made, a process that will then take place continuously.

The step by which the child comes to reinform their understanding of the interactional setting will include a constant assessment of the image of 'the child' that they perceive within that space. Children come to internalise this constructed image and use it as part of shaping meanings. This can be seen in relation to illustrations in Chap. 8 Additional examples might be the way in which children give meanings to different spaces within a school[1] and the extent to which perceived adult understandings of age and competence become factors that the children use to define the way in which they come to understand their personal access to certain spaces. Taking the example of school, the process of reinforming is limited. The opportunities provided by the setting are restricted, so children's meaning-making and related actions simply reflect the ongoing maintenance of the status quo. However, as well as such closed opportunities creating 'confromity' on the most part, it does not stop children questioning and re-assessing as they continually reflect on this very particular structural backdrop. Indeed, it is only by recognising what is expected that efforts to resist and subvert really take on meaning (A further example of this aspect of the framework is shared in Appendix 2). Notably, the nature of the opportunities (whether those are restricted, as in school, or more open) has a direct impact on the dynamic nature of the structure of a setting. Indeed, it can mark a contrast between a setting in which the focus is one of contnuity (maintaining the status quo) or change.

The final chapter, therefore, considers the relevance of each part of the framework and what this means for the way in which children come to be positioned in relation to moral discourses. How does a recognition of children as social partners change the way in which we consider them in relation to the dominant attitudes that have shaped, and continue to shape, their experiences? Indeed, does this offer alternative images of the child, that reflect a vision for childhoods in which children and adults actively co-construct the interactional settings within which everyday life is experienced?

Note

1. A connection that was well documented in an unpublished final year project by a student at Kings at Western University.

9

Restructuring Moral Discourses

Margaret Mead quote? Chapter 8 illustrated the extent to which children as social agents are engaged in shaping moral meaning as part of their everyday lives. As Chaps. 3 and 4 suggested, these individual processes are situated within an interactional setting that is shaped and defined by certain constructed images of the child (see Chaps. 5–7). These images themselves carry assumed moral understandings that have implications for the practices that come to shape children's experiences within that space. This chapter seeks to show, by way of some concluding thoughts, how those spaces might turn adult-defined practices into opportunities, and by doing so, see moral order as becoming co-constructed, with consequences for the way in which we come to think about those key interactional settings. In short, this chapter argues that redefining adults' images of the child (or, indeed, those that children perceive) within interactional settings can have implications for how we come to construct childhoods.

© The Editor(s) (if applicable) and The Author(s) 2017
S. Frankel, *Negotiating Childhoods*, Studies in Childhood and Youth,
DOI 10.1057/978-1-137-32349-1_9

9.1   Participation

Structure, as presented in this book, must be recognised as changing. This is particularly obvious in relation to the different interactional settings that children find themselves in. The way in which these spaces come to be structured cannot be seen in one-dimensional terms that solely reflect social directives on what a school, for example, should be like. Rather, such settings only come to take on a form when considered through the lens of the individual.

To understand children's engagement with morality, we not only need to recognise the way in which a backdrop for interaction comes to be constructed, but also the way in which the individual responds to this backdrop and continues to respond to it in establishing meanings that inform actions. Chapter 3 suggested that the way in which we come to frame an image of the child within a given interactional setting should be seen in relation to a membrane that is created by those within that space. Recognising people as the membrane through which structure comes to take on 'form' explains why the practices in one home differ from those in another, despite the fact that these two homes might be side by side. The fact that the membrane that shapes how a setting comes to be 'informed' by those wider social themes is made up by people means that it carries the potential to be dynamic. Chapters 4 and 8 have suggested that agency is made up of a number of processes that include the individual engaging with structure as part of shaping meanings that lead to actions and reactions. However, it is important to realise that these actions and reactions do not need to be seen to continue within the same ongoing and unchangeable structure, but rather the structure of an interactional setting can itself change.

As such, the individual becomes a force for change within any interactional setting, including an institution such as home or school. The starting point for this discussion lies in illustrations of participation that are increasingly emerging within childhood studies (Percy Smith and Thomas 2010a). In short, these studies explore how a recognition of agency carries the potential for children to be seen as part of change. Significantly, the extent of that change is defined by the opportunities that the individuals are given or are able to establish. Opportunities are therefore a major feature in this final chapter as we consider how the themes of earlier chapters have ongoing application.

One issue in relation to morality is that it is an area of children's lives that has been so completely controlled that any opportunities for children to reinform those dominant images is, at best, restricted. The final chapter of this book seeks to argue that the recognition by adults and children of the mutuality of agency can impact on the meanings that evolve within settings, with very real implications for the way in which children come to experience their everyday lives.

9.1.1 Children as Agents of Change

The following example offers a useful illustration of the extent to which children can act as agents of change in reframing the contextual backdrop (with reference to image and practices) that informs their experiences of childhood. Notably, this example recognises that a key part of any social change is the adult. In the same way that children are acting as agents, so are adults. It is therefore within the ability of adults to establish a range of meanings in relation to the interactional settings which they share with children. These meanings can change, and in so doing, so can the image of the child that the adult holds.

In an engaging piece of research, Meintjes (2014) reflects on a project in South Africa. South African society has faced a number of significant challenges over many years. As a society, it has had an interesting relationship with children (which was touched on in Chap. 7). This relationship contains a tension between traditional views of childhood and the image of the child that was reflected in children's participation in the changes that led to democracy. However, it is the view of the child in terms of more dominant moral images that has created the societal backdrop, in front of which children were seeking to make sense of the destructive impact of HIV/AIDS. For example, children are the focus of news stories that simply reiterate a perceived moral image, reaffirming adult practices that do little to acknowledge the voice of the child,

Analysis of South African media reporting critique a tendency to 'use the voices of children' to support preconceived stories rather than to inform the account: 'children are enlisted as characters to enrich and confirm the journalist's stake on the situation, rather than brought in as active participants in creating their own representations. (Bird and Rahfald 2011: 54, cited in Meintjes 2014: 150)

This illustration can be related to children's place in society more widely. In the context of South Africa, it simply highlighted the extent to which images of the child reflected children's passivity because adults controlled how those images came to be constructed.

Meintjes (2014) study highlighted some of the cultural barreirs that were impacting on the relationships between children and adults in South Africa. In particular it made visible an awareness that children had of these cultural forces and their place in shaping the wider 'context' within which they (and adults) were operating. These reflections on structure were illustrated, for example, through children's observations that there were limited ways in which they could express themsevles to adults. These reflections on structure were illustrated through children's observations that there were, for example, few ways in which they could express themsevles to adults. Without such opportunities, there was no vehicle through which children could challenge or change the images of the child and the related practices that were established within settings such as home and school. As such, the wider context remained static and adults maintained control of the way in which social knowledge was used to define childhoods. It was through giving children microphones that the imbalance was challenged. It created an opportunity for children to share, and more importantly, for their voices to be heard. As such, it added an 'additional factor' (see Part 3 of the framework) for consideration in assessing how the individual related to the setting that they were in.

Through considering how adults responded to this project, one can see how it challenged perceived images of the child, with direct implications for the way in which interactional spaces came to be structured. As such, it marks a move from an adult-assumed image to one that is directly informed by a recognition of the agency of children. The impact of this change of attitude, and the implications it has for images of the child, is reflected in the following comments by a head teacher.

What I have learnt is that we look at kids or think about kids as not being aware of issues, or of issues not affecting them. But after hearing programs I've realised that children know about things we think they don't know about. I realised that they know, and if given a chance to speak about those things, they speak. I realised that they think deeply about these things and these issues that they raise…I no longer look at children as mere children who do not know anything. I look at them as people who know something and who have something to say to me, and who can speak freely and be just as confident as an adult. (Meintjes 2014: 163)

As a result of children being given an opportunity to participate, adult thinking changes. This is one of a number of examples that highlight how, through acknowledging children's agency, the potential for change is created. Here, a key adult within the community finds her moral image of the child challenged as she is forced to rethink themes of competence, with very real implications for the way in which themes relating to 'virtue' come to be considered. Here, children move from being a concern to being collaborators. It is the sense of children as participants (Percy-Smith and Thomas 2010b)[1] that provides the basis for challenging the moral images that have been and continue to be so dominant.

9.2 A Partnership?

An ongoing theme of this final chapter is to consider how far an awareness of children's agency impacts on the structure that defines and shapes children's everyday experiences. It establishes a foucs on participation and the related opportunties that are created as one considers the joint construction by children and adults in shared interactional spaces and the implciations this carries. This way of thinking challenges the roots of the assumed relationship that children and adults have had within society. Lee's (2005) discussion of separation and independence reflects on the relationship and the tensions within it. Lee argues that adults' approach to children has been to mark that separation between adult and chlid and to promote a need for increasing independence. However, it is a flawed ambition. For separation and independence are impossible within society. Children can never be fully separate from adults and they can never be completely independent. It is a more realistic aim to focus on the need to recognise the strains within society that 'bind together'. In looking at a range of philosophical positions in relation to the child, Lee foresees no problem with having an approach to the child that sees the adult and the child having social lives that are interlinked. Rather, it is through embracing the nature of that link that one can look to develop a more effective understanding of this key relationship, with implications for the way in which both adults and children experience social life. In a review that carries many themes that are relevant to the moral images of the child discussed in this book, Lee acknowledges that adult desires to protect and care for the child are not necessarily to be seen as separate from a call to see them as equals.

The intention of bridging a divide in which both parties have value is central in challenging the hold of dominant moral discourses and the impact they have on the image of the child. This final chapter will seek to offer alternative images of the moral child as it reflects on the creation of participatory opportunities in light of themes from Chap. 8, as it loooks at the integrity of children's personhood (in terms of their ownership of the elements that make up their identity), perceiving them as learners who are both beings and becomings (like all of us in society) and as collaborators or partners in change. This review will use the framework to reflect on dominant structural themes, images and practices on its way to considering settings that are increasingly co-constructed.

9.3   Integrity of Personhood

Although each of these themes can be applied in the different settings in which children find themselves, the first one will be considered in relation to home. One of the characteristics of a deeper understanding of children's engagement with morality is the extent to which they are drawing on personal 'elements' of self in order to make meanings. It is the personalised nature of those meanings that should be the focus for thinking about alternative images and opportunities.

9.3.1   Dominant Structural Themes

As the previous chapters have shown, dominant structural themes in the home see the parent developing moral images (with reference to themes of reason, virtue and social harmony) that are shaped by a need to ensure effective management of the child. This is built not only on a personal level because parental roles draw on a legacy that reflects a hierarchical, indeed patriarchal, structure, but also in terms of the way in which the home is positioned within society as whole. In Chap. 5 we saw the extent to which home provided society with a means for macro control that could be reinforced at a micro level through the role of adults within that family. As such, the family not only provided a 'holding pen' for the developing child, it also offered a site through which key social attributes could be communicated as part of a wider moral agenda and the threat posed by the unsupervised child was controlled (Durham 1991).

Today, the home continues to be judged by its effectiveness in producing the compliant citizen, just as it was some 3000 years ago. In 2011, there were pop-up riots in many large cities in England, particularly affecting London (Ministry of Justice 2012). These riots, directed through social media and shared through video and photo, saw the media focus particularly on the role of children. Significantly, a report into what happened highlighted the role of the family as a key factor in why the riots took place (Department for Communities and Local Government 2013). The suggestion that what happens in the home can offer society a level of control was observed by Parton (2006) in examining the way in which UK governments from the mid-1990s, linked rising crime rates to the family as 'both the source and solution to a range of social problems' (James 2013: 49). This stance has been reinforced through a number of legislative policies[2] focused on 'responsible parenting' (see Muncie 2015: 257). It is simply not accurate to suggest that the link between fears about the potential of young people and incomplete parenting is a feature of the past. The home remains an important focus for the state, just as it was used in earlier societies for managing social order (Donzelot 1980; Guldberg 2009).

9.3.2 Interpretation of Structure and Images of the Child

This drive towards control comes to be represented in the moral images that are constructed within homes. As a result, a defining feature in shaping perceptions of the child draw on the need for the adult to take control, reinforcing links to the hierarchical models of the past. This is illustrated in the work of popular parenting writer, Alfie Kohn. From a psychological perspective, Kohn identifies two models of parenting. The first is the 'conditional parent', who overwhelmingly reflects the dominant themes discussed previously by managing the child and taking on the position of enforcer over every aspect of their lives.

The conditional parent, therefore, relates to themes that have been presented in earlier chapters because parental ambitions to do what is 'best' for the child sees them relying on adult assumptions of a connection between social success and adult domination. The conditional parent is driven by an image of the child and their ability to reason that results in the mechanical application of moral principles, which rely on praise on the one side and pain on the other, as children's behaviour within the home becomes *the* focus. Indeed the nature of the parents' relationship with the child is shaped as a response to how they judge the actions of their child. It creates a one-dimensional view which Kohn suggests is reflected in the tone of many parenting books and the extent to which very few of these books look beyond actions to recognise and engage with feelings (Cagan 1980). The result is that parenting books 'define a successful strategy as anything that gets kids to follow directions' (2005: 5).

High-profile examples of conditional parenting include the television shows *Super Nanny* and *Nanny 911*, in which an outsider offers parents a hierarchical structure that is defined by the adult knowing (and doing) what is 'best' (Channel 4 2005). This model draws on a developmental view of the child as a project rather than a participant within the process of managing the home. It is reiterated in other mainstream parenting models as well because many parenting techniques not only look to establish a sense of hierarchy within the home, but also complete parental control over every aspect of children's lives. Some parenting programmes define every aspect of a baby's life from when they eat and sleep to when they can be touched (Hogg and Blau 2001). This model denies any form of children's agency because their cries are perceived simply as a biological response rather than a desire to communicate. It might ensure parents have a good night's sleep, but how does this come to be reflected in the way their children make meaning about the social world and the role of their parents. What impact does this moral image of the child have on their experiences?

9.3.3 Practices

The practical reality is that home, therefore, remains a space in which morality is experienced through practices that continue to rely on roles that place adults as both the teacher and the enforcer of moral knowledge. Popular works on parenting, such as the aptly named *Mummy Coach*, focus on building up the parent, giving them the confidence to be a leader and a motivator (Thomas 2010). However, at the same time this role is continually being questioned by researchers (Silva and Smart 1999). It establishes an atmosphere in which the pressure to act and to be seen to act in a certain way towards one's children is rife. It is perhaps not surprising, therefore, that 'discipline' (as a reflection of adult dominance – see Chaps. 5 and 6) is a key theme for the home today because it is supposed to provide 'a framework within which our children can grow and flourish' (Thomas 2010: 22). The popular, conditional parenting model also reflects the ongoing reality of the way in which children and adults come to be positioned.

The ongoing place of discipline as a focus for effective parenting has been captured to some extent in the international debate around corporal punishment. It is a polarising issue, reflected by the Chair of the UN Committee on the Rights of the Child reporting that only 48 states have signed up to its provisions on ending corporal punishment (OHCHR 2016). The intensity of attitudes towards corporal punishment in many western countries, drawing from those historical representations, remains high (Saunders and Goddard 2010). Indeed, a 2015 report by the UN Human Rights Committee in the UK highlighted the continued practice of corporal punishment, and called on it to be banned in words that could not be clearer.

The state party should take practical steps, including through legislative measures where appropriate, to put an end to corporal punishment in all settings, including the home, throughout United Kingdom and all Crown dependencies and overseas territories, and repeal all existing legal defences across the state party's jurisdiction. It should encourage non-violent forms of discipline as alternatives to corporal punishment, and conduct public information campaigns to raise awareness about its harmful effects. (*Daily Telegraph* 23/7/15)

However, the following extract from a New Zealand newspaper stresses that, even when smacking is banned, practices still appear to be shaped by 'discipline' that is defined by aggression towards the child's body.

It was quite disturbing to recently hear parents on talk back radio say that now that they 'couldn't smack' they were forcing their children to eat soap, mustard or even chilli. Or they screamed and yelled at their children to get their attention. How can this help a child learn to behave? (*NZHearld* 2009)

Of course, not all children are exposed to such practices.[3] However, it is important to be actively investigating the way in which a 'curriculum of virtue' is pursued in the home, and to ask questions such as whether the child's body remains an ongoing focus for the transmission of an understanding of what is right and wrong. It is a historic way of thinking that has a strong legacy, one in which 'virtue' is something to be 'taught' by adults to the un-reasoning child. Even in homes where corporal punishment does not exist, one must still be conscious of the pervading context that encourages parents to provide an effective moral foundation through direction rather than negotiation, as seen in techniques such as 'time out', 'grounding' and many others.

9.3.4   Alternative Images: Creating Opportunities

An alternative image is offered by Kohn's (2005) second approach to parenting: the 'unconditional parent'. The unconditional parent is one who looks beyond the behaviour of the child and seeks to understand the motive and meaning behind the action. Rather than seeking to repress feelings, this approach encourages parents to engage with the child. Although the conditional parent is recognised as wanting the best for their child, Kohn views their desire to attach this to certain behaviours as essentially negative because self-esteem becomes contingent: 'the real problem may not be self esteem that's too low (I don't feel very good about myself) but self esteem that's too contingent (I feel good about myself only when)' (2005: 44). The consequence, as Kohn argues, is children lacking the ability to regulate their own feelings, which has implications for their success as a 'moral child'. If the child is encouraged, cared for, given examples and opportunities to engage then they are more likely to manage effectively the moral decisions that they are continually making (2005: 192). This connection has been noted in other research which has uncovered a link between effective engagement with children's emotions and the learning opportunities that children find the most positive (Davidov et al. 2012).

It is from that sense of engagement that one is encouraged to consider what children's participation within the home means with reference to discourses around, for example, discipline. This was considered in Chap. 8, where, for example, Solberg's work on negotiation within the home highlights approaches that reflect roles that are built on an initial recognition of equality. From this starting point, the aim is not therefore to manage the child, but rather to engage children in the management of *their* home. It moves a conversation of children's space within the home away from perceptions that their room is their only space (Lincoln 2013) to a perspective in which their house is their space. As such, 'order' within the home comes to be structured through a joint process of decision-making. It reiterates those themes from Chap. 8 in which children, when opportunities were provided, demonstrated their ability to construct meanings that informed the 'practices' within the home.

Here, by recognising that sense of individual personhood and the integrity of social agency, an alternative image of the child within the home is presented. The images vary, but the foundation on which they are based has direct implications for the nature of the practices within those spaces and the extent to which children will continually be part of reinforming the nature of the space itself. As such, we move from a traditional model of 'discipline' that is characterised by adult authority to one that more directly reflects the origins of the word itself, one in which learning is key and the adult plays the part of navigator or guide.

9.4   A Learning Process

The previous section described how embracing the notion of children as learners can challenge the dominant discourses around morality within the home. This argument is pursued here in relation to school. It is ironic that learning within schools continues to be interpreted in a similar way to discipline within the home. The relationship between corporal punishment and the child as a learner (Chap. 6) offers an illustration of this. Here, in pursuing the ideas of agency from Chap. 8, and their implications for how we think about the nature of what it means for a child to be a learner, further emphasis can be given to an alternative image, one that reflects the extent to which the individual (both adult and child) is both a being and a becoming.

9.4.1   Dominant Structural Themes

One of the major issues with challenging the moral images of the past is that schools continue to see children in terms of an evolving capacity for competence. At the end of the nineteenth century, there were challenges to the dominant thinking behind the drive for compulsory schooling. These ways of doing school, fuelled by the romantic image of the child, sought to reposition the child away from the 'mechanical learner' (Cockburn 2013) of the past. Thinkers such as Johann Pestalozzi and Fredrich Froebel proposed a different way of thinking about education (Stone 1999). This process of education did not rely on punishment, rather it recognised the child's capacity to self-regulate their learning, through a focus on the 'whole' child.[4] Tolerated while their reach was limited, these ideas were certainly not considered suitable for the masses.[5] Rather education policy can be more clearly linked to those constructed images of the child as a project that were considred in previous chapters, setting a train of thought that was to continue through the twentieth century.

Although assessing schools more than 20 years ago, Mayall (1994) concludes that children are merely objects within an institution that is preparing them for the adult world. Under the heading of 'Contextual factors influencing learning and behaviour' (1994: 125), she describes schools as spaces of:

- Socialisation as prescription
- Adult authority in context of institutional norms
- Adult construction of child as project
- Child construction of self as object

- (ibid.)

Notably, despite this assessment being dated, these factors still have relevance to the researcher, practitioner and wider society (Brooks 2012; Wrigley et al. 2012). As such these headings present schools in terms of an ongoing one-dimensional model of socialisation, one that is firmly rooted in a understading of reason that limits or restricts children's capacity. Consequently, Mayall's analysis highlights succinctly how the processes for doing school continues to be influenced by a set of assumptions that can be related directly to themes from the past.

9.4.2   Interpretation of Structure and Images of the Child

The view in the previous section reflects school as a corporate project. However, it is also really important to note the extent to which individual schools have a unique structure, with particular constructed meanings that shape children's experiences. This is reflected in Connolly's work (1998, 2004) on racism and class within schools (see Chaps. 3 and 4). It investigated the extent to which the teachers drew on the wider culture of the community in structuring the culture within school and the classroom in a London primary school.

[I]t appeared to be …that the broader discourses on 'race', crime and the inner city that were manifest within Manor Park had a tendency to influence and shape some of the teachers' practices. The difficulties faced by these teachers in relation to order and control appeared at times to resonate quite closely with their general perception of the street-wise and harden male living in the estate. Arguably these in turn provided the discursive frame through which some teachers' experiences came to be lived and understood. To the extent that these discourses were themselves refracted through the racist stereotypes relating to the perceived troublesome and violent nature of the Black male in particular, it was not surprising that Black boys in the school tended to be rendered acutely visible at times of crisis. In this, it could be argued that the more the teacher was forced to act spontaneously and thus was denied the opportunity to investigate and discern which child was the main culprit for any misdemeanour, the more these radicalised discourses had a tendency to encourage some teachers to focus on Black children in the sea of faces at assembly or in the classroom. (Connolly 1998: 78)

It is the association between 'context', 'setting' and the moral image of the child which stands out so clearly. Not only does the institution of school allow such thinking, in many ways it encourages it, because it offers a means to ensure continued management through a perspective, based on a particular image of the moral child, that this is the most appropriate 'educational' course of action to take. Indeed a 2015 report by the Institute of Education reflected on the pervasiveness of teachers' assessments of performance based on perceptions of the child's background: 'the research found that pupils from disadvantaged backgrounds tend to be perceived by teachers as less able than their more advantaged peers, despite getting equivalent scores in tests' (*Guardian* 9/6/15).

By positioning children as objects affected by a one-dimensional socialisation perspective that fundamentally draws on a particular understanding of children's capacity to reason, schools become more about managing the child rather than any real attempt to further them as learners (Dweck 2006; Brooks 2012). From a moral perspective, this is powerfully summed up in John Taylor Gatto's (2005) challenge to the education system: 'the truth is that schools don't really teach anything except how to obey orders' (2005: 21). Gatto suggests that this view extends throughout the education system,[6] creating a particular structural reality within which children experience school.

9.4.3 Practices

A consequence of this image, for Gatto, is the extent to which it results in an ongoing desire to see supervision as the key focus of children's learning. As such, Gatto reflects on just how much time children actually have left to themselves.

> Out of 168 hours in each week my children sleep 56. That leaves them 112 hours a week out of which to fashion a self. According to recent reports children watch 55 hours of television a week. That leaves them with 57 hours a week in which to grow up. My children attend school for 30 hours a week, use about eight hours getting ready for and travelling to and from school, and spend an average of seven hours a week in homework – a total of 45 hours. During that time they are under constant surveillance. They have no private time or private space and are disciplined if they try to assert individuality in the use of time or space. That leaves them 12 hours a week out of which to create a unique consciousness. (2005: 25–26)

The need for supervision and its place in a 'learning environment' sits alongside a range of other discussions: for example, the age at which children should start school, the length of the school day (*Guardian* 17/3/2016) and the role of after-school activities (*Telegraph* 2007). In a similar way to the discussion on discipline in the previous section, fears about children's potential as a threat to the status quo become a defining feature in how learning comes to be structured, and indeed practised.

This is illustrated in a policy initiative in England that sees troubled families 'turned around'. A successful family is a family in which 'all children have been back in school for a year when they were previously truanting or excluded, and youth crime and antisocial behaviour has been significantly cut across the whole family' (*Guardian* 10/3/2015). The implication of this report is conveyed in the association between children attending school and a reduction in crime, satisfying the dominant discourse about the threat that children pose. Notably, despite an investment of £1.3on a follow up report has suggested this approach has had 'no discernable impact' (Guardian 8/8/2016). A determination in Western society to see children in school was highlighted by another case of a US women who died whilst in prison for non-payment of truancy fines (*Guardian* 2014). Not only does this case show the state's desire to see that attendance is maintained, but also that the blame for non-compliance should be focused on the parent.[7] The fear, reflected in these illustrations, is that without school society opens itself up to the threat that the child poses. The link between school and its role in protecting the child (and most importantly us) from their own bad behaviour is clear. It invites further questions about the desire of some governments to continue to reduce the age that children start school (*Guardian* 16/4/2014). Yet again, these policies are particularly focused around lower-income families (*Guardian* 4/11/2013).

It is the message of this book that much of education practice today should be examined through the lens provided by the framework in this book because it focuses on a determination to maintain social harmony, as well as the themes of virtue and reason. It is not that governments are necessarily misplaced in wanting a sense of harmony within their communities. The issue is what images of the child they are using to frame policy and practice, and how that impacts on the way in which school then comes to be structured and ultimatly experienced.[8]

9.4.4   Alternative Images: Creating Opportunities

The approach in the previous section is all about establishing separation and independence in adult–children relationships (Lee 2005). It is not surprising that Illich refers to school as the worst place for transformation: 'school is the advertising agency which makes you believe that you need the society as it is' (1972). What is surprising is that Illich was writing in 1970s. The extent to which school is still about maintaining the status quo means that the only true learning environment is one that is 'free of institutional norms' (Teamey and Hinton 2014: 31). This presents a massive challenge for the way in which we think about learning communities and the role of adults and children within them.

Lave and Wenger (1991) talk about creating 'communities of practice', which are framed by a recognition of joint enterprise, a shared repertoire of resources and mutual engagement, in order to create an environment for change. Watkins (2005) uses that sense of coming together in presenting his model for a learning community.

> [A] learning community operates on the understanding that the growth of knowledge involves individual and social processes. It aims to enhance individual learning that is both a contribution to their own learning and the group's learning, and does this through supporting individual contributions to a communal effort. (2005: 57)

What is significant about both of these models is the extent to which they challenge the roles that teacher and pupil come to play. No longer are these roles orientated by a desire for control, instead learning becomes something that is achieved in collaboration as teacher and pupil work together. It is a model that only works through recognising the bi-directional nature of the relationship between the social agent and the structure in which they find themselves, an approach in which the pupil is as much a driver in shaping the structure as the adult. The role of the adult, in keeping with arguments in Chap. 8, moves from a director of children's knowledge to a facilitator for it, as the teacher act as interpreter and guide.

This approach demands that schools do more than simply provide tokenistic opportunities for pupils to be involved. Davies et al's *Inspiring Schools* (2006) describes efforts to integrate participation into a school community. A reflection on this work highlights three ways in which children can be more involved in shaping the structure of school (Yamishita and Davies 2010). First, communication needs to involve all students. Second, the themes children are able to engage with need to be 'serious' and not secondary issues that are of not perceived importance. Third, children are to be seen as 'professionals', they are to be consulted and involved (for example, children being part of teacher evaluations). Approaches like this are a step in the right direction, but they highlight the challenge of overcoming the assumptions that shape practices in school. It is a discussion that needs to be taken further, as one considers it in relation to the curriculum of virtue that was a key focus in Chap. 6. In short, school needs to re-orientate the way in which it defines learning and to re-approach it on the basis that those who are learning are social agents (Frankel and Fowler 2016). As a result, moral curriculums become more about engaging with an understanding of what it means to participate (Cockburn 2013) in building a shared community, rather than simply about taking on character attributes that are handed down from adults. That is not to say that elements of these attributes are not of value, but they need to be recognised in the practical context of children making sense of the world around them as they manage structure in light of their agency – as they are given opportunities to 'learn to be' rather than simply being 'taught to do'.

9.5   Collaborative Citizenship

The idea, discussed above, of children and adults having joint influence in shaping the structure of settings such as school is signficant as we think about children's everyday lives. This section will consider how these themes can also be considered in relation to the neighbourhood. Beyond the confines of home and school, the neighbourhood represents a complex space, one that is full of variables and open to a range of influences. Identifying those 'opportunties', therefore, through which adults and children can establish a shared vision becomes key.

9.5.1 Dominant Structural Themes

Moral images of the child have come to direct practices largely by focusing on the need for children to be prepared for the adult world. The notion of the child as a future citizen marks the effort to see children move away from moral ignorance to 'be seen as members of society…with a legitimate and valuable voice and perspective' (Roche 1999: 479). An interesting illustration of this can be provided through looking at the UK's flirtation with the notion of a Big Society. The Big Society was a political project that had been pushed as part of an election drive by the Conservative Party approaching the 2010 elections. It offered a model for society that was about 'working hard for the common good and the national interest' (Cameron 2010). It sought to usher in a society in which politicians truly served the public and communities rather than leaving the state to solve the problems (Wells

2011). At its heart was the need to engage with and respond to the notion of the common good, one that directly extends the arguments around rights and citizenship introduced earlier in the chapter. Sandel (2010: 7), writing for a newspaper pamphlet, stated that 'if a just society requires a strong sense of community, it must first cultivate in citizens a concern for the whole, a dedication to the common good'. However, this sense of the common good was not predefined. Instead, in a similar approach to the model of structure and agency that is being presented in this book, the common good was co-produced.

> To achieve a just society, we have to reason together about the meaning of the good life and create a public culture hospitable to the disagreements that will inevitably arise. (Sandel 2010: 7)

A historical theme (see Chap. 7) is the extent to which children have been excluded from moral discourses; rules or laws were and are developed without children's input. The Big Society model seemed to be suggesting that its members should shape their notion of society together (for more, see Bacon and Frankel 2013). It, therefore, appeared to be presenting a real chance for society to engage with the child, whether on the basis of a rights agenda or indeed by treating children as social agents.

9.5.2 Images

As part of this specific effort for change, the newly elected Conservative party and its Coalition partners designed a flagship programme to promote the Big Society. By 2015, the notion of the Big Society had significantly waned, but its flagship programme, the National Citizen Service (NCS), remains (2016). In a content analysis of a range of NCS materials, Bacon, Frankel and Faulks (2013) considered the way in which these documents constructed an image of the child. Their analysis showed that the NCS programme, although well intentioned, continued to demonstrate a perception of the child that was driven by legacy fuelled discourses in which the 'image' was summed up by the word 'lack'.

9.5.3 Practices

In effect, the NCS creates a perception of virtue in which the child is being inducted into a way of thinking and being that they were previously outside of. This falls a long way short of a co-produced sense of the common good. The child needs to go through some experience if they are to reach the point where they can be fully anointed as a citizen of the Big Society or its successor. This is characterised by the sense in which the NCS presents a process that reflects a traditional rite of passage (see Van Gennep 1960) in which 16-year-old children are invited to leave their families and join a short training programme before being re-placed into their community with the task of running a project that makes a positive difference. However, rather than children's previous competence and skills being acknowledged, the model uses language that focused on 'change' and 'transformation' as their lack was replaced by knowledge that would serve them in taking up a role as a positive member of their communities, and in preparing them for the work place. Through the training programme, children would develop virtues such as resilience, confidence, respect and responsibility. Thus equipped, they could 'graduate' and by doing so be granted a passport that would grant them access to society.

> [W]e hope business will work with us on incentives and reward schemes for successful NCS graduates ... NCS graduation should eventually be a passport to the next stage of a young person's life. An essential mark on anyone's CV that employers look for. (cited in Bacon et al. 2013)

It is clear that the rhetoric surrounding the NCS was about allowing children entry into an adult world. It was about children taking on the virtues and the shared ambitions of the current members of society (those who were already citizens). After reaching a defined age and having been through this 'experience', they were recognised as 'ready' to serve society as a 'citizen'. It raises questions about the value of the education that children had previously received, despite it being a statutory part of the curriculum,[9] because this clearly was not seen as sufficient. Rather, it seems to suggest that it is only through experiencing the NCS programme that change can take place. In short, it simply reinforces an image of the child as a citizen–in-waiting, with wide-ranging implications for children's involvement and partnership in the neighbourhood (for more. see Bacon et al. 2013).

This aspect of policy represents the extent to which (moral) images of the child pervade the way society seeks to engage with children, reinforcing the sense that adults see children in terms of their 'lack'. The way of talking about the child is clearly based on a constructed notion of childhood, one that continues to limit opportunities for children's engagement. Rather, the neighbourhood (as with other settings) is a space in which adults seek to manage 'participation'. As a result, 'participation' within society is used as a building block for the future citizen who, after instruction, may then be ready to take on their part as an effective (financial) contributor to society. It is a model that is some way from viewing children as collaborators; a step that would take a fundamental reassessment of those features that inform perceived moral images of the child.

9.5.4   Alternative Images: Creating Opportunities

So are children citizens? In Chap. 7, consideration of this question informed the discussion, which has been played out in practical terms above. The discussion highlights a sense in which adults are unsure about bestowing the title of 'citizen'. Indeed, it is a title that they see as requiring some form of formal training, training that notably can only be taken once children reach a particular stage of their development. Perhaps, therefore, we need to reconsider the question. Maybe the question should be: 'Do children see themselves as citizens?'. This moves us away from a top-down approach to one that looks at children and their place in the neighbourhood from the bottom up. It is a consideration that sits at the heart of the way in which children are placed within society. The UN Convention on the Rights of the Child (UNCRC) and the rights agenda, despite their focus on the child, cannot get away from the fact that they are written from a top-down approach, with adults offering a range of 'articles' that they think reflect an acceptable childhood. Unsurprising, as discussed in Chap. 7, this agenda is defined by images of the child that

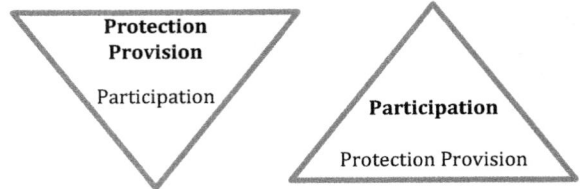

Fig. 9.1 Inverted participation triangles

have been primarily driven by provision and protection and the accompanying adult assumptions.

If the UNCRC was not driven by those adult agendas of protection and provision, but rather participation, it would offer a different perspective. In considering the relationship between children and the law, specifically in relation to Article 6, McNamee et al. (2016) suggested inverting the triangle that has dominated our approach to children and citizenship, and their place within the legal system, for so long (Fig. 9.1).

The triangle on the left shows how protection and provision have come to define participation and how it enables a model in which adults maintain control over the nature of children's engagement in society. However, by fundamentally reconfiguring this approach to one in which participation becomes the primary focus, children through their participation, become involved in shaping a collaborative agenda for *their* protection and *their* provision. By asking whether children see themselves as citizens demands that we reflect on the image of the child that we acknowledge within the neighbourhood. In effect, it offers a new starting point, one that begins with a consideration of the child's agency, providing a foundation for collaboration that has previously not existed.

This way of thinking has implications for how we view children within, for example, the justice system or in respect of high-profile social issues. An illustration of this is to ask whether the most appropriate way to engage in a moral discourse around gun ownership in the United States is through providing children with doctored accounts of fairy tales in which the key characters, rather than using their wits (or not) to escape the villains, are given guns (NRA 2016). In this approach, the image of the child relies on a traditional socialisation perspective in which children's thinking is swayed simply by their exposure to a particular point of view. This can be contrasted with the other side of the argument by which protection becomes the defining theme in terms of restricting children from any connection with guns. Both sides' approaches are too simplistic. Both are framed by a relationship with the child that is dominated by a uni-directional arrow (Chap. 2). Instead, these issues need children to be given an acknowledged role as competent social agents, one that recognises the wider structural issues that children face as they seek to make sense of the world around them. Within this, gun ownership moves from simply being understood in terms of a 'constitutional right' to an issue that is framed more by identity. It becomes a discourse that can only be addressed by engaging with the way in which people make sense of themselves in the wider context of the world around them. Fundamentally, it demands that it is only by recognising the processes of children's agency, and inviting their meaningful participation, that one can even start to understand the issues, let alone come up with a solution.

From the starting point that children are recognised with the capacity to engage, we need to acknowledge children's role in other areas of the neighbourhood. For example, in Chap. 7, we touched on children's relationship with the police and the justice system more widely. Applying the above arguments, we recognise that it is not sufficient, in searching for a response to a child's criminal behaviour, to be driven by an adult agenda. Rather, it is a process of enquiry that must be framed by the child's participation, as steps are taken to make sense of the way in which the child as a social agent has acted in the context of a particular interactional setting. It represents an approach to youth justice that challenges directly the retributive models that reflect a desire for adults to demonstrate that they are 'tough on crime', and calls for a more radical model instead. Nils Christie (1977) is one of a number who argue that, if we are to truly establish a system of justice, crime needs to be reclassified. These classifications should focus therefore on conflict, troubles, disputes, problems, harms. What is compelling about this approach is the extent to which it repositions justice in the realms of the everyday. Rather than seeing justice in terms of the need to define someone as a 'criminal', it recognises the extent to which such actions reflect wider social issues. These can be linked to a desire to acknowledge that the social agent is seeking to negotiate different interactional settings, recongising that certain actions have had a negative impact, which can only be resolved if the aggressor, the victim and society more widely can come together.

This way of thinking fundamentally challenges the reliance on age that sits at the heart of measures of responsibility within the system. Indeed, within this approach it can be argued that the age of criminal responsibility becomes meaningless. Rather, society is presented with a set of interventions that are framed within the context of the individual child's everyday, and which demand and respect the competence of the individual, as both a meaning-maker and a learner, in which difference from adults is framed by degree and not kind. As such, the engagement of the individual is not reflected by a presumed moment of moral awakening, but rather is one that can be invested in. Knowledge, therefore, should no longer simply be seen as belonging to adults; knowledge is something that children too can 'own'. This notion directly challenges the practical realities of the justice system in which models of discretion, for example, simply highlight an approach in which knowledge is power. Recognising children's agency should create opportunities to invite children to embrace *their* part in *their* communities.

The closest we have come to this approach are 'pure' models of restorative justice. The challenge for governments around the world, though, is how to incorporate such a model alongside an ongoing agenda to be seen as tough on crime. As a result, restorative justice comes to be a subsidiary of a wider model, one that allows options for 'diversion' of minor offences or as a way of restoring some sense of equilibrium for either victim or offender following sentence. Part of the issue here is that 'restorative' justice, by definition, is about trying to restore a sense of social order. However, in practice, restorative justice has demonstrated in countries such as New Zealand that it does far more than simply restore. It transforms. For such change to occur, restorative justice must be seen as much more than a 'instructional tool', rather it needs to bring social agents together with the opportunity for participation and potential transformation that that meeting provides. Within this, the image of the offender is significantly different. Rather than sitting on the edge of a process that tests the nature of their actions, they become central, and with that move a powerful statement is made about the purpose of justice and attitudes towards strengthening a sense of social harmony.

The aim here is not to paint a picture of happy endings because applying this model to themes such as child soldiers, for example, exposes additional layers that need to be understood. Instead, this book suggests that, if we are to be more effective in engaging with such issues, then the starting point must be through an image of the child that recognises their social agency and their potential as collaborators, inspiring the search for meaningful opportunities for co-operation. In many ways, it simply reflects an example that children themselves are offering through online games in which collaboration is key. In assuming online identities, children take a collaborative role in structuring their 'worlds' through games such as Minecraft. It is important that children do not feel that a virtual community is the only place where their participation is valued, as images are reconsidered and children's value to their 'real' community is acknowledged.

9.6 Closing Thoughts

By pursing the five steps set out in the Introduction (Chap. 1) this book hopes to have repositioned the child in relation to moral discourses. Perhaps both the starting point and indeed our finishing point are realisations of the implications of a bi-directional relationship between the agent and the social structure around them. For not only does this allow the researcher to pursue the way in which the individual makes sense of settings, and draws meanings from them through those elements of self, but also the extent to which the individual has the potential to contribute to structure. As such, the nature of 'opportunities' really matter because consideration is given to how far those opportunities create the space for children to truly participate.

Children's participation through meaningful opportunities creates change which has the potential to provide more relevant policy and practice. The framework offered within this book provides a basis on which that change can be considered by exploring how interactional settings come to take on constructed meanings, how the individual responds to them and the extent to which this then reinforms the wider context, with the potential to influence how that setting is experienced. The discussion has focused on a conceptual application of the framework, but it must be noted that the framework can be applied to individual settings in order to extend the analysis in relation to children's everyday interactions. An example of this is offered in Appendix 2, although extending the application of the framework marks an important next step (McNamee and Frankel forthcoming). Both conceptually and practically, therefore, the framework allows us to see, through the moral filters, the means for furthering our understanding of children's lives, whether a historical or contemporary investigation, or at a macro or micro level.

This book has shown the extent to which social constructions of childhoods carry a moral dimension, one that can be considered in relation to reason, virtue and social harmony. The results are images which informed and inform the settings in which children find themselves. An image of the child, whether children are seen as co-constructors or not, will always be present in any setting. In the same way, a setting will carry a constructed image of any adults that are present: for example, what it means to be a father within a home, what it means to be a woman in the boardroom – both of which will have an impact on how the individual makes meanings in those social arenas. The question here, however, is the extent to which those settings remain a province in which adults control the wider contextual themes and forces that are allowed to permeate, framing any experiences.[10] Indeed, adults maintain control over the structural form of so many of the settings that children find themselves in. Adults position themselves as the membrane through which wider social forces or parameters (see Chap. 3) come to have meaning in shaping images of the child and related practices. For change to happen, children need to share in the role of defining social settings and creating the contextual backdrop – children need to be seen as collaborators in shaping childhoods. An illustration of this was given in Chap. 9 in relation to the South African radio project. It reflected interactional spaces that were initially marked by adults limiting children's opportunities to collaborate because such practices were adult-defined, based on adult-assumed images of the child. However, as a result of the project and the opportunities it created, adults repositioned children so that they were increasingly recognised as offering a valid contribution (they became part of the membrane) that informed how both the image of the child and the practices towards them took shape in both homes and school.

Throughout writing this book what has become increasingly clear to me is the extent to which any investigation of childhoods must be seen through a lens in which childhoods are negotiated; negotiated by adults and negotiated by children. This has become particularly obvious in relation to the three recurring themes of reason, virtue and social harmony, and their treatment in Chaps. 5, 6 and 7 . This investigation was then followed up in Chaps. 8 and 9 through the themes of personal integrity, children as learners and children as collaborators have offered a means to reflect on the reality of this daily negotiation and its relevance to children's everyday lives.

To challenge dominant discourses of children and morality, one must first recognise the extent to which a framework for analysis must be focused by an active engagement with children's personal lives. Here those personal elements, including emotions, offer a means to consider how children are responding to the social world through a consideration of self and others. Within this, there are many layers that can be attached to an investigation of emotions, and how these need to be read with reference to both the 'context' of the interactional setting and the range of personal elements that the individual brings to the interaction. Through seeking to position these elements, the child makes meanings in relation to what is seen as acceptable. As a socialising process, it demands adult attention to, first, an acknowledgement of children's personal lives and, second, an understanding of how they interact with it, recognising that the individual will be drawing on a body of 'emotional' experiences in assimilating a sense of social order and making sense of the world around them.

Another key theme in challenging traditional discourses to morality is a consideration of the importance of 'learning'. This book promotes an approach to learning that is driven more by the individual seeking to make sense of their complex social world than the need for direct adult instruction. It reflects a model in which children are given opportunities to 'learn to be' (in contrast to simply being 'taught to do'). Within this, relationships are important because children perceptively recognise that much of an understanding of the world is related to their ability to manage the social. Relationships, therefore, provide a means for not only building experiences implicitly, but also for developing knowledge explicitly. A relationship with an adult who is perceived as having a good understanding of the individual is, therefore, an important ingredient for children in developing their sense of social awareness. Moral images of the child need to take into account key relationships and, as a result, question their effectiveness as channels through which the child feels they can gather the knowledge about right and wrong that they need to successfully navigate their social world. This was considered with reference to adults in the three key spaces of home, school and the neighbourhood. It raises questions, for example, in relation to school, and the extent to which we continue to rely on it as a site for virtue education via a defined curriculum. Perhaps a more personalised programme of learning is needed, one that accommodates focused opportunities for individuals to work with adults with whom they have a relationship of mutual respect, to develop understandings that reflect how they as an individual draw on their 'personal elements' in responding to the interactional settings that they find themselves in. This is just as relevant to the neighbourhood. For in such settings, as we have seen, right and wrong (in its applied form) comes to be seen through a unique prisim of individual factors. It is, therefore, only by engaging with the individual on that basis that virtue education can be truly effective as the individual comes to give meaning to what is 'right' through specific reference to their personal life in the context of a particular interactional setting.

In a formal environment, this has implications for our approach within, for example, the legal system. Already a more personalised model is forming part of court procedures. However, as the arguments in this book suggest, these initiatives must continue to be encouraged, in terms of 'justice' and the child's voice carrying the weight that it should. But, perhaps this is most important in facilitating the way in which the individual child is able to relate to the relevance of the legal system. Is it an infrastructure built by adults for adults? This is a question that can be posed in relation to the practices in the range of arenas within which children live their lives. This, of course, is linked to the third theme that makes up the challenge to the dominant images of the child that have impacted moral discourses: alongside agency one must look for children's participation in setting moral agendas. This is to be considered at a range of levels, from a moral framework that makes sense at home, to a more active awareness that children must be seen to be involved in framing community-wide conceptions of a 'common good'. That is not to say that children do not inform structure at present. However, because of particular images of the moral child, the extent to which children's agency is able to reinform the policies and practices through which a community agenda is expressed is at best limited. The fact is that children are informing a moral agenda within the settings where they interact and as a society we need to find ways that allow children's participation to have an effect on those wider structural forces that inform social life. The continuity of a moral order is not simply the job of passing a baton of virtues from one generation to the next, adult to future adult. Rather, it is about each society finding ways to communicate so that one might learn from the past, but also from the present as adults and children both take their place in these discourses.

Moral images of the child must change. By applying a moral filter to structure we can trace the moral images of the child through history and assess their place in thinking today. This analysis provides a defined foundation on which to mount a challenge. What this book has argued, adding to a developing body of work, is that a recognition of the child as a social agent offers a *new* way of thinking about children and morality. Within this, we begin to recognise the child's skills and also the learning processes with which they are engaged as they seek to extend their knowledge in response to different interactional settings. A moral dimension to our understanding of children and society must find a place at the centre of our desire to engage with children's everyday lives, because only then can we ever hope to make sense of the processes that inform, shape and produce social action.

It is by recognising agency as the *contextually mediated capacity of the individual to make meanings that inform their actions, that are relationally situated and morally constituted and which are framed within a range of elements that make up children's personal lives* that one can start to really understand what it means to negotiate childhoods.

Notes

1. In the final chapter of their edited collection they reflect on seven key themes linked to children's participation (2010: 356).
2. James and James (2004) reflect on the extent to which government demonstrated its concerns for the effectiveness of the family in fulfilling their role towards managing the child. With reference to 'Supporting Families', a 2002 initiative, they highlight how, for the first time, the government sought to take on a role within the family (notably in contrast to the position of state and family discussed at the start of Chapter 5).
3. Jutengren and Palmerus (2002) highlight the differences in approaches to parenting techniques between US and Swedish fathers. Although there are significant similarities, their research reflects on the greater tendency of fathers in the US to resort to 'punishment', a way of practising that, the authors argue, is shaped to an extent by US legislation.
4. A minority report as part of a Royal Commission in 1888 referred to the need to educate the 'whole' child. Cockburn underlines this by quoting James Roscoe's argument for the need to 'supplement our present one sided system of education, which relies on books and on authority, by the introduction of studies which can call into activity mental and physical capabilities that have hitherto lain dormant' (quoted in Cockburn 2013: 95).
5. Cockburn (2013) links this to a desire to assert national identity at the start the twentieth century. In France, this movement saw Durkheim's Sociology of Education as a tool to support educators in teaching children conformity to moral codes. In Britain, it manifested itself in the continuing domination of the working classes through the education system, as well as through the promotion of empire and in the virtues of glory: 'children in schools and homes were taught about heroes and glories of the homeland' (Cockburn 2013: 97), repeating a very similar approach to the use of stories in ancient Greece.
6. Gatto reflects on this through seven different 'lessons', starting with confusion. The others are class position, indifference, emotional dependency,

intellectual dependency, provisional self esteem and the fact that 'one can't hide' (Gatto 2005).

7. A similar theme has emerged in England over parents wishing to take their children on holiday during the school term, with 16,430 prosecutions in 2014 (*Guardian* 12/8/2015).

8. Gatto (2005) notes the extent to which home school is offering children the opportunity to direct their learning with implications for levels of attainment, which he argues are far higher than the state system. It is an area, however, that needs further investigation.

9. In 1999 citizenship was added to the curriculum in England, making it statutory for all secondary school pupils from 2002.

10. It is only in the last 60 or so years that women have been seen as having a valid place in managing those parameters and shaping social institutions in a more formal and accepted way. It is important to make the distinction between the formal and informal nature of interactional settings. In a formal sense, settings have been defined by a hierarchical model of social roles. However, this does not necessarily reflect what has happened in specific interactional spaces themselves. Informally, children and women have always had the capacity as social agents to shape the settings that they are part of, although these would have had to be negotiated or managed in the context of particular social norms.

Bibliography

ABC Online. (2015, September 8). *South Australia Government working on Stolen Generation compensation scheme.* http://www.abc.net.au/news/2015-09-09/south-australia-working-on-stolen-generation-compensation-scheme/6760460.

Alanen, L. (2011). Generational order. In J. Qvortrup, W. Corsaro, & M. Honig (Eds.), *The Palgrave handbook of childhood studies.* Basingstoke: Palgrave Macmillan.

Alanen, L., & Mayall, B. (Eds.). (2001). *Conceptualizing child adult relations.* London: RoutledgeFalmer.

Alexander, J. (1988). *Action and its environments.* New York: Columbia University Press.

All Party Parliamentary Group for Children. (2014). *"It's all about trust": Building good relationships between children and the police.* London: National Children's Bureau.

Allen, M. (1997). *Textbook on criminal law* (4th ed.). London: Blackstones.

Amos, H., & Laing, A. (1979). *These were the Greeks.* Cheltenham: Stanley Thornes.

Aquinas, T. (1880). *Summa Theologica.* Paris: Bloud.

Archard, D. (2004). *Children: Rights and childhood.* London: Routledge.

Archer, M. (1982). Morphogenisis versus structuration: On combining structure and action. *British Journal of Sociology, 33,* 455–483.

© The Editor(s) (if applicable) and The Author(s) 2017

265

S. Frankel, *Negotiating Childhoods*, Studies in Childhood and Youth,

DOI 10.1057/978-1-137-32349-1

Aries, P. (1962). *Centuries of childhood: A social history of family life*. New York: Vintage Books.

Aristotle. (1999). *The Nicomachean ethics* (Rev. ed.). Cambridge, MA: Harvard University Press.

Arthur, J. (Ed.). (2010). *Citizens of character: New directions in citizenship and values education*. Exeter: Imprint Academic.

Arthur, J., Harding, R., & Godfrey, R. (2009). *Citizens of character – The values and character dispositions of 14–16 year olds in the Hodge Hill constituency*. Project Report. University of Birmingham, Birmingham. http://www.learning-forlife.org.uk/research-projects/learning-for-life-research-reports/view/?id=20.

Axtell, J. L. (Ed.). (1960). *The educational writings of John Locke*. Cambridge: Cambridge University Press.

Aye Maung, N. (1995). *Young people, victimisation and the police* (Home Office Research Study No. 140). London: HMSO.

Ayers, W. (1997/98). The criminalisation of youth. *Rethinking Schools, Online 12*(2, Winter). http://www.rethinkingschools.org/archive/12_02/kids.shtml.

Aynesley-Green, A. (2007). *11 million reflections on children in conflict with the law*. Speech given 27 November 2007.

Bacon, K. (2010). *Twins in society: Parents, bodies, space and talk*. New York: Palgrave Macmillan.

Bacon, K., & Frankel, S. (2014). Rethinking children's citizenship: Negotiating structure, shaping meanings. *The International Journal of Children's Rights, 22*(1), 21–42.

Bacon, K., Frankel, S., & Faulks, K. (2013). Building the 'Big Society': Exploring representations of young people and citizenship in the National Citizen Service. *International Journal of Children's Rights, 21*, 1–22.

Bailey, R. (2011). *Letting children be children*. London: Home Office.

Bainham, A. ([1998] 2005). *Children and the modern law*. Bristol: Jordan.

Ball, C. (2004, March). Youth justice? Half a century of responses to youth offending. *Criminal Law Review*, 167–180.

Bandalli, S. (1998). Abolition of the presumption of Doli Incapax and the criminalisation of children. *The Howard Journal of Criminal Justice, 37*(2), 114–123.

Barrie, J. M. (1989). *Peter Pan*. Richmond Hill: Scholastic-TAB Publications.

Barton, J. (2003). *Understanding old testament ethics*. London: John Knox Press.

BBC. (2010, February 18). *Stop sexualising children, says David Cameron*. http://news.bbc.co.uk/2/hi/uk_news/politics/8521403.stm.

BBC. (2015, July 13). *Can a school prevent extremism?* http://www.bbc.com/news/uk-33486339.

BBC. (2016, January 20). *Lancashire terrorist house row not a mistake.* http://www.bbc.com/news/uk-england-lancashire-35354061.

Bell, J. (1999). Appealing for justice for young people: A critical analysis of the Crime and Disorder Bill. In B. Goldson (Ed.), *Youth justice: Contemporary policy and practice.* Aldershot: Ashgate.

Bell, S. (2007). *Young offenders and youth justice.* Toronto: Nelson.

Bentham, J. (1879). *An introduction to the principles of morals and legislation.* Oxford: The Clarendon Press.

Bergmann, T. (1998). Introduction morality in discourse. *Research on Language and Social Interaction, 31*(3 and 4), 279–294.

Bernstein, B. (1975). Open schools, open society. In *Class codes and control* (Vol. 3). London: Rutledge and Paul and Kegan.

Bird, W., & Rahfaldt, M. (2011). Children and the media: Voices worth hearing? In L. Jameison, R. Bray, A. Viziers, L. Lake, S. Pendlebury, & C. Smith (Eds.), *South African child gauge 2010/11.* Cape Town: Children's Institute, University of Cape Town.

Birnbaum, R., Canada Department of Justice, & Canadian Electronic Library (Firm). (2009). *The voice of the child in separation/divorce mediation and other alternative dispute resolution processes: A literature review.* Toronto: Canada Department of Justice.

Blackburn, S. (2008). *The Oxford dictionary of philosophy* (2nd, rev. ed.). Oxford: Oxford University Press.

Blake, W. (1971). *Songs of innocence.* New York: Dover Publications.

Bluebond-Langner, M. (1978). *The private world of dying children.* Princeton: Princeton University Press.

Bonner, K. (1998). *Power and parenting.* Basingstoke: Macmillan Press.

Bourdieu, P. (1971). *Knowledge and control: New directions for sociology of education.* Oxford: Macmillan.

Bourdieu, P. (1977). *Outline of a theory of practice.* Cambridge: Cambridge University Press.

Bourdieu, P. (1990). *The logic of practice.* London: Polity.

Bradley, K. (1991). *Discovering the Roman family.* Oxford: Oxford University Press.

Brandt, R. (1996). *Facts, values and morality.* Cambridge: Cambridge University Press.

Brofrenbrenner, U. (1994). Ecological models of human development. In *International encyclopaedia of education 3.* Oxford: Elsevier.

Brooks, D. (2012). *The social animal: The hidden sources of love, character, and achievement* (Random House trade pbk. ed.). New York: Random House Trade Paperbacks.

Brown, S. (1998). *Understanding youth crime: Listening to youth?* Buckingham: Open University Press.

Brunson, R., & Miller, J. (2006). Gender, race and urban policing: The experience of African American youths. *Gender and Society, 20*(4), 531–552.

Buckingham, D. (1993). Television and the definition of childhood. In D. Buckingham (Ed.), *Reading audiences*. Manchester/New York: Manchester University Press.

Buckingham, D. (1996). *Moving images*. Manchester: Manchester University Press.

Bunting, L., Webb, M., & Healy, J. (2010). In two minds? – Parental attitudes towards physical punishment in the UK. *Children and Society, 24*(5), 359–370.

Burman, E. (1995). *Deconstructing developmental psychology*. London: Routledge.

Burnyeat, M. (1980). Aristotle on leaning to be good. In A. Rorty (Ed.), *Essays on Aristotle's ethics*. Berkley: University of California Press.

Butler, I., Robinson, M., & Scanlan, L. (2005). *Children and decision making*. London: National Children's Bureau.

Cagan, E. (1980, January/February). The positive parent: Raising children the scientific way. *Social Policy, 10*, 41–48.

Calhoun, G. (1927). *The growth of criminal law in ancient Greece*. Berkley: University of California.

Cambridge Primary Review. (2009). *Children, their world, their education*. London: Routledge.

Cameron, D. (2010). *Big society speech*. Available at: http://www.number10.gov.uk/news/ big-society-speech/.

Carlen, P., & Morgan, R. (1999). *Crime unlimited? Questions for the 21st century*. Macmillan: Basingstoke.

Casey, J. (1989). *The history of the family*. Oxford: Basil Blackwell.

Catholic Church. (2016). *Amoris Laetitia, Joy of Love*.

Cavidino, P. (1997). Goodbye Doli we must leave you. *Child and Family Law Quarterly, 9*(2), 165–171.

Centre for Social Justice. (2014). *Girls and gangs*. London: Centre for Social Justice.

Channel 4. (2005). *Supernally*. London: Hodder and Staughton.

Children's Society. (2015). *The good childhood report 2015*. London: The Children's Society.

Christensen, P. (2002a). Why more quality time is not on the top of children's lists: The qualities of time for children. *Children and Society, 16*, 77–88.

Christensen, P. (2002b). Why more quality time is not on the top of children's lists: The qualities of time for children. *Children and Society, 16*, 77–88.

Christensen, P., & James, A. (Eds.). (2000). *Research with children: Perspectives and practices.* London: Routledge.

Christie, N. (1977). Conflicts as property. *British Journal of Criminology, 17*(1), 1–15.

Chua, A. (2011). *Battle hymn of a tiger mum.* New York: Penguin.

CNN. (2011). *Corporal punishment polices around the world.* http://www.cnn.com/2011/WORLD/asiapcf/11/08/country.comparisons.corporal.punishment/.

Cockburn, T. (1998). Children and citizenship in Britain: A case for socially interdependent model of citizenship. *Childhood, 5*(1), 99–117.

Cockburn, T. (2013). *Rethinking children's citizenship.* Basingstoke: Palgrave Macmillan.

Cohen, A. K. (1955). *Delinquent boys: The culture of the gang.* New York: Free-Press.

Cohen, S. ([1972] 2002). *Folk devils and moral panics.* London: Paladin.

Cohen, A. P. (Ed.). (1986). *Symbolising boundaries.* Manchester: Manchester University Press.

Cohen, A. P. (1994a). *Self consciousness: An alternative anthropology of identity.* London: Routledge.

Cohen, A. P. (1994b). *Self consciousness: An alternative anthropology of identity.* London: Routledge.

Collingwood, R. G. (2013). In D. Boucher & T. Smith (Eds.), *An autobiography and other writings, with essays on Collingwoods life and words.* Oxford: Oxford University Press.

Connolly, P. (1998). *Racism, gender identities and young children: Social relations in a multi ethnic, inner city primary school.* London: Routledge.

Connolly, P. (2004). *Boys and schooling in the early years.* London: RoutledgeFalmer.

Connolly, P. (2006). The masculine habitus as distributed cognition: A case study of 5- to 6-year-old boys in an English inner-city, multi-ethnic primary school. *Children & Society, 20*(2), 140–152.

Cook, D. (2011). Children as consumers. In J. Qvortrup, W. Corsaro, & M. Honig (Eds.), *The Palgrave handbook of childhood studies.* Basingstoke: Palgrave Macmillan.

Cooley, C. H. (1964a). *Human nature and the social order.* New York: Schocken.

Cooley, C. H. (1964b). *Human nature and the social order.* New York: Schocken.

Corsaro, W. (1985). *Friendship and peer culture in the early years.* Norwood: Ablex.

Corsaro, W. (2005). *The sociology of childhood* (2nd ed.). Thousand Oaks: Pine Forge Press.

Coveney, P. (1957). *Poor monkey: The child in literature*. London: Rockliff.

Crick, M. (1976). *Explorations in language and meaning*. London: Malaby Press.

Cromdal, J., & Theolander, M. (2015). *Morality in practice: Exploring childhood, parenthood and schooling in everyday Life*. Sheffield: Equinox.

Cunningham, H. (1995). *Children and childhood in Western society since 1500*. London: Pearson Longman.

Cunningham, H. (2006). *The invention of childhood*. London: BBC.

Cunningham, S., & Lavalette, M. (2004). Active citizens or irresponsible truants? School students strike against the war. *Critical Social Policy, 24*(2), 255–269.

Curtis, S., & Boultwood, M. (1977). *A short history of educational ideas*. Slough: University Tutorial Press.

Daily Mail. (2011, August 10). *British youths are 'the most unpleasant and violent in the world': Damning verdict of writer as globe reacts to riots*. http://www.dailymail.co.uk/news/article-2024486/UK-RIOTS-2011-British-youths-unpleasant-violent-world.html.

Damon, W. (1990). *The moral child: Nurturing children's natural moral growth*. New York: The Free Press.

Danby, S., & Theobald, M. (2012). *Disputes in everyday life: Social and moral orders of children and young people*. Emerald Group Publishing Ltd: Bingley.

Darwin, C. (1877). A biographical sketch of an infant. *Mind, 2*(7), 285–294.

Das, M., Verma, R., Ghosh, S., Ciaravino, S., Jones, K., O'Connor, B., & Miller, E. (2015). Community mentors as coaches: Transforming gender norms through cricket among adolescent males in urban India. *Gender & Development, 23*(1), 61–75.

Davidov, M., Grusec, J., & Wolfe, J. (2012). Mothers' knowledge of their children's evaluations of discipline: The role of types of discipline and misdeed, and parenting practices. *Merrill Palmer Quarterly, 58*(3), 314–340.

Davies, L., Williams, C., & Yamashita, H. (2006). *Inspiring schools: Impact and outcomes: Taking up the challenge of pupil participation* (Review for Carnegie young people initiative). London: Carnegie Trust.

Davis, K. (2011). *"Turning out": Young people, being and becoming*. Unpublished PhD Thesis, University of Manchester.

Davis, P., & Park, D. (1987). *No way: The nature of the impossible*. New York : W.H. Freeman.

de Mause, L. (1974). *The history of childhood*. New York: Psychohistory Press.

Department for Communities and Local Government. (2013). *Government response to the riots, communities and victims panel's final report*, London.

Department of Education. (2013a). *Citizenship programme of study*. London: Department for Education. https://www.gov.uk/government/publications/national-curriculum-in-england-citizenship-programmes-of-study.

Department of Education. (2013b). *National curriculum in England: Primary curriculum*. London: Department for Education. https://www.gov.uk/government/collections/national-curriculum.

Devine, D., & Kelly, M. (2006). I just don't want to get picked on by anybody: Dynamics of inclusion and exclusion in a newly multi-ethnic Irish primary school. *Children & Society, 20*(2), 128–139.

Dixon, S. (1992). *The Roman family*. Baltimore: John Hopkins University Press.

Dobash, R. E., & Dobash, R. (1979). *Violence against wives: A case against the patriarchy*. New York: Free Press.

Dobash, R. E., & Dobash, R. (1992). *Women, violence, and social change*. New York/London: Routledge.

Donaldson, M., & Hughes, M. (1979). The use of hiding games for the studying co-ordination of viewpoints. *Educational Review, 31*, 133–140.

Donaldson, M., & McGarrigle, J. (1975). Conversation accidents. *Cognition, 3*(34), 1–50.

Donzelot, J. (1980). *The policing of families*. New York: Pantheon Books.

Douglas, M. (1966). *Purity and danger*. London: Routledge and Kegan.

Douglas, M. (1972, March 9). Speech, class and Basil Berstein. In *e Listener no 2241*. London: BBC.

Douglas, M. (1973a). *Rules and meaning*. Harmondsworth: Penguin.

Douglas, M. (1973b). *Natural symbols*. London: Barrie and Rockcliff.

Drotner, K. (2011). Children and digital media: Online, on site, on the go. In J. Qvortrup, W. Corsaro, & M. Honig (Eds.), *The Palgrave handbook of childhood studies*. Basingstoke: Palgrave Macmillan.

Dunn, J. (1988). *The beginnings of social understanding*. Oxford: Blackwells.

Dunn, J. (1999). Young people understanding of other young people. In A. Woodhead (Ed.), *Making sense of social development*. London: Routledge.

Durham, M. (1991). *Moral crusades: Family and morality in the Thatcher years*. Washington Square, N.Y.: New York University Press.

Durkheim, E. (1951). *Suicide, a study in sociology*. New York: Free Press.

Durkheim, E. (1964). *The division of labour in society*. London: Macmillan.

Durkheim, E. (1978). *On institutional analysis* (ed. & trans: Traugott, M.). London: University of Chicago Press.

Durkheim, E. (1979). *Essays on morals and education*. London: Routledge.

Durkheim, E., & Lukes, S. (1982). *The rules of sociological methods: And selected texts on sociology and its methods*. London: Macmillan.

Dweck, C. (2006). *Mindset*. London: Constable and Robinson.

Elias, N. (1978). *What is sociology?* London: Hutchinson.

Elkin, F. (1960). *Children and society: The process of socialisation*. New York: Random House.

Emirbayer, M., & Mische, A. (1998). What is agency? *American Journal of Sociology, 103*, 962–1023.

Euripides. (1963). *Medea and other plays* (trans: Vellacott, P.). London: Penguin.

Faulks, K. (1998). *Citizenship in modern Britain*. Edinburgh: Edinburgh University Press.

Faurehold, J. (2010). Children and their life experiences. In G. Llewellyn, R. Traustadóttir, D. McConnell, & H. Björg Sigurjónsdóttir (Eds.), *Parents with intellectual disabilities: Past, present and futures*. Chichester: John Wiley & Sons, Ltd.

Fielding, S. (2001) Walk on the left. In S. Aitken (Ed.), *Geographies of young people*. London: Routledge.

Finch, J. (1989). *Family obligations and social change*. Cambridge: Polity Press.

Finch, J., & Mason, J. (1993). *Negotiating family responsibilities*. London: Routledge.

Fingerson, L. (2005). Agency and the body in adolescent menstrual talk. *Childhood, 12*(1), 91–111.

Fletcher, A. (2008). *Growing up in England: The experience of childhood, 1600–1914*. London: Yale University Press.

Fortin, J. ([1998] 2009). *Children's rights and the developing law*. London: Macmillan.

Foucault, M. (1977). *Discipline and punish: The birth of prisons*. London: Penguin.

Foucault, M. (1988). *Madness and civilization: A history of insanity in the age of reason*. New York: Random House.

Fox, M. (Ed.). (1949). *Fundamental principles of the metaphysics of morals*. Indianapolis: Merrill.

Franchi, V. (2008). The rights of the child and the good of the learners. *Childhood, 15*(2), 157–176.

Frankel, S. (2009). *Streetwise*. London: Jessica Kingsley.

Frankel, S. (2012). *Children morality and society*. Basingstoke: Palgrave Macmillan.

Frankel, S. (2014). Researching social agency and morality. In O. Saracho (Ed.), *Handbook of research methods in early childhood education* (Vol. II). Charlotte: Information Age Publishing.

Frankel, S., & Fowler, J. (2015). 'The social learning agenda – Briefing paper – For All Party Parliamentary Group For children. *Scholarship at Western*.

http://ir.lib.uwo.ca/do/search/?q=sam%20frankel&start=0&cont
ext=674312.

Frankel, S., & Fowler, J. (2016). *How to take your school on a journey to outstanding*. Church Stretton: EquippingKids.

Frankel, S., McNamee, S., & Pomfret, A. (2015). Approaches to promoting ideas about children's rights and participation: Can the education of undergraduate students contribute to raising the visibility of the child in relation to child participation in Canada? *Canadian Journal of Children's Rights, 2*(1), 26–47.

Franklin, B., & Petley, J. (1996). Killing the age of innocence: Newspaper reporting of the death of James Bulger. In J. Pilcher & S. Wagg (Eds.), *Thatchers children*. London: Falmer.

Freeman, M. (1997) *The moral status of children*. The Hague: Martinus Nijhoff Publishers.

Frost, N. (2011). *Rethinking children and families: The relationship between childhood, families and the state*. London: Continuum. See Photo of useful page.

Garnier, P. (2014). Childhood as a question of critiques and justifications: Insights into Boltanski's sociology. *Childhood, 21*(4), 447–460.

Gatto, J. T. (2005). *Dumbing us down: The hidden curriculum of compulsory schooling*. Gabriola Island: New Society Publishers.

Gennep, A. v. (1960). *The rites of passage*. Chicago: University of Chicago Press.

Gert, B. (2011). The definition of morality. *Stanford Encyclopaedia of Philosophy*. http://plato.stanford.edu/entries/morality-definiton. Accessed 28 May 2013.

Giddens, A. (1979). *Central problems in social theory*. London: Macmillan.

Gilligan, C. (1982). *In a different voice: Psychological theory and women's development*. Cambridge, MA: Harvard University Press.

Globe and the Mail. (2015, October 1). *Sex education protests five birth to new private schools in Toronto*. http://www.theglobeandmail.com/news/national/sex-education-protests-give-birth-to-new-private-schools-in-toronto/article2 6608144/?service=mobile.

Goebel, J. (1976). *Felony and misdemeanor: A study in the history of criminal law*. Philadelphia: University of Pennsylvania Press.

Goffman, E. (1969). *The presentation of the self in everyday life*. London: Allen Lane.

Goodwin, M. (2006a). *The hidden world of girls: Games stance status and exclusion*. Oxford: Blackwell.

Goodwin, M. (2006b). *The hidden world of girls: Games stance status and exclusion*. Oxford: Blackwell.

Green, C. (2006). *New toddler training*. London: Vermillion.

Guardian. (1993, February 20). *Heysel, Hillsborough and now this*.

Guardian. (2012, March 1). *Accusations of witchcraft are part of a growing pattern of child abuse in UK.* http://files.ccpas.co.uk/presscuttings/010312TheGuardianSP.pdf.

Guardian. (2013a, November 4). *School should admit children at age of two or three, says Ofsted chief.*

Guardian. (2013b, November 4). *Schools should admit children at age of two or three says Ofsted.*

Guardian. (2014, April 16). *Compulsory school age in danger of becoming two, survey shows.*

Guardian. (2015a, March 10). *More than 105,000 households 'helped by troubled families programme.*

Guardian. (2015b, August 12). *More parents in England prosecuted for taking children out of school.* http://www.theguardian.com/education/2015/aug/12/increase-parents-england-prosecuted-taking-children-out-of-school.

Guardian. (2015c, June 9). *Children from poorer families perceived by teachers as less able says study.*

Guardian. (2015d, June 9). *All schools must promote 'British Values' says Michael Gove.*

Guardian. (2015e, March 5). *Islamic state trains per child soldiers in doctrine of hate.* http://www.theguardian.com/world/2016/mar/05/islamic-state-trains-purer-child-killers-in-doctrine-of-hate.

Guardian. (2016a, August 8). *Troubled families scheme has had no discernible impact.* https://www.theguardian.com/society/2016/aug/08/13bn-troubled-families-scheme-has-had-no-discernible-impact.

Guardian. (2016b, March 17). *Longer school hours.* http://www.theguardian.com/commentisfree/2016/mar/17/longer-school-hours-george-osborne-budget.

Guldberg, H. (2009a). *Reclaiming childhood: Freedom and play in an age of fear.* New York: Routledge.

Guldberg, H. (2009b). *Reclaiming childhood: Freedom and play in an age of fear.* New York: Routledge.

Gutman, L., & Schoon, I. (2013). *The impact of non-cognitive skills on outcomes for young people.* London: Institute of Education.

Guttormasson, L. (2002). Parent child relations. In D. Kertzer & M. Barbagli (Eds.), *The history of the European family* (Vol. 2). New Haven: Yale University Press.

Habermas, J. (1987). *The theory of communicative action vol. 2. Lifeworld and system: A critique of functional reason.* Boston: Beacon Press.

Hanawalt, B. (1979). *Crime and conflict in English communities 1300–1348.* London: Harvard University Press.

Hanawalt, B. (1993). *Growing up in medieval London: The experience of child-hood in history*. New York: Oxford University Press.

Handel, G., Cahill, S., & Elkin, F. (2007). *Children and society: The sociology of children and childhood socialisation*. Los Angeles: Roxbury Publishing Company.

Hansard. (2014, January 28). Ammendment 53ZA volume 751, column 1141–1153.

Hardman, C. (1973). Can there be an anthropology of children? *Journal of the Anthropology Society of Oxford, 4*(1), 85–99.

Harrison. (2010). *Citizens of character: New directions in citizenship and values education*. Exeter: Imprint Academic.

Haste, H. (1999). Moral understanding in socio-cultural context. In M. Woodhead (Ed.), *Making sense of social development*. London: Routledge.

Hebdige, D. (1979). *Subculture: The meaning of style*. London: Methuen.

Helpern, D. (2005). *Social capital*. London: Polity Press.

Hendrick, H. (1997). Construction and reconstruction of British childhood: An interpretive survey, 1800 to the present. In A. James & A. Prout (Eds.), *Constructing and reconstructing childhood*. London: Falmer Press.

Hendrick, H. (2000). The child as a social actor in history. In P. Christensen & A. James (Eds.), *Research with children*. London: Falmer.

Hendrick, H. (Ed.). (2005). *Child welfare and social policy: An essential reader*. Bristol: The Policy Press.

Herlihy, D. (1978). Medieval children. In B. Lackner & K. Philip (Eds.), *Essays in medieval civilisation: The Walter Prescott Webb memorial lectures*. Austin: University of Texas Press.

Herlihy, D. (1985). *Medieval households*. Cambridge, MA: Harvard University Press.

Hersh, D., Paolitto, J., & Reimer, J. (1979). *Promoting moral growth: From Piaget to Kholberg*. New York: Longman.

HM Government. (2015). *Prevent duty guidance*. London: *Home Office*.

Hobbes, T. ([1651] 2008). *Leviathan*. Oxford: Oxford University Press.

Hodgkinson, T. (2010). *The idle parent*. London: Penguin.

Hogg, T., & Blau, M. (2001). *How to speak your baby's language*. San Francisco: Bonnier Corporation.

Høgh-Olsen, H. (Ed.). (2010). *Human morality and sociality*. Basingstoke: Palgrave Macmillan.

Hollingsworth, K. (2012). Youth justice reform in the 'big society'. *Journal of Social Welfare and Family Law, 34*(2), 245–259.

Homer. (1991). *Odyssey* (trans: Rieu, E. V. & rev. trans: Rieu, D. C. H.). London: Penguin.

Howard League. (2007). *Children as victims: Child sized crimes in a child-sized world.* London: Howard League for Penal Reform.

Hunt, D. (1969). *Parents and children in history.* London: Basic Books.

Hunt, A. (1978). *The sociological movement in law.* London/Basingstoke: Macmillan.

Hutchby, I., & Moran Ellis, J. (Eds.). (1998). *Children and social competence: Arenas of action.* London: Falmer Press.

IAPC. (2016, April 21). *Institute for the advancement of philosophy for children.* http://www.montclair.edu/cehs/academics/centers-and-institutes/iapc/#d.en.9966. Accessed 21 Apr 2016.

Illich, I. (1972). *Deschooling society* (1st Harrow ed.). New York: Harrow Books.

Independent. (2015, June 18). *16 and 17 year olds given the vote in Scotland on the same day they are banned from voting in EU.* http://www.independent.co.uk/news/uk/politics/16-and-17-year-olds-given-the-vote-in-scotland-on-the-same-day-they-are-banned-from-voting-in-eu-10330223.html.

James, A. (1993). *Childhood identities.* Edinburgh: Edinburgh University Press.

James, A. L. (2010). Competition or integration? The next step in childhood studies? *Childhood, 17*(4), 485–499.

James, A. (2013). *Socialising children.* Basingstoke: Palgrave Macmillan.

James, A., & James, A. L. (2004). *Constructing childhood.* Basingstoke: Palgrave Macmillan.

James, A., & Prout, A. (1995). Hierarchy, boundary and agency: Towards a theoretical perspective on childhood. *Sociological Studies of Children, 7,* 77–99.

James, A., & Prout, A. (Eds.). (1997) [first published 1990]. *Constructing and reconstructing childhood.* London: Falmer Press.

James, A., Jenks, C., & Prout, A. (1998). *Theorising childhood.* London: Polity.

Jans, J. (2004). Children as citizens: Towards a contemporary notion of child participation. *Childhood, 11*(1), 27–44.

Jenkins, R. (2004). *Social identity.* London: Routledge.

Jenkins, R. (2010). Beyond social structure. In P. J. Martin & A. Dennis (Eds.), *Human agents and social structures* (pp. 133–151). Manchester: Manchester University Press.

Jenks, C. (1992). *The sociology of childhood.* London: Batsford.

Jenks, C. (1996). *Childhood.* London: Routledge.

Jensen, A., & McKee, L. (Ed.). (2003). *Children and the changing family: Between transformation and negotiation.* London/New York: RoutledgeFalmer.

Jordonova, L. (1989). Children in history: Concepts of nature and society. In G. Scarre (Ed.), *Children, parents and politics.* Cambridge/New York: Cambridge University Press.

Jordonova, L. (1999). Baturalising the family: Literature and the bio-medical sciences in the late eighteenth century. In L. Jordonova (Ed.), *Nature displayed: Gender, science and medicine 1760–1820*. Harlow: Longman.

Jutengren, G., & Palmerus, K. (2002). A comparison of Swedish and US fathers' self reported use of parental discipline. *Children and Society, 16*, 246–259.

Kagan, J. (1984). *The nature of the child*. New York: Basic Books.

Kagan, J. (1986). Introduction. In J. Kagan & S. Lamb (Eds.), *The emergence of morality in young children*. Chicago: University of Chicago Press.

Kamur, K. (1978). *Prophecy an progress*. Harmondsworth: Penguin.

Kant, I. (1949). *Fundamental principles of the metaphysics of morals*. Indianapolis: Bolts-Merril.

Kantor, R., Elgas, P., & Fernie, D. (1998). Cultural knowledge and social competence within a preschool peer-culture group. In M. Woodhead, D. Faulkner, & K. Littleton (Eds.), *Cultural worlds of early childhood*. London: Routledge.

Kholberg, L. (1984). *The psychology of moral development*. San Fransico: Harper and Row.

Killen, M., & Smetna, J. (2010). *Handbook of moral development*. London: Psychology Press.

Kingsley, C. (1900). *Water babies*. New York: H. M. Caldwell Co.

Kirchberg, V. (2007). Cultural consumption analysis: Beyond structure and agency. *Cultural Sociology, 1*(1), 115–135.

Kirtzinger, J. (1997). Who are you kidding? In A. James & A. Prout (Eds.), *Constructing and reconstructing childhood*. London: Falmer Press.

Kohn, A. (2005). *Unconditional parenting*. New York: Atria Books

Kuefler, M. (2003). A wyred existence: Attitudes toward children in Anglo-Saxon England. *Journal of Social History, 24*(4), 823–834.

Laing, R. D. (1969). *The divided self* Harmondsworth: Penguin.

Lave, J., & Wenger, E. (1991). *Situated learning: Legitimate peripheral perception*. Cambridge: Cambridge University Press.

Layard, R., & Dunn, J. (2009). *A good childhood*. London: Penguin.

League of Nations. (1924). *Geneva declaration on the rights of the child*. United Nations. http://www.un-documents.net/gdrc1924.htm.

Lee, N. (2001). *Children and society: Growing up in an age of uncertainty*. Buckingham: Open University Press.

Lee, N. (2005). *Childhood and human value: Development, separation and separability*. Maidenhead: Open University Press.

Lee, D., & Newby, H. (1983). *The problem of sociology*. London: Routledge.

Lichtheim, M. (1997). *Moral values in ancient Egypt*. Fribourg/Göttingen: University Press.

Lincoln, S. (2013). 'Styling' teenage private space: Identity, fashion and consumption in girls' bedrooms. *Film, Fashion & Consumption, 2*(2), 121.

Locke, J. (1772). *Two treatises of government: By Iohn Locke,* London printed MDCLXXXVIIII reprinted the seventh time by J. Whiston, W. Strahan, J. and F. Rivington, L. Davis, W. Owen [and 18 others in London], London.

Lukes, S. (1973). *Emile Durkheim.* Stanford: Stanford University Press.

Lukes, S. (2005). *Power: A radical view.* Basingstoke: Palgrave Macmillan.

MacIntyre, A. (1998 [1966]). *A short history of ethics.* London: Routledge.

MacIntyre, A. (2007). *After virtue.* London: Duckworth.

Macleans. (2015, February 6). *How safe is sexting.* http://www.macleans.ca/society/how-safe-is-sexting/.

Madehose, W. (1996). Nurturing danger: High medieval medicine and the problem(s) of the child. In J. Cormi Parsons & B. Wheeler (Eds.), *Medieval mothering.* London: Garland Publishing.

Marshall, T. H. ([1950] 1995). *Citizenship and social class.* London: Pluto Press.

Martin, K., & Franklin, A. (2010). Disabled children and participation in the UK. In B. Percy Smith & N. Thomas (Eds.), *A handbook of children and young people's participation.* London: Routledge.

Matthews, M. H. (2002). The street as a liminal space: The barbed spaces of childhood. In P. Christensen & M. O'Brien (Eds.), *Children in the city: Home, neighbourhood and community.* London: RoutledgeFalmer.

May, V. (Ed.). (2011). *Sociology of personal life.* Basingstoke: Palgrave Macmillan.

Mayall, B. (1994). Children in action at home and school. In B. Mayall (Ed.), *Children's childhoods.* London: Falmer.

Mayall, B. (2002). *Towards a sociology for childhood.* Buckingham: Open University Press.

McBride, T. (1997). As the twig is bent. In A. Wohl (Ed.), *The Victorian family: Structures and stresses.* London: Croom Helm.

McDiarmid, C. (2013). An age of complexity: Children and criminal responsibility in law. *Youth Justice, 13*(2), 145–160.

McGinley, B., & Grieve, A. (2010). Maintaining the status quo. In B. Percy-Smith & N. Thomas (Eds.), *A handbook of children and young people's participation: Perspectives from theory and practice.* New York/London: Routledge.

McLaughlin, M. (1974). Survivors and surrogates children and parents from the ninth to thirteenth century. In L. De Mause (Eds.), *The history of childhood.* New York: Psychohistory Press.

McNamee, S. (1998). *Questioning video game use: An exploration of the spatial and gender aspects of children's leisure.* Unpublished PhD Thesis, University of Hull.

McNamee, S. (2016). *The social study of childhood: An introduction.* Basingstoke: Palgrave Macmillan.

McNamee, S., & Frankel, S. (forthcoming). Subverting the research encounter: Context, structure and agency in the creative analysis of research data in researching kids and teens: Methodological issues, strategies, and innovations. In *Sociological studies of children and youth* (Vol. 22).

McNamee, S., Frankel, S., Birnbaum, R., & Pomfret, A. (2016). Article 6 of the UNCRC and holistic development. CBA Toolkit: Canadian Bar Association.

McRobbie, A. (1994). *Postmodernism and popular culture*. London: Routledge.

Mead, G.-H. (1934). *Mind, self and society: From the standpoint of a social behaviourist*. Chicago: University of Chicago Press.

Meintjes, H. (2014). Growing up in time of AIDS: The shining recorders of Zisize. In K. Tisdall, A. Gadda, & U. Butler (Eds.), *Children and young people's participation and its transformative potential*. Basingstoke: Palgrave Macmillan.

Mill, J. S. (1910). *Utilitarianism: Liberty, representative government*. London: Dent.

Minisitry of Education. (2015). *Sex education in Ontario*. http://www.ontario.ca/page/sex-education-ontario.

Ministry of Justice. (2012). *Statistical bulletin on the public disorder of 6th to 9th August 2011–September 2012 update*. London: Ministry of Justice.

More, H. (1840). *Stories for young persons*. London: Allman.

Morgan, D. H. J. (1996). *Family connections: An introduction to family studies*. Cambridge: Polity Press.

Morgan, D. H. J. (2011). *Rethinking family practices*. New York/Basingstoke: Houndmills/Palgrave Macmillan.

Muncie, J. (2015). *Youth & crime* (4th ed.). London: SAGE.

Murdoch, I. (1971). *The sovereignty of good*. New York: Schocken Books.

Musgrave, P. (1987) *Socialising contexts*. Sydney: Allen and Unwin.

Nahwegahbow, B. (2015). *Feds appeal nod to Sixties Scoop class action*. Aboriginal Multi-Media Society of Alberta (AMMSA).

National Post. (2013). B.C. kindergarten no-touch rule includes ban on hand holding, lightsabre duels Nov 5.

National Post. (2014). When one New Zealand school tossed its playground rules and let students risk injury, the results were surprising March 21st.

National Post. (2015, December 14). *Terminally ill children as young as 12 should have euthanasia choice expert panel urges*. http://news.nationalpost.com/news/canada/terminally-ill-children-as-young-as-12-should-have-euthanasia-choice-expert-panel-urges.

Newell, P. (1997). *Listening to the heartbeat of god*. London: SPCK.

NRA. (2016). *Hansel and Gretel (Have Guns)*. http://www.nrafamily.org/articles/2016/3/17/hansel-and-gretel-have-guns/. Accessed 21 Apr 2016.

NZHearld. (2009, April 3). A positive spin on parenting – Jan Pryor.

Oakley, A. (1994). Women and children first and last. In B. Mayall (Ed.), *Children's childhoods: Observed and experienced*. London: Falmer Press.

Ofsted. (2014). *Below the radar: Low-level disruption in the country's classrooms*. London: Ofsted.

OHCHR. (2016, March). Prohibiting all corporal punishment of children: progress and delay. Briefing prepared by the Global Initiative to End All Corporal Punishment of Children March 2016 edition. http://www.endcorporalpunishment.org/resources/global-reports/global-progress-and-delay-leaflet-march-2016.html.

Omer, A. (2011) *The new authority*. New York, Cambridge University Press.

Ontario Catholic School Board. (2011). Ontario Catholic school graduate expectations.

Orme, N. (2006, June). What did medieval schools do for us. *History Today*.

Oswell, D. (2013). *The agency of children: From family to global human rights*. Cambridge: Cambridge University Press.

Ozment, S. (1983). *When fathers ruled: Family life in reformation Europe*. Cambridge, MA: Harvard University Press.

Paget, J.-P., & Fronchi, V. (2008). The rights of the child and the good of the learners. *Childhood, 15*(2), 157–176.

Parents as First Educators. (2016). http://www.p-first.com. Accessed 1 Mar 2016.

Parsons, T. (1951). *The social system*. London: Routledge and Kegan Paul.

Parton, N. (2006). *Safeguarding childhood*. Basingstoke: Palgrave Macmillan.

Pateman, C. (1988). *The sexual contract*. Cambridge: Polity.

Pattison, R. (1978). *The child figure in English literature*. Athens: University of Georgia Press.

Pearson, G. (1983). *Hooligans: A history of respectable fears*. London: Macmillan.

Pendlebury, S., Henderson, P., & Jamieson, L. (2014). Unsettling notions of participation: A view from South Africa. In K. Tisdall, A. Gadda, & U. Butler (Eds.), *Children and young people's participation and its transformative potential*. Basingstoke: Palgrave Macmillan.

Percy Smith, B., & Thomas, N. (Eds.). (2010a). *A handbook of children and young people's participation*. London: Routledge.

Percy-Smith, B., & Thomas, N. (2010b). Conclusion. In B. Percy-Smith & N. Thomas (Eds.), *A handbook of children and young people's participation: Perspectives from theory and practice*. New York/London: Routledge.

Piaget, J. ([1935] 1975). *The moral judgement of the child*. London: Routledge and Kegan Paul.

Piaget, J. (1967). *Six psychological studies*. London: University of London Press.

Pinchbeck, I., & Hewitt, M. (1969). *Children in English society*. London: Routledge & K. Paul.

Plato, & Halliwell, S. 1988, *Plato: Republic 10*. Warminster: Aris & Phillips.

Plutach. (1898). (trans: Shilleto, M. A.). 26/27. http://www.gutenberg.org/files/23639/23639-h/23639-h.htm.

Pollard, A. (1985). *The social world of the primary school*. London: Holt Rinehart and Winston.

Pollard, A. (1994). Towards a sociology of learning in primary schools. In A. Pollard & J. Bourne (Ed.), *Teaching and learning in the primary school*. New York/London: Routledge in Association with the Open University.

Pollard, A. (2014). *Reflective teaching in schools*. London: Bloomsbury.

Pollock, L. (1983). *Forgotten children: Parent–child relations from 1500 to 1900*. Cambridge: Cambridge University Press.

Pomeroy, S. (1997). *Families in classical and hellenistic Greece: Representations and realities*. Oxford: Clarendon Press.

Postman, N. (1983). *The disappearance of childhood*. London: W.H. Allen.

Public Health England. (2014). *The link between pupil health well being and attainment*. London: Public Health England.

Punch, S. (2005). The generation of power: A comparison of child–parent and sibling relations in Scotland. In *Sociological studies of children and youth, 10* (pp. 169–188). Amsterdam: Elsevier.

Qvortrup, J. (1994). Childhood matters: An introduction. In J. Qvortrup et al. (Eds.), *Childhood matters: Social theory practice and politics*. London: Falmer.

Qvortrup, J. (2011). Childhood as a structural form. In J. Qvortrup, W. Corsaro, & M. Honig (Eds.), *The Palgrave handbook of childhood studies*. Basingstoke: Palgrave Macmillan.

Ranson, B. (1997). The iconography of Roman childhood. In B. Ranson & P. Weaver (Eds.), *The Roman family in Italy*. Oxford: Clarendon Press.

Ranson, B., & Weaver, P. (Eds.). (1997). *The Roman family in Italy*. Oxford: Clarendon Press.

Rapport, N. (1995). Migrant selves and stereotypes. In S. Pile & N. Thrift (Eds.), *Mapping the subject*. London: Routledge.

Rapport, N. (2003). *I am dynamite: An alternative anthropology of power*. New York/London: Routledge.

Rawson, B. (2003). *Children and childhood in Roman Italy*. Oxford: Oxford University Press.

Rayner, J. (1926). *The complete Newgate Calendar*. London: Navarre Society.

Rietveld, C. (2005). Classroom learning experiences of mathematics by new entrant children with Down syndrome. *Journal of Intellectual & Developmental Disability, 30*(3), 127–138.

Ritzer, G. (2011). *Sociological theory*. New York: McGraw Hill.

Robb, M. (2014). *Children, morality and society, children and society*. Hoboken: Wiley-Blackwell.

Roche, J. (1999). Children: Rights, participants and citizenship. *Childhood, 6*(4), 475–493.

Rose, N. (1989). *Governing the soul*. London: Routledge.

Rosier, K. (2011). Children as problems, problems of children. In J. Qvortrup, W. Corsaro, & M. Honig (Eds.), *The Palgrave handbook of childhood studies*. Basingstoke: Palgrave Macmillan.

Rousseau, J.-J. ([1762] 1911). *Emile*. London: JM Dent and Sons.

Russell, P. (2003). "Access and achievement or social exclusion?" Are the governments policies working for disabled children and their families? *Children and Society, 19*, 385–396.

Ryan, P. (2013). *Master-servant childhood*. New York: Palgrave Pivot.

Sadler, R. (1994). *Patriarchy, property and death in the roman family*. Cambridge: Cambridge University Press.

Sandel, M. (2010). We need a public life with purpose. *Citizen Ethics (Pamphlet distributed with the Guardian)* 20th February 2010.

Sargeant, J. (2014). Prioritising student voice: 'Tween' children's perspectives on school success. *Education 3–13, 42*(2), 190–200.

Saunders, B., & Goddard, C. (2010). *Physical punishment in childhood: The rights of the child*. Oxford: Wiley- Blackwell.

Savyasaachi, & Butler, U.-M. (2014). Decolonizing the notion of participation of children and young people. In K. Tisdall, A. Gadda, & U. Butler (Eds.), *Children and young people's participation and its transformative potential*. Basingstoke: Palgrave Macmillan.

Schaffer, H. R. (1996). *Social development*. London: Blackwell.

Scraton, P. (1997). Whose childhood? What crisis. In P. Scraton (Ed.), *Childhood in crisis*. London: UCL Press.

Semel, S., & Sadovnik, A. (Eds.). (1999). *"Schools of tomorrow" schools of today*. New York: Peter Lang.

Sereny, G. (1998). *Cries unheard*. Basingstoke: Macmillan.

Shakespeare, W. (1986). *William Shakespeare, the complete works* (Original-spelling ed.) – Wells, S., Taylor, G., & Salmon, V. Oxford [Oxfordshire]/ Toronto: Clarendon Press.

Sherwood, E. (1869). *The Fairchild family*. London: Hatchards.

Short, G. (1999). Children's grasp of controversial issues. In M. Woodhead (Ed.), *Making sense of social development*. London: Routledge.

Shorter, E. (1976). *The making of the modern family*. Harmondsworth: Penguin.

Silva, B., & Smart, C. (Eds.). (1999). *The new family*. London: Sage.

Smale, I. (1998). *A history of children*. London: Silver Fish.

Smart, C. (2007). *Personal life*. Cambridge: Polity Press.

Smout, T. (1969). *History of the Scottish people: 1560–1830*. London: Fontana Press.

Solberg, A. (1996). The challenge in child research: From being to doing. In J. Brannen & M. O'Brien (Eds.), *Children in families: Research and policy*. London: Falmer.

Solberg, A. (1997). Negotiating childhood: Changing constructions of age in Norwegian children. In A. James & A. Prout (Eds.), *Theorising childhood*. London: Falmer Press.

Sommer, D. (2012). *A childhood psychology*. Basingstoke: Palgrave Macmillan.

Spilsbury, J. C. (2002). If I don't know them, I'll get killed probably: How children's concerns about safety shape help-seeking behavior. *Childhood, 9*(1), 101–117.

Steedman, C. (1994). *Strange dislocations: Childhood and the idea of human interiority, 1780–1930*. Cambridge, MA: Harvard University Press.

Sterponi, L. (2009). Accountability in family discourse: Socialization into norms and standards and negotiation of responsibility in Italian dinner conversations. *Childhoods, 16*(4), 441–459.

Stone, L. (1979). *The family, sex and marriage in England 1500–1800*. London: Penguin.

Tamanaha, B. (2001). *General jurisprudence in law and society*. Oxford: Oxford University Press.

Taylor, D. (1998). *Crime, policing and punishment in England, 1750–1914*. Basingstoke: Macmillan.

Teamey, K., & Hinton, R. (2014). Reflections on participation and its link with transformative processes. In K. Tisdall, A. Gadda, & U. Butler (Eds.), *Children and young people's participation and its transformative potential*. Basingstoke: Palgrave Macmillan.

Telegraph. (2007, July 26). After school clubs 'will combat yob culture'.

The Hindu. (2016, April 21). *UK expresses concern over gender violence in India*. http://www.thehindu.com/news/international/uk-expresses-concern-over-gender-violence-in-india/article8505464.ece.

Thomas, L. (2010). *The mummy coach*. London: Hamlyn.

Thompson, E. P. (1975). *Whigs and hunters*. London: Penguin.

Thompson, M. (2005). *Ethical theory*. Coventry: Hodder Murray.

Thompson, K., & Tunstall, J. (1971). *Sociological Perspectives*. Middlesex: Penguin.

Thornberg, R. (2008). 'It's not fair!' – Voicing pupils' criticisms of school rules. *Children and Society, 22*(6), 418–428.

Thorne, B. (1993). *Gender play*. Buckingham: OUP.

Tierney, J. (1996). *Criminology: Theory and practice*. London: Prentice Hall.

Times, The. (2016, January 12). *All children should have tiger mums*. http://www.thetimes.co.uk/tto/news/politics/article4662945.ece.

Tisdall, E. K. M., Gadda, A. M., & Butler, U. M. (2014). *Children and young people's participation and its transformative potential: Learning from across countries*. New York: Palgrave Macmillan.

Tomanovic, S. (2004). Family habitus as the cultural context for childhood. *Childhood, 11*(3), 339–361.

Torstenson-Ed, T., Linköpings universitet, Institutionen för samhälls- och välfärdsstudier, Lärande, E., Naturvetenskap (LEN), & Utbildningsvetenskap. (2007). Children's life paths through preschool and school: Letting youths talk about their own childhood – Theoretical and methodological conclusions. *Childhood, 14*(1), 47–66.

Turner, J. (1986). *The structure of sociological theory*. Chicago: Dorsey Press.

Twum-Danso Imoh, A. (2013). Children's perceptions of physical punishment in Ghana and the implications for children's rights. *Childhood, 20*(4), 472–486.

UN Geneva Declaration on the Rights of the Child. http://www.un-documents.net/gdrc1924.htm.

UNICEF. (2007). *An overview of child well being in rich countries Florence*. UNICEF.

Valentine, K. (2011a). Accounting for agency. *Children & Society, 25*(5), 347–358.

Valentine, K. (2011b). Accounting for agency. *Children & Society, 25*(5), 347–358.

Victim Support. (2014a). bedfordshire uni

Victim Support. (2014b). *Suffering in silence: Children and unreported crime*. https://www.victimsupport.org.uk/sites/default/files/Hidden%20Victimisation%20of%20Children_low%20res.pdf.

Vygotsky, L. (1978). *Mind in society: The development of higher psychological processes*. Cambridge, MA: Harvard University Press.

Wells, P. (2011). Prospects for a big society? Special issue of people place and policy online. *People, Place & Policy Online, 5*(2), 50–54.

White, L. (2014). Understanding Canada's lack of progress in implementing the UN convention on the rights of the child. *International Journal of Children's Rights, 22*, 164–188.

WHO (World Health Organisation). (2016). *Female genital mutilation*. http://www.who.int/mediacentre/factsheets/fs241/en/.

Wilson, E. K. (1966). *Sociology: Rules, roles, and relationships.* Homewood: Dorsey Press.

Winlow, S., & Hall, S. (2006). *Violent night.* Oxford: Berg.

Wooden, W. (1995). *Renegade kids and suburban outlaws.* London: Wadsworth.

Wrigley, T., Thompson, P., & Lingard, B. (Eds.). (2012). *Changing schools.* London: Routledge.

Wrong, D. (1961). The oversocialized conceptions of man in modern sociology. *American Sociological Review, 26*(2), 183–193.

Wyness, M. (2012). *Childhood and society.* Basingstoke: Palgrave Macmillan.

Xenophon 14: 50. (1897). Cryopaedia – On eduaction (trans: Dakyns, H., & Stawell, F.). https://ebooks.adelaide.edu.au/x/xenophon/x5cy/.

Yamashita, H., & Davies, L. (2010). Students as professionals. In B. Percy Smith & N. Thomas (Eds.), *A handbook of children and young people's participation.* London: Routledge.

2008. Yougov poll see wyness for more.

Cases

Gillick v West Norfolk and Wisbech Area Health Authority and Another (1986) 1 FLR 224.

Mullins v Richards. (1998). 1 WLR 1304.

Stephen (Malcolm R). (1984). 79 Cr App R 334.

Index[1]

A

aboriginal, 154
'adult child', 72, 226n3, 242–4
adult-child relationships. *See also*
    fathers; mums; stranger danger;
    trust
  as authority figure, 198, 213, 244
  changing relationships, 92, 125
  child as participant, 23, 34, 36,
    62, 63, 127, 184, 221, 225,
    226, 227n7, 235, 237, 243,
    254, 255, 257, 260–1
  political responses, 251, 258
  responding to children as a threat,
    94, 172, 176, 179
agency. *See also* moral agency

children as social agents, 5, 42,
    75, 203, 230, 251, 255, 261
  definition of, 7, 79, 80, 95–7
  processes of, 3, 6, 44, 69, 78, 84,
    96, 98, 234, 255
age of criminal responsibility,
    169–70, 188, 256
ages and stages, 127. *See also* age of
    criminal responsibility
Alanen, Lina, 55, 74–5, 102n2
alcohol use, 173, 206
Ancient Egypt, 166–7
Ancient Greece, 106, 130n1, 262n5
Ancient Rome, 110
antisocial behaviour, 187, 188, 247
antisocial child, 188

---

[1] Note: Page number followed by 'n' refers to notes.

Aquinas, Thomas, 112–13, 119, 159n6
Archard, David, 27, 120, 121, 185
Aries, Philippe, 48–9, 145
Aristotle, 112, 119, 122, 141–2, 159n4, 165, 168
Arthur, James, 155, 156
authority, 107, 153, 177, 191, 198, 213, 218, 244
autonomy, 60, 65, 218

B
babies, 79, 121, 240
backdrop, 1, 5–6, 15, 33, 41–4, 47, 55–7, 64, 66, 69, 70, 75, 92, 101, 103–5, 117, 129, 134, 145, 151, 152, 157, 176, 195, 196, 230, 234–6, 258
Bacon, Kate, 76, 79, 165, 185, 219, 226, 227n7, 251, 252
Bainham, A., 186
baptism, 115, 117, 131n11, 146
Barnardo's, 182
behaviour. *See also* antisocial behavior; guilt
in a moral context, 15, 27, 36, 37, 156, 240, 242–3
the nature of, 135, 240
as social concerns, 164, 177
unpredictability of, 23
Bell, Mary, child murderer, 3
belonging, 61, 84–7, 135, 164, 199, 201, 203, 204, 227n7, 256
Bentham, John, 165
Bergman, T., 36–8, 77
Big Society, 250–2

biology, 19, 30, 120, 139
Black Act, 177
Blake, William, 180–2
blank slate, 121, 122
Bluebond-Langner, Myra, 31
body
actual body, 85
as a focus for control, 158n2
physical contact, 94
a site for negotiated power, 88
styled body, 85
Bonner, K., 117–18, 147–8
Boultwood, M.
history of education, 137–8
boundary, 12, 66, 75–6, 91, 120, 220
Bourdieu, Pierre, 29, 30, 50, 72, 91
boy bishops, 116
Brofrenbrenner, U., 57
Bulger, Jamie, murder of, 170, 187
bullying, 87, 202, 203

C
Canada, 64, 154, 185, 227n5
caning, 151
capital, 84, 91–5, 99, 155, 205–6
change, 252
constructions of childhood, 6–7, 42, 49, 64, 125, 153
societies, 19, 20
as stage in life course, 23
Chicago School, 22
child abuse, 108
childhood
changing constructions, 6–7, 42, 49, 64, 125, 153
childhoods, 16

representations of, 52, 59, 60, 62,
168, 169
social construction, 4, 32, 43, 47,
48, 258
as stages in life course, 35
childhoods, 16
children, 185
competence, 12, 26, 28, 30, 32, 64,
70–2, 101n1, 109, 111, 116,
126, 166, 170, 173, 244
moral agency, 35–6
as participants, 23, 34, 36, 62, 63,
127, 184, 221, 225, 226,
227n7, 235, 237, 243, 254,
255, 257, 260–1
Children Act 1989, 62
Children, Morality and Society, 2, 4,
7, 89, 195, 207, 209, 211,
222–4
child safety orders, 188
Church
Catholic, 19, 113, 117, 160n9
Pope Francis, 119
Protestant, 159n6
citizenship, 164, 168, 183, 184, 190,
191, 250–7, 263n9
education, 161n15, 191
city states, 106, 135, 138
civic society, 225
civil law, 171
class, 33, 77, 106, 108, 124, 131n7,
132n18, 136, 137, 141,
149, 152–4, 176, 177, 180,
212, 245
clothes, 85, 120
Coalition government, 251
Cockburn, Tom, 106, 113, 119–20,
141, 152, 153, 159n5, 164,
185, 244, 250, 262n4,
262n5

Cohen, Anthony, 81, 85
Cohen, Stanley, 63, 186, 187
commitment, 3, 76, 177, 219
common good, 51, 165, 166, 221–2,
226, 250–2, 261
community, 18, 19, 61, 82, 115,
135, 143, 158n1, 166, 167,
184, 197, 223–5, 237, 245,
249–2, 256, 257, 261
competence, 2, 11, 12, 20, 26, 28,
30, 32, 54, 63, 64, 70–2,
77, 79, 101n1, 106–9, 111,
116, 119–20, 122, 124,
126–8, 129n1, 133, 166,
170, 171, 173, 175, 180,
183, 186, 190, 204, 225,
226, 231, 237, 244,
252, 256
Connolly, Paul, 63, 79, 91, 92, 94,
95, 245–6
consent
everyday giving of, 221
constructions
of childhood, 4, 6–7, 32, 38,
42–4, 47–52, 54, 56–7, 59,
61, 64, 97, 105, 107, 109,
112, 117, 134, 136, 140, 153,
154, 157, 158, 163–5, 169,
171, 179, 182, 185–7, 217,
233, 240, 244,
253, 258
moral, 38–9, 44, 47, 54, 59, 60,
63, 86, 106, 107, 151. 164,
171, 182, 184, 188, 240
social, 4, 32, 43, 47, 48, 258
context
contextual backdrop, 5, 6, 103–5,
129, 134, 145, 151, 152, 196,
230, 235, 258
contract, social, 119

control
  educationally, 137, 190
  legal, 173, 174, 176
  parental, 240
corporal punishment, 119, 125, 148,
  157, 160n13, 160n14, 209,
  212, 241–2, 244
Corsaro, W., 79, 189, 221
court, 97, 114, 151, 171, 172, 260
Covey, Stephen, 156
Crick, Malcolm, 28
crime, 19, 63, 118, 159n3, 168–70,
  177–9, 208, 239, 246, 247,
  255, 256
Crime and Disorder Act 1998, 170
criminal law, 167, 169, 171, 179,
  188, 215, 216
criminology, 226n1
cultural units, 85–6
Cunningham, H., 113–16, 122,
  131n10, 147, 154, 176,
  180–3, 191
curriculum, 66n1, 147, 156, 191,
  249, 260
  curriculum of virtue, 144, 148,
  149, 152–5, 157–8, 166, 210,
  214, 217, 242, 249
Curtis, S.
  history of education, 137–8

Danby, Susan, 37, 77
decision makers, 186
de Mause, L., 49, 148, 151, 160n10
developmentalism, 16, 25, 36, 76,
  115, 119, 126–9, 223
deviancy, 19, 86, 186, 220
differences, 84–6, 99, 103, 204, 217
disability, 62–3, 200

discipline, 21, 126, 138, 145, 147–8,
  157, 197, 241–4
doli incapax, 170, 179, 188
domestic violence, 54
Douglas, Mary, 66n1, 75, 84, 86,
  87, 164, 168
Durkhiem, Emile, 19
duty, 148, 155, 219

education, 136–43
  children's agency, 244
  curriculum, 191, 260
  expulsion and suspension, 211
  policies, 154
Emile (Rousseau), 123
Emirbrayer, M., 72
emotions, 7, 27, 80, 82, 91–5,
  158n2, 196–211, 214, 219,
  243, 259
equality, 70, 120, 243
  establishing a sense of, 72
Euripides, 135
euthanasia, 66
Every Child Matters, 62
everyday
  children's lives, 5, 7, 8, 10, 12,
  16, 18, 37, 39, 43, 50, 55,
  64, 66, 87–8, 96, 101,
  130n3, 153, 195–227, 236,
  259, 261
  home, 196–201, 207–10, 217–20
  morality, 7, 38, 44, 78, 94, 95,
  100, 209
  neighbourhood, 204–6, 214–17,
  222–5
  school, 201–4, 210–14, 220–2
evil, 60, 116, 123, 146, 147, 150,
  151, 167, 169

evil child, 52, 64
experiences, 1, 2, 17, 19, 27, 31, 32,
        34, 39, 41–2, 44, 48–50,
        55–6, 59, 62, 64, 67n3, 82,
        86, 91–5, 104, 105, 113,
        117, 121, 125, 126, 128,
        131n9, 132n18, 136, 140,
        141, 144, 151, 152, 157,
        158, 166, 176, 200, 201,
        203, 209, 223, 226n3, 235,
        237, 238, 241, 245, 252,
        259
extremism, 66, 119

F
Fairchild Family, The, 118
faith, 14, 119, 167
family
    in current discourse, 109, 119,
        218, 222
    historical view, 107–9
    as place of moral learning, 145
fathers, 108, 109, 125, 147, 166,
        199, 258, 262n3
feelings, 26, 27, 76, 142, 159n2,
        173, 198, 200, 204, 206,
        209–12, 223, 240, 243
female genital mutilation, 65
fields, 22, 29, 92
figuration, 92
Finch, J., 219
flogging, 151
Fortin, Jane, 185–6
Foucault, Michel, 88, 102n6, 109,
        191n3
free will, 12, 22, 122
Freud, S., 19, 26, 126

friendship
    consent, 203–4
    dares, 204–5
    naming, 202–3
    peer pressure, 89–90
Frost, N., 218
fun, 198, 205, 206, 222

G
games, 27, 49, 90, 96, 189, 22⁻, 257
gangs, 67n3, 176, 220
gender differences, 224
gender violence, 66
generationing, generational order,
        55, 74–5, 101n2
Geneva Declaration on Children's
        Rights, 184
Giddens, Anthony, 29, 30, 32,
        58, 72
Gillick ruling, 174
Gilligan, C., 53, 77, 102n3
Goffman, E., 28, 36, 85
Good Childhood Report, 211
Greek writing, 147
grid group theory, 75
guilt, 76, 167, 171–2
guns, 216, 254–5

H
Habermas, J., 29
habitus, 29, 72, 91, 92, 95
happiness, 132n17, 141, 165, 181
Hardman, Charlotte, 31
Haste, H., 36, 77
Hendrick, H., 50, 68n5, 123, 153
hierarchy and boundary, 75, 76, 91

Hobbes, Thomas, 119, 122
home
    building commitment, 219
    positive relationships, 124, 207–8
    responsibilities within, 219
    as space for negotiated meaning,
      218–19
Homer, 14–15, 135
hoodies, 187
House of Lords/House of Commons
    Joint Committee on
    Human Rights, 156

I

identity, 33, 39, 79–95, 151, 154,
    193, 206, 210, 221, 224,
    227n7, 255, 257
images, 1, 6–7, 38, 43, 44, 47, 49,
    50, 52, 54–7, 59–65, 69,
    71, 94, 95, 97, 105–12,
    114–18, 120, 121, 123,
    125, 128–9, 134–6, 140,
    146, 155, 157, 158, 164,
    167, 169, 171, 172, 174–6,
    179–82, 184–90, 196,
    198–9, 203, 206, 207, 214,
    219–20, 222, 225, 230–1,
    233, 235–8, 240–51,
    253–7, 260, 261
individual, 2, 4, 6, 7, 10, 13–15, 17,
    19–21, 23–6, 29–30, 32–6,
    38, 39, 41, 43–5, 49, 58, 66,
    67n3, 69–70, 72–88, 90–2,
    95, 96, 98–101, 106, 108,
    112–13, 117, 119, 120,
    126–8, 151, 165, 167, 195,
    199–201, 204, 205, 208,
    209, 214, 222, 229, 230,
    234–5, 256, 257, 259, 260

individualism, 33, 38
injustice, 212
'innocent child', 52, 60, 64, 122,
    124, 180–3, 190
institutionalisation, 57, 62, 154, 165
institutions, 9, 24–5, 55, 59, 60, 70,
    129, 149, 151, 157, 203,
    217, 222,
    229–30, 245
interaction, 3, 6, 11, 29, 32, 33,
    35–8, 41, 42, 47, 72, 74,
    75, 77, 80, 82–4, 87–90,
    92, 94, 95, 98–100, 150,
    177, 193, 195, 198, 199,
    205, 210, 220, 225,
    229, 258
    interactional settings, 5, 33, 44,
      56–62, 64, 78, 81, 83, 90,
      92, 97, 112, 113, 119, 129,
      134, 189, 194, 196, 197,
      199–201, 203, 204, 206, 209,
      210, 214, 217–19, 221,
      227n7, 230, 233–5, 255,
      257, 259–61

J

James, Adrian, 5, 16–17, 32, 57, 62,
    71, 85, 91, 157, 165, 171,
    186, 262n2
James, Allison, 24, 31–6, 38, 39, 42,
    48, 52, 57, 60, 62, 71, 72,
    75–6, 79, 81, 84–7, 91, 96,
    111, 157, 165, 171, 186,
    209, 214, 229,
    239, 262n2
Jenkins, Richard, 83–4
Jenks, Chris, 21, 23, 25, 48–50,
    66n1, 187
Jordonova, 50

K

Kant, Immanuel, 19, 26, 54,
        125–7, 171
Kholberg, L., 76, 127, 128
knowledge, 2, 12, 35, 61, 64, 78,
        121, 129n1, 135, 144, 153,
        155, 158, 158n1, 158n2,
        166, 171, 207, 215, 216,
        241, 249, 252, 256, 259–61
Knox, John, 54, 145
Kohn, Alfie, 240, 242–3

L

lack, lacking, 11, 31, 62, 63, 111,
        141, 145, 156, 157, 159n2,
        166–8, 185, 191n3, 216,
        223, 243, 251–3
language, 28, 37, 80, 84, 86, 88, 99,
        143, 160n7, 179, 188, 252
law. See civil law; criminal law
League of Nations, 184
learning, 7, 24, 26, 82, 121, 123,
        124, 136, 138, 140, 143,
        145, 156, 158–9n2, 203,
        207, 209–12, 214, 216–18,
        222, 223, 225, 243–50,
        259–61, 263n8
Lee, N., 18, 31, 53, 237–8, 248
literature, 14, 48, 92, 130n3, 134–5,
        147, 176, 181, 226n2
Locke, John, 120–2, 125
love, 148, 199–200
Lukes, Steven, 19, 21, 39n2, 88,
        102n5
Lutheran, 117
Luther, Martin, 54, 117

M

MacIntyre, Alistair, 51–2, 112
Mayall, Berry, 2, 3, 35–6, 55, 72, 74,
        79, 245
May, Teresa, 33, 82
meaning, 1, 5–6, 20, 21, 23, 25, 31,
        33, 35–9, 42–5, 49, 58–9,
        66, 71, 73–9, 81–9,
        96–100, 151, 169, 137,
        194, 196, 199–202, 205–7,
        209, 215, 217–21, 224,
        230–1, 234, 235, 238, 241,
        243, 245, 255, 257–8
    creating, 1–2, 29, 59, 67n3, 81,
        84, 86, 94, 100, 151, 215,
        221, 225
Meintjes, Helen, 235–7
Menno Simons, 148
Mill, John-Stuart, 165
minority group, 3, 53, 54
Mische, A., 72
moral agency, 35, 36, 96
moral agent, 35–6, 77
moral citizens, 32, 250, 253
moral codes, 23, 131n9, 152, 262n5
moral development, 28, 76–7, 115,
        123, 127, 129, 131n6
moral discourses
    classical traditions, 119, 121
    criminological traditions, 22
    the individual, 52, 112
    Kantian traditions, 19, 26, 125–7
    Piagetian traditions, 26–8, 76–7,
        126–7
    sociological traditions, 5, 18, 21, 36
moral education, 54, 124, 129, 145,
        152, 154

morality
   as part of the everyday, 7, 38, 44,
      78, 94, 95, 100, 209
   as social construct, 4, 17, 19, 50–2
moral judgements, 20, 27, 37, 67n3,
      91, 96, 224
   formation of, 127–8
moral panic, 63, 186–90
moral philosophy, 14, 37, 39n1, 51,
      67n3
Mullin v Richards, ruling, 172
mums, 109, 200, 224
mundane interaction, 66
mutuality
   with adults, 209, 260
   amongst child peer friendships, 204

N
nanny, 111, 131n7
National Citizen Service, 251
nationalism, 153
natural law, 112, 119, 159n6
neighbourhoods, 2, 6, 7, 103, 155, 163,
      164, 166, 168, 175, 178, 188,
      189, 204–6, 214–17, 222–5,
      250, 253–5, 260
new paradigm, 29, 32, 36, 38, 41, 42

O
'ominous child', 168–86
online games, 189, 257
order, 5, 12, 18, 20, 22–4, 26, 27,
      38, 48–51, 55, 74–5,
      78–80, 83–4, 86, 94, 107,
      108, 110, 111, 128, 136,
      141, 158, 164–9, 176–8,
      219–21, 225, 226, 233,
      239, 243, 256, 259, 261

original sin, 117. See also sin
Oswell, David, 67n2, 70, 71, 101n1
otherness, 85, 135

P
Paine, Thomas, 13
panics. See moral panic
parenting, 61, 109, 115, 118, 124,
      148, 196, 239–42, 262n3
parents. See family; fathers; home;
      mums
Parsons, Talcott, 23–5, 28, 30, 33,
      95
participation, 26, 62, 63, 184, 186,
      221, 225, 227n7, 234–7,
      243, 249, 253–7, 261
patriarchy, 107–9, 113, 120, 131n9,
      132n16, 149, 239
pedagogues, 111, 142
personal life, sociology of, 33, 81,
      82, 96
personhood, 33, 38, 95, 227n7,
      238–44
Philosophy for Children, 156–7
Piaget, Jean, 26–8, 30, 71, 76–7,
      126–7, 171
   challenges to, 31
Plato, 106, 122, 137–41, 158n2,
      159n3, 159n4, 165
play, 49, 90, 92, 94, 215, 221. See
      also games
police, 178, 187, 190, 223–4, 255
policy, 17, 34, 62, 64, 65, 74, 150,
      154, 173, 176, 185, 187,
      188, 191, 239, 248, 253,
      257, 261
Pollard, A., 156, 161n16,
      207, 220
pollution, 86, 87, 168, 178

power
mutuality, 209
powerfulness, 89, 90, 168
powerlessness, 89, 90
press, 177, 178, 187, 188, 192n5, 192n10
protest, political, 191
Prout, Alan, 31, 36, 38, 48, 71, 75–6
psychology, 19, 35, 82, 155
public school, 149–50
punishment, 20, 23, 60, 108, 110, 119, 125, 128, 131n15, 139, 140, 142, 148, 153–4, 157, 160n10, 160n13, 160n14, 167–8, 173, 176, 179, 183, 192n3, 196, 198, 207–9, 212, 218, 241–2, 244, 262n3

Q
Qvortrup, Jans, 16, 57

R
race, 13, 106, 154, 246
Rapport, N., 80–1, 86
reason, 6, 12, 13, 26–7, 30, 31, 51, 54, 61, 62, 64, 65, 77, 101, 103, 105–33, 137, 138, 140, 142, 144–6, 152, 158–9n2, 164–6, 168–9, 171–2, 179, 180, 185, 190, 191n3, 196–207, 215, 239, 240, 245, 246, 248, 251, 258, 259
recklessness, 172
Reformation, 52, 117–19, 144, 145
regulation, 106, 166–8, 183, 220, 225

relationships. *See also* family; friends; mutuality; neighbourhoods; school
adults, 3, 6, 16, 42, 51, 55, 74, 109, 111, 123, 125, 149, 151, 200, 214, 223, 237, 240, 248, 259–60
changing nature (parental), 125
peers, 30, 89, 90, 220, 222
rescuing, the child, 182, 183
research, 17, 37, 42, 48, 57, 70, 72, 76–8, 200, 203, 204, 208, 212, 218, 224, 225
respect, 94, 97, 127, 145, 155, 156, 213, 218, 223, 252, 260
restorative justice, 256
rights, 27, 31, 54, 122, 149, 174, 176, 179, 183–6, 223, 251, 255
rights agenda, 175, 183–6, 251, 253
riots, 239
rite of passage, 149, 252
romanticism, 123
Rousseau, Jean-Jacque, 54, 122–3, 125, 180
rules, 21, 23, 26, 27, 29, 40n5, 40n6, 75, 112, 127, 156, 158n1, 164, 166, 158, 251
within everyday spaces, 197, 215–16, 218, 2 20, 224

S
sanctions, 197, 209, 212
Sandel, P., 251
school
as space for moral learning, 211, 212
as space for negotiated power, 222

self, 6, 15, 26, 27, 33, 38, 78–81,
        83–7, 94, 96, 100, 125,
        194, 199–202, 204, 205,
        209, 210, 212, 217, 220,
        257, 259. *See also* power
self-esteem, 80, 243, 263n6
self-identity. *See* self
settings, 5, 8, 33, 35, 36, 44, 55, 56,
        58–60, 64, 66, 74, 76, 97,
        112, 119, 129, 134, 174,
        196, 197, 201, 204, 210,
        214, 222, 225, 230, 233–5,
        238, 255, 257–8, 260, 261,
        263n10
sex education, 64–5, 119, 131n15, 190
Sherwood, Mary, 118, 131n14, 182
siblings, 11, 36
similarity, 84–6, 99, 103, 204, 217
sin, 115, 117, 118, 124, 145, 146,
        160n9. *See also* original sin
smacking, 62, 197, 209, 242
Smart, Carol, 33, 81–2, 95, 199,
        201, 219, 227n6, 241
social capital, 155. *See also* capital
social harmony, 6, 54, 61, 64–6,
        101, 103, 163–93, 196,
        198, 217–25, 248, 257–9
social interaction, 32, 36–7, 88, 127
socialisation, 5, 7, 19, 22–6, 28,
        32–5, 37, 38, 41–2, 50, 65,
        79–81, 96, 130n6, 189,
        198, 200, 207, 210, 220,
        226, 246, 254
social media, 189, 224, 239
social order, 5, 12, 18, 20, 22–4, 26,
        27, 38, 48–50, 55, 74, 75,
        78–80, 84, 86, 110, 111,
        136, 167, 173, 179, 226,
        239, 256, 259

sociology of childhood, 5, 13
Socrates, 106, 139
Solberg, A., 217, 243
soul, of the child, 112–13, 145,
        158n2
South Africa, 173–4, 212, 235–6
space. *See* home; neighbourhood;
        school
Sparta, 107, 166
spirit, of the child (spirituality), 114,
        115, 117, 125
Squire, P., 188
state school, 157
Stephen Malcolm, R v, ruling, 171–2
stereotypes, 86, 217, 246
Sterponi, L., 37–8
Stone, L., 108–9, 176–7, 244
stranger danger, 176
strategic decision making, 205
strike, 191
structuration, 32
structure, 3–5, 7, 10–42, 44, 47–69,
        73–8, 81, 82, 88, 91, 95–7,
        99–101, 108, 113, 189,
        198, 200, 204, 214, 218,
        222, 229–31, 234, 236,
        237, 240–1, 244–7, 249,
        250, 257, 261. *See also*
        agency, grid group theory;
        hierarchy and boundary
substance misuse, 206
surveillance, 154, 247

T

teachers, 1, 11, 58, 74, 94, 122, 150,
        151, 156, 157, 160n8, 203,
        211–13, 220, 227n5, 236,
        241, 245–6, 249

teaching, 11, 31, 112, 114, 115, 117, 118, 129n1, 136, 138, 139, 142, 144, 147, 155, 156, 159n3, 159n6, 159n7, 191, 262n5
teenagers, 190, 216, 223
television, 216–17, 240, 247
Theobald, M., 37, 77
Thompson, E. P., 177
Thorne, B., 86, 87
threat. *See also* violence
    to children, 222
    children as, 23, 94, 152, 166, 168–72, 174–6, 179, 180, 182, 183, 189–91, 222–3, 239, 247, 248
    to girls, 151–2
    and policy, 176, 191
time, 32, 48, 49, 52, 59, 73, 111, 118, 247
tokenism, 249
transportation, 179
trust, 142, 185, 218, 222, 223

U
unfair, 213
United Nations Convention of the Rights of the Child, 31, 170, 175, 185
universality, 16

V
Valentine, K., 70–2, 78–9
victims, 189, 190, 256
violence
    depictions of, 149–51, 176
    perceptions of, 150
virtual worlds, 189, 257
virtue, 6, 54, 61, 62, 64, 65, 101, 103, 106, 107, 110, 133–61, 163–5, 167, 168, 185, 190, 196, 207–17, 237, 242, 248, 252, 258, 259
virtue education, 140–3, 146–52, 156, 207, 214, 260
voices, 7, 8, 16, 174, 184, 191, 195, 235–6, 260
voting, 173–4, 190
vulnerability, 153, 182, 189
Vygotsky, L., 36, 77

W
women, 53–4, 65–6, 102n3, 109, 116, 120, 146–7, 248, 263n10
Wyness, M., 22, 71, 186, 189

X
Xenophon, 107, 140, 159n4

Z
zones for reflection, 83, 84

Printed by Printforce, the Netherlands